T0318468

THE EVOLUTION OF LUXURY

This book offers a unique analysis of how our definitions of luxury have changed over the ages, and with that the role and actions of both suppliers and buyers of luxury products. It traces the way luxury was seen as avarice and emblematic of morally corrosive behavior in past societies, to being viewed in more virtuous terms as the inevitable outcome of structural changes that legitimize the acquisition and display of wealth. It examines the origins of the shift from criticism to acceptance, and traces these changes to fundamentally different notions of what constitutes the basis for social order.

Whereas pre-industrial hierarchies cloaked inequality in various secular and sacred guises to mitigate its presence, capitalism justified and reified inequality as a measure of individual success and initiative through interdependent market behavior. The result of this transformation is that status markers have become aspirational tools as hierarchies became porous and self-identity less ascriptive.

Correspondingly, as demand for luxury became legitimized, the supply side underwent dramatic changes. Such changes are explored fully in the sectors of fashion, art and wine. As demand for high priced and scarce goods in each of these sectors has increased, in each case key actors have manipulated markets to purposefully either consolidate their pre-eminence or manufacture the requisite scarcity that affords them canonical status.

The demand for and supply of luxury goods is now global; consumers seeking validation and affirmation of their status whilst producers engineer scarcity. Luxury is seen not only as good; it is virtuous, its demand possibly insatiable and extremely profitable.

Ian Malcolm Taplin is Professor of Sociology and International Studies at Wake Forest University and Visiting Professor at Kedge Business School, Bordeaux. He is the author of numerous articles and books on the organization of work in the clothing industry and the evolving structure of markets in the wine industry in Napa California, North Carolina and Bordeaux. He is the North American editor of the *Journal of Fashion Marketing and Management*.

THE EVOLUTION OF LUXURY

Ian Malcolm Taplin

Routledge
Taylor & Francis Group

NEW YORK AND LONDON

First published 2020
by Routledge
52 Vanderbilt Avenue, New York, NY 10017

and by Routledge
2 Park Square, Milton Park, Abingdon, Oxon, OX14 4RN

Routledge is an imprint of the Taylor & Francis Group, an informa business

© 2020 Taylor & Francis

The right of Ian Malcolm Taplin to be identified as author of this work
has been asserted by him in accordance with sections 77 and 78 of the
Copyright, Designs and Patents Act 1988.

Library of Congress Cataloging-in-Publication Data
A catalog record for this title has been requested

ISBN: 978-0-815-38651-3 (hbk)
ISBN: 978-0-367-35122-9 (pbk)
ISBN: 978-0-429-32990-6 (ebk)

Typeset in Bembo
by Lumina Datamatics Limited

To the memory of my parents without whose support and encouragement early in my life, none of this would have been possible.

CONTENTS

List of Tables viii

Acknowledgments ix

1 Introduction 1

2 Luxury in Historical Context 22

3 Industrialism, Materialism and the Birth
of a Consumer Society 42

4 Mass Production, Mass Consumption and New
Consumers of Luxury 65

5 At Home in the Fields of Luxury: From Artisan Production
to Global Brands 84

6 Art: From Aesthetics to Investment Grade Collateral 103

7 Fine Wine: Creating Luxury in a Bottle 125

8 Conclusion: Pilgrims on the Luxury Road 148

Bibliography 159

Index 166

LIST OF TABLES

5.1 Brand value of the top ten luxury brands worldwide   93
5.2 Sales of leading luxury goods companies worldwide in
     million euros, 2012–2016   93

ACKNOWLEDGMENTS

I have learned much from conversations with friends and colleagues about the topic of luxury. Some have made humorous suggestions about researching and writing about a topic such as this; others have offered their opinions and reflections on why they embrace or reject the materialism on offer today. In almost every case though, their comments have caused me to pause and deliberate about how something so ubiquitous continues to intrigue and fascinate. To everyone who has had such conversations with me, I extend my thanks. When asked what I was writing and I responded, there was always a genuine interest in the topic and a desire to know what angle I was taking in my discussion and analysis.

Many specific people have aided me as I embarked upon this project. In the wine industry where much of my recent research has focused I am particularly grateful to Russ Weis, Bill Harlan, Delia Viader and Doug Shafer, all of whom have extensive experience in the Napa Valley wine industry and with whom I have had many conversations about that region's storied history. I have learned much from them, and their insights have been most edifying. I am grateful to Joanne Roberts of the Luxury Research Group at Winchester College of Art for inviting me to give several presentations there and be part of an ongoing dialogue about the evolving nature of luxury in contemporary societies. These conversations have been stimulating, and it has been exciting to be part of an embryonic research agenda that attempts to situate the role of all facets of luxury in contemporary society.

I have benefitted in my understanding of art markets from conversations with gallery owners and museum directors in the United States, France and England. Each in their own way provided often nuanced interpretations of trends as well as basic operational issues that I otherwise would not have considered.

The imperatives of any marketplace are often shrouded by imponderables that an outsider can find bemusing and fascinating. Art markets fit neatly into this category!

Christopher Dandeker and David Yamane read drafts of the manuscript and made valuable comments; thanks to you both and I hope the current finished version adequately reflects their suggestions.

Early versions of chapters were presented in lectures and presentations at University of Surrey, School of Management; Winchester College of Art; Kedge Business School, Bordeaux; SECCA (South Eastern Center for Contemporary Art) (NC); Cameron Art Museum (NC); Sonoma State University, Wine Business Institute; and the Southern Sociological Society Annual Conference, Charlotte NC. I am grateful to all of the people in these institutions who made useful comments on my presentations.

Finally, I owe a huge debt of gratitude to my wife Cindy, mathematician, artist and musician whose range of talents always surpass mine. She has been patient and gracious in tolerating the amount of travel away from home to conduct this research and enthusiastic about its progress. My thanks to her is immeasurable.

1

INTRODUCTION

In 1982 American artist Jean-Michel Basquiat painted a skull (*"Untitled"*), and two years later it was sold at auction to a private collector for $19000. In May 2017, that same painting was at auction again, this time sold by Sotheby's in ten minutes of bidding for $110 million (the pre-sale estimate was $60 million) to a Japanese e-commerce entrepreneur named Yusaku Maezawa. He intends to build his own museum to display this and other paintings. In May 2015 a mystery buyer (speculated to be former Qatari Prime Minister Hamad bin Jassim bin Jaber Al Thani) paid $179.4 million for Picasso's *Les Femmes D'Alger (version O)* at a Christie's auction. The piece remains the most expensive work ever sold at an auction. Whether it will be displayed to the public or stored in a warehouse remains to be seen, as does the motive behind the purchase. No matter what aesthetic beauty resides in this or any painting, the high price paid is part of a recent trend whereby auction houses position art as an investment grade commodity aimed at a select few, often anonymous individuals, who often sequester the painting away until a future date when it can be resold at a presumed higher price.

Leaving the world of fine art, imagine being seated at the dinner table with an august group of friends, partaking of an impeccably prepared meal, you sip on a fine glass of red wine from an outstanding vintage and notable producer. Perhaps you paid $30–40 for the bottle, even $100 if it was a truly celebratory meal. Or if you are a true oenophile, with unlimited funds, you stumped up for a *2014 Domaine de la Romanee Conti, La Tâche* for $2808. After all this wine is available without buying at auction – that is if you can find someone to sell it to you. It comes from one of Burgundy's most famous estates and is characterized by "finesse, balance and refinement." But also, as Vinfolio's online wine store notes in their "Collectibility Index," it has 30 out of 30 for an overall score, 10 out of 10 for price/appreciation, 10 out of 10 for critical acclaim, and 10 out of 10 for scarcity.[1] Perfect scores and not just for its taste. In other words, whatever doubts you had about the wine and your discerning palate its provenance was impeccable. On the other hand, if you have a preference for new world wines then obviously you pour a bottle of *2010 Screaming Eagle* ($3129) ("utter perfection...opulent and full-bodied with a multidimensional personality, gorgeous purity and a stunning, flawless texture"[2]) or if your means are more modest then a *2011 Harlan Estate* ("super expressive and textured in the glass") at $699.[3] Apparently there is something magical about wines from Napa, but limited availability, waiting lists for wine allocation that you will probably never get on, and high price elevate such wines to a level usually seen for classified growths in Bordeaux and Burgundy. How did a beverage, drunk to complement a meal, assume almost iconic status through its high price and extremely limited availability?

Let's go back a few hours to when your guests arrived for dinner. They come from different backgrounds but one of the women appears splendidly stylish with her Hermés *Birkin* bag. You know of it but perhaps didn't realize that it costs somewhere between $10,000 and $129,000. After all it is made from real leather by skilled craftsmen and named after the actress Jane Birkin and launched in 1984. Even though the chief executive of Hermés, Axel Dumas, claims that "it's not about creating scarcity," it's hard to image that the market is flooded by these bags or that this particular one provides a storage function lacking in other bags! This product, like so much of what the firm produces is a quintessential luxury product. It's a high quality, very expensive, extremely difficult to obtain material product that for the lucky owner denotes status, wealth, prestige and all of the other trappings of exclusivity that are perceived to inhere in such goods.

Each of the above is a product that has exhibited different functional properties throughout a long and storied history. But in these cases they have acquired a distinctive status by entering the rarified pantheon of becoming luxurious, available to a select few, treasured by them and envied by others. How this transformation has occurred and why, in an age of mass consumption and mass production, we remain enamored of luxury products and the various manifestations of wealth and status is the subject of this book. Put slightly differently, in an increasingly secular age, why do so many people continue to worship at the altar of conspicuous consumption in the service of class distinctions? Yet if the essence of mass production is the provision of mass commodities, there nonetheless remains a niche marque for the exclusive. Niche products are produced by niche producers – viz Rolls Royce, Bentley and Ferrari in the automobile market.

The concept and reality of *luxury* continue to confound, anger, intrigue, titillate, motivate and demarcate. References to it abound in the daily press, whether it be about extravagant lifestyles, lavish properties or the improbable price paid for a particular item at an art auction. Scholarly debates often invoke Veblen's comments on conspicuous consumption as a defining feature of modern society: they also reference how *luxury* was viewed in derogatory terms as excess in ancient cultures. *Luxury* has, and continues to be, associated pejoratively with indolence, extravagance and often greed. Yet despite the sometimes heated rhetoric over what many feel is ostentatious behavior, we are acutely aware that today it is merely part of the consumer economy that is pervasive, albeit as a niche that attracts disproportionate attention from those seeking to demonstrate and enjoy their enhanced status. It remains controversial because it explicitly deals with goods that are unavailable to the majority of the population. By offering a tantalizing glimpse into the lives of a select few, it implicitly acknowledges that doing so generates lust as well as admonition.

In previous centuries, indulgence in luxuries was seen as a vice and thus a moral problem. It implied extravagance and even sinful behavior. Such sentiments are less resonant in a more secular age where private behavior, particularly consumption, lacks public accountability. Furthermore, society's embrace of the pursuit of self-interest as a motivating force privileges those who are seen to be successful. Adam Smith was quite forthright in acknowledging the motivating rationale of wealth for the select few, even though he had reservations about the morality of excessive inequality. He argued that avarice and ambition, the pursuit of wealth, power and privilege enable one to be observed, noticed and attended to, thus allowing the rich man to glory in his riches.[4] For him, wealth was virtuous since it was a manifestation of one's own ambitions. Its impact was most effective, however, when it contained a powerful "display" function – one's wealth had to be seen and thus acknowledged. As Montgomery and Chirot state in summarizing Smith's argument, "we want to be wealthy to be admired and desired because this is how we feel about the wealthy ourselves."[5] A consumerist ideology that views material gain as a measure of success thus diminishes even informal norms of frugality that occurred in the distant past.

Whatever its connotations luxury has always been a manifestation of basic class differences in society and thus an almost inevitable outcome of a broader issue, that of inequality. As class structures become more fluid, luxury might be viewed less problematically as avarice and thus regulated through sumptuary laws. The pursuit of luxury for a contemporary elite becomes a means to differentiate oneself from the masses and thus a reasonably legitimate form of consumer behavior. The centuries-old decline of fixed hierarchies does not mean the end of inequality, merely a different way in which it becomes legitimized and systematized. Luxury now has lost many of its negative connotations and is seen merely as an expression of desire by those who can afford significant above average standards of living.[6] Ultimately then, luxury is still about inequality, albeit a form that differs in its modus operandi from the past. It continues to be a refuge for the fantasies of the rich and the means whereby they can differentiate themselves from the majority. No matter what detractors say it eulogizes and glorifies excess and remains a vibrant cornerstone in most advanced economies. Wealth and class are synonymous but so-called "genuine" class means style. As such it merits continued investigation.

Despite a widespread implicit understanding of what the term luxury means, it is nonetheless fraught with conceptual ambiguity. It can differ widely according to historical context, cultural reference and the situational experience of particular consumers. At one level it is the vehicle whereby *individuals* situate themselves relative to others in society. It also exists through the activities of *organizations* that produce the goods that are eagerly sought after. Finally, there is a broader *global/societal/institutional* context in which both of the above are deployed. This is where the activities of markets are important in framing and structuring interactions that play off the persistence of inequality. Using this tripartite conceptual framework will allow us to dissect the rare and the familiar that pervade consumer behavior in an age where material well-being for many is greater than at any time in history, but also where heightened riches for a few continue to demarcate the "haves" from the "have lots more."

The urge to differentiate oneself is grounded in consumers' desire for uniqueness – a product of self-perception and a demonstration of material success.[7] The fact that an item is expensive can be a justification in itself for a wealthy person to purchase the product. For as Kapferer has argued, "this is luxury's core, latent sociological role, despite the overt excuses or rationalizations that consumers may provide when asked in surveys why they purchase luxury items for themselves."[8] No matter what continent they live on, wealthy people want to enjoy their wealth and also signal that wealth to others as a mark of their status. Essentially they are purchasing an identity commensurate with their new found wealth. In regions where economic growth has resulted in significant wealth creation and more pronounced inequality, newly rich consumers are responsible for much of the increase in global luxury goods sales. For it is this group that is most actively asserting their new identity and thus exploiting (for them) the benefits of growing inequality. For example, upper income families in China have become empowered as consumers, seeking, as Luca Solca recently argued, "to mark, crystallise and communicate their freshly acquired status. This is where the luxury industry steps in."[9] Consequently, it is this pervasive issue of inequality that continues to frame much of the discussion and analysis of luxury in both emerging and advanced economies.

Luxury continues to figure prominently in the press, albeit in very different and often indirect ways. On the one hand there has been much coverage of issues that are a testament to the continued strength of ultra-wealthy, high net worth (UHNW) individuals. Conversely there have been sobering comments on the persistence of inequality and the growing sense of frustration amongst large swathes of the population who face increased uncertainty over so many aspects of daily life. The plight of the latter has become a central platform for politicians in many western societies with policies pitched at less-educated white males whose jobs have disappeared following the decline of the manufacturing sector. This is the voter rage that underlies Trump's success in the United States as consumers lash out at politicians for apparently failing them. The June 2016 Brexit vote in Britain followed a similar trajectory. In this case many felt their lack of opportunity, limited access to education, lower life expectancy and a visceral feeling that immigrants were taking their jobs and crowding social services, resulted in a "protest" vote to leave the institution that was felt to be, if not directly responsible for such malaise, at least could be identified as a major culprit.

In both countries generalized anger is directed at structural changes in the economy that have left many clinging desperately to the middle class life line that sustained earlier generations but which is now slipping away. It also focuses upon politicians who are deemed insensitive or indifferent to the plight of such individuals. In the United States a 2015 Harris poll showed that 85 percent of Americans believe the people running the country do not care about them and 81 percent thought that the rich were getting richer whilst the poor became even poorer.[10] The "happy citizen consumer" that drove economic growth in the 1970s and 1980s is increasingly disillusioned, certainly not happy, and fraught with anxiety over exactly how much they can afford to consume. As long as US median household incomes remain flat, as they have been for the past two decades, it is difficult to see a silver lining to this collective angst.

In stark contrast to the above, the wealthy continue to become effectively more segregated from the masses, enjoying personalized services in ways that the average person can only vaguely remember. From personalized banking, concierge health services and the ability to interact with an actual human being rather than an automated response system, this group enjoys dramatically different rules and experiences from the average person. The lifestyle benefits of wealth transcend mere acquisition of material goods; they encapsulate a de facto segregation that is cultural as well as socio-economic. Much of the current debate on inequality is referencing this trend.

There have always been those whose wealth singled them out from others so why is this different today? Exactly what sort of wealth levels are we talking about? To give several examples: UK FTSE 100 chief executive salaries have risen by a third since 2010 with an average take home pay of £4.1 million in 2015 – a ratio of 140 times that of average employee's wages. In the US, the median pay of S&P chief executives in 2015 was $10.8 million – 204 times their employees' median compensation.[11]

Inequality, however, is not a twenty-first-century phenomenon. Disparities in income and wealth have always existed but what is salient here is the feeling that a few continue to benefit whilst the majority become progressively excluded from such largesse. The much-maligned 1 percent are perceived to be increasingly insulated from the economic and social uncertainty that bedevils others in society. In other words the reversal of decades of upward mobility has left an increasing segment of the population questioning the meritocratic ideology that sustained social and cultural coherence in western societies. The tremendous increases in living standards in the post-World War II decades, a result of productivity improvements associated with widespread application of Fordist manufacturing principles and then micro-electronic technology have dissipated in the last decade.[12] Now we have increased polarization following the dramatic rise of low wage service sector work as an emerging employment norm accompanying a significant increase in incomes of a select group, notably bankers, health care workers, and senior executives plus some in the legal profession.

While inequality has been pervasive in the past, its underlying rationale was different to that of contemporary times. Autocratic, monarchic and authoritarian societies in the past exhibited vast differences in wealth between rich and poor. But while the underprivileged majority might have harbored considerable grievances, their expectation of a better life was minimal. That has changed in the past 150 years. The growth of industrial capitalism and economic development plus participatory democracy from the late nineteenth century onwards not only unleashed opportunities for many, it also led to a culture of material expectations and consumerism. As a consequence the current criticism of elites is as much a cultural narrative as an economic one inasmuch as it invokes notions of fairness and equity. For the majority non-wealthy, the perception is one of diminishing returns in a system that had implicitly promised material gain in reward for effort and determination. In other words inequality was seen as acceptable as long as one had a chance to elevate one's position and status. When that dissipates, reality sets in and a collective angst emerges and takes center stage.

Part of this narrative of despair is the specter of globalization, which has been seen as contributing to shifts in income distribution. Globalization does appear to have been responsible for increased income inequality in rich countries as many previously well-paid manufacturing jobs have disappeared (relocated to emerging nations) whilst a vigorous growth of service sector work is notable for low wages. As Kay argues, "while it (globalization) enabled people with unique or distinctive skills...to deploy these skills in a wider market, it also intensified competition and depressed earnings for unskilled labour as low-tech manufacturing was able to relocate to low-wage countries."[13] For him the direct and indirect effects of financialization are key to this process or globalization, especially in the US and UK where extraordinary levels of remuneration are in place for high paid financial and corporate executives.

At the same time however, economic growth in China and India has lifted more people out of poverty in the past decade than in any other period of history.[14] In addition to giving many people opportunities hitherto unavailable in these societies, it also fueled further inequality and a concomitant obsession with luxury goods. Whilst an emerging middle class has enthusiastically embraced consumerism in such countries, an increasing number of very wealthy have sought to differentiate themselves through purchasing expensive products and practices, thus mirroring their western elite counter-parts. Chinese consumers (including those in Hong Kong, Macau and Taiwan) purchased 29 percent of total luxury goods worldwide in 2013, ahead of North American (22 percent) and European (20 percent) consumers.[15] Gender plays a role in China, with Chinese women obsessing over their designer bags whilst their male counterparts have provided the German luxury car segment with their most devoted buyers.

Here as well as in countries such as Brazil, India and Russia, rising inequality appears to be a crucial factor in the growth of luxury consumption. Not only is there an increased number of rich people, many are exhibiting the same desire as their Western and Japanese counterparts to accumulate goods that are unique, exclusive, of high quality and very expensive–possessing things that others don't and cannot have. To give an example, just recently in China we have seen the start-up of a luxury ride-hailing service called UCAR Inc. that offers a dedicated fleet of rental cars driven by chauffeurs.[16] This niche market is very different from the cut-throat ride-hailing mass market fought over until recently by Uber and Didi, whose strategies were often to go lower in prices than the competition with the result that both racked up sizable losses since their inception. UCAR unambiguously has targeted the wealthy for whom transportation is not just a means of getting places but essentially the style in which one travels there.

The idea of elite separation from the masses, a singular feature of pre-industrial societies where such distinction was believed to be ordained, has assumed a more fluid form in contemporary society. In pre-industrial societies there was an implicit recognition of a hierarchy that afforded an elite due deference and removed a conscious demarcation effort on their behalf. Luxuries were seen as dangerous and potentially corrupting for the mass of society and thus forbidden by sumptuary laws that restricted such items to the aristocracy and rulers.[17] The Church provided the religious rationale for such actions and cemented its cultural acceptance. The gradual decline of this hierarchical order following industrialization, secularization, democratization and subsequent increased consumption legitimized new classes of wealthy. Lacking the sort of normative and moral justification that kept elites distinct, contemporary societies embrace distinction that is earned rather than inherited (although the latter continues to play a large size role). Fixed, immutable hierarchies were replaced by more fluid ones in which new groups more assertively announced their new position. Perhaps this is why the status markers adopted by the current wealthy are more overt and numerous. The visible markers that are entailed are the logical extension of consumer culture as well as a product of new production systems. Luxury has been reinvented without the medieval moral opprobrium and instead is indicative of transcendence and longing through the experience of buying. It is simultaneously a symbol of power for those who have experienced social and economic ascendency, as well as a legitimating tool for the newly privileged whose cultural insecurity often necessitates acknowledged markers.

Evidence of these modernizing trends can be seen in the organizations that operate in global markets producing the requisite luxury goods to satisfy the needs of eager consumers. Luxury fashion (clothing and accessories), the market for art and fine wine are each a material manifestation of the products that have assumed such normative distinction in the lives of the few who can afford them. These are the three themes that will be investigated in this book inasmuch as each reveals a dimension on how luxury has been become an integral commodity in an age of sustained inequality. These various facets of luxury consumption are part of a process whereby contemporary elites and the super-rich assert and reinforce their status. By enjoying the benefits of privilege and exclusivity, and in larger numbers than ever before, they have transformed the way goods are made and given others iconic status. The manufacturing of luxury has become an industry itself; a system that is increasingly global in scale and scope and technologically sophisticated. Pervasive marketing campaigns have created "brands" that emphasize the uniqueness of tradition combined with the effectiveness of a modern business.[18]

Luxury Fashion

Fashion is synonymous with style and refers to a way of behaving, specifically here in terms of what one wears and how accepted that is by many members of a group.[19] We communicate through clothing and it becomes a visual narrative of our life. The prevailing sense of dress at a particular place and time is also a product of accepted cultural values.[20] It has also been used as a marker of one's identity, whether oppositional by deliberately deviating from the sartorial norm, or as a way of demonstrating distinctive signs of authority.[21] We use clothes in multiple ways: to protect ourselves, make work easier, to attract attention and to proclaim or disguise our identity.[22]

Fashion is one of the sectors easily associated with luxury and inequality since the dress of elites unambiguously demonstrated their elevated position and those of the working poor told everything about their status. For most people traditionally clothes were homespun garments made by and for the people who wore them. The wealthy had their clothes custom made, generally by local skilled artisans. The industrial revolution transformed the textile and eventually clothing industry by introducing factory production and scale economies that lowered the price of fabric and ultimately that of garment manufacture. More and more people bought ready-made clothing. For the wealthy, clothing remained custom made but gradually assumed a less parochial and more systematized production form. This is exemplified in women's wear by the development of so-called "fashion houses."[23]

The transformation in the late nineteenth century intimated above presaged the business model of haute couture, attributed by many to Charles Frederick Worth around 1858, that rationalized dress making techniques and laid the foundations for today's industry.[24] Specifically, Worth offered his clients something that was distinctive which could demonstrate their importance. This was consistent with the ways elites in the past had used clothes to signal their status difference but here was an evolving industry based upon originality and uniqueness that was nonetheless embracing a more commodified production system. Alongside the high level of craftsmanship, Worth offered, according to Dirix, "luxurious, innovative and exquisite garments" all at a price well beyond the reach of normal consumers.[25] Arguably an artisanal industry at its inception, increasingly it adopted the practices and production systems that characterize industrial capitalism. It did this in order to meet the growing demand for luxury products amongst the twentieth-century elite.

As the twentieth century progressed, increasing consumerism was the outgrowth of technological and organizational changes associated with Fordist mass production and mass distribution. Advertising created consumer desire and newly affluent groups were able to break away from the stylized conformity of previous generations. The Department Store became the emporiums for the masses; clothing brands became ubiquitous, often displayed proudly by logos on garments that easily communicated who you are by what brands you wear. The qualitative expansion of available clothing, plus its increased quantity at an affordable price facilitated using clothes for more fluid identity construction. But the more egalitarian access to fashion became, the more a parallel growth of a luxury goods sector that explicitly catered to the rich evolved.

While mass produced fashionable clothing has been successfully marketed through simple yet often provocative advertising, small luxury goods companies relied upon the elusive nature of their product. Their scale was limited, products highly crafted in artisanal settings, and often sold to a select group of individuals "in the know." They were selling lifestyles rather simply appealing to the more fluid identities of young consumers. Hitherto the domain of small family run firms, by the 1980s a process of consolidation started that continues today. There is a parallel here between the mass and niche market for automobiles, even though many of the niche players are part of mass producing conglomerates.[26]

Faced with the prospect of a larger global market for luxury goods, two significant events occurred. First many of the smaller firms were acquired by conglomerates who introduced new staff and a corporate mindset that focused more on profitability derived from rationalized supply chains and synergistic production efficiencies. Second, they embraced global retailing ambitions, marketing extensively and expensively worldwide in an effort to build the brand. An increasingly globalized marketplace required greater capital investments and organizational resources behind brand building. This has resulted in a smaller number of firms who account for a large share of the multi-billion dollar luxury industry. LVMH, Hermes, Kering (owners of Gucci and Bottega Veneta) Prada and Burberry are a few of the best know examples. Each has a similar business model that emphasizes craftsmanship and uniqueness plus non-comparability and charging a high price for the experience.[27]

In many respects Frenchman Bernard Arnault epitomized this transformation when he set about designing the *business* of fashion.[28] Acquiring small fashion houses he was eventually able to build the LVMH conglomerate that relied upon a multi brand strategy to ensure constant growth with a stable of newer acquisitions offsetting any slack in its other brands. A similar strategy was pursued by other conglomerates such as Richemont and Kering.

In the past decade the sales growth of the top ten conglomerates has been superior to that of the other major companies in this sector.[29] The scale efficiencies in areas such as sourcing, distribution and marketing are clearly beneficial to such conglomerates. Their strategies have embraced diversification and the creation of a broad portfolio of signature brands. This broad portfolio, often in diverse sectors such as wine, watches, luggage and clothing sustain their legitimacy by placing emphasis upon long traditions of craftsmanship, quality and exclusivity.

In catering to the wealthy, they were offering an elite product, whose scarcity and high-price limited consumption to a small select group of individuals. This form of referential self-identification means luxury goods companies simultaneously cater to the elite demand for status as well as shaping that market. But does exclusivity inevitably become diluted with increased market share following their global reach and scale? Brand positioning, continuing to build product rarity as the market place expands, and manufacturing larger quantities without sacrificing the supposed artisanal heritage are all problems many luxury goods firms face. Can they continue to be purveyors of distinctive goods when the market has grown so fast? Should they look to new customers with lower priced entry level products (so-called aspirational luxury) or does this diminish the value of the brand? Finally, have such strategies transformed luxury goods into a commodity?

These are questions that continue to confound some in the industry. One answer, however, takes us back to our original discussion of inequality. Rolex unambiguously asserts that the goal of its advertisements is not to sell Rolexes but make those who have the means to buy a Rolex happy that others, who do not have the means, nonetheless know what Rolex means. Or perhaps even less subtly put, a recent television commercial features a passenger in the coach section of the plane enviously eyeing the first-class section. When he approaches that section an officious flight attendant brusquely closes the curtain separating the section and the caption on the screen reads "The purpose of first class is to remind most people that they are not first class." If ever there were paeans to status envy, these are clearly them.

Market for Art

Art is another area with a unique market where one of a kind objects have acquired commercial status, thus transforming a longstanding patron–client relationship into a cash nexus mediated by auction houses and mega galleries.

For centuries painters had patrons who sustained them financially by providing stipends or who commissioned works that were then dispatched to religious institutions as indulgences or even penance for earlier sins. The painters and sculptors were willing to oblige by producing images inspired by sacred texts that would encourage reverential contemplation in churches and public spaces. Occasionally they were able to meet the demand for erotic art, often salacious nude depictions that aristocrats commissioned for their "private" viewing. Titian's "Venus of Urbino" (1538), painted for the Duke of Urbino to hang in his bedroom and to be viewed by a select number of guests is a perfect example of this and was deemed sufficiently sensual that it led to further commissions of a similar "genre."[30] A similar sentiment existed in the world of music where Mozart, who apparently disliked the flute as an instrument, nonetheless wrote flute concertos because he was paid a considerable amount of money to do so. For all their aesthetic splendor, Renaissance painters had clearly delineated markets for their product and were enthusiastic adherents to a system of clientelism that was unambiguously supply and demand structured. Eventually the church was replaced by wealthy merchants and landowners who wanted depictions of themselves to display their power and wealth. Artists such as Gainsborough, Holbein and Van Eyck were more than happy to oblige with such commissions.

By the nineteenth century artists started to liberate art from the conventional forms and realistic depictions of nature and in doing so shocked and surprised clients and the establishment. Although individuals and institutions continued to acquire art, there was greater uncertainty as to its aesthetic status and even its intrinsic value became more circumspect. It was as if artists were freeing themselves from the received aesthetic dictates of the past, casting aside convention and embracing a freedom of form that was a reaction to industrialism as well as its embrace. For collectors who increasingly made up the ranks of patrons, the challenge was self-referential – identifying someone you liked and justifying that decision on looser aesthetic grounds than in the past.

More dramatic changes occurred during the early decades of the twentieth century. Industrialized warfare, technological changes, massive unemployment and socio-political unrest resulted in an erosion in the earlier confidence of modernization and the presumed socio-economic benefits of industrialization. Artists positioned themselves at the cross roads of this cultural crisis. Some opposed, excoriated and sought to subvert the process; others affirmed its vitality and glorified its implicit rationale. In their own ways they were questioning the function of art and its market. For whom were the paintings or sculptures intended? Was the supreme purpose that of shock, as the Dadaists claimed, with evident disregard for any commercial value to be attributed to art? Or was all of this mere propaganda designed to bring attention to artists so they could sell more in a marketplace where traditional patronage had dissipated and new types of buyers were emerging?

Modernism in particular had attempted to redefine the purpose of art by conceiving it as an overt vehicle for ideological expression and protest (Duchamp's "Urinal" and Picasso's "Guernica" being good examples of this trend). There was confusion about what paintings meant (titles were often as mystifying as the paintings themselves) and the "shock of the new," to use Robert Hughes book title,[31] confounded many who assumed that art should not be visually challenging and of uncertain cultural provenance. The intellectual and aesthetic poverty of modernism provided fuel for critics but it did little to dampen the enthusiasm of many who were eager to embrace new ideas in a changing marketplace. In fact artists were often denigrated for not embracing a critical, oppositional stance to the received aesthetic culture. For example American painter Andrew Wyeth was dismissed as a purveyor of regional nostalgia because of his realistic depictions of rural America.

The past few decades have seen greater acceptance of non-conventional forms and oppositional art, with movements such as Abstract Expressionism, Pop Art and most recently conceptual art such as that by Damien Hirst and Jeff Koons entering the mainstream. Arguably the counter-cultural beast has been tamed and commodified like their counterparts in the past. This is precisely what literary scholar Frederic Jameson argued when he claimed "aesthetic production...has become integrated into commodity-production" and high and low culture synthesized to have the broadest appeal possible.[32] Restored consumer confidence in contemporary art's marketability also mirrors subtle change in the motivations of buyers as well as continuing changes in the marketplace for art. Art's one-of-a-kind status continued to confer a symbolic value providing there were enough people willing to take a chance.

By the late 1970s art had begun to assume status as a formal investment tool; a way of diversifying and hedging ones portfolio away from normal financial products. Wealthy people in the past bought art because it spoke to them in visual terms; now many purchasers were looking for a return on their investment. Auction houses and mega galleries now position themselves as arbiters of taste by simultaneously commodifying the product as well as restricting its supply. They cater to a select global group of "super rich" whose acquisitive drive for art is often top of their needs list – true trophy products because of their uniqueness and rarity.[33] This group and the institutions that cater to them are driving interest in and demand for certain types of art.[34] Such individuals treat art as an investment grade product that nonetheless confers the requisite status on their new found wealth. Art markets have thus been transformed with the product itself granted a more ambiguous status (visual icon or illiquid asset that can yield future profit). But even if art has become a tool or a place to park one's money, there remain many people who use it to display to select peer audiences as a visual marker of their position and power.

Historically art occupied the realm of exclusivity inasmuch as it was in finite supply. It has been a product that the wealthy acquired to keep for themselves or donate to religious institutions to salve their conscience. It became a valuable aesthetic commodity because of this differential demand and its status as luxury good solidified when certain artists proved more popular than others. Increasingly art was used to validate the status of the newly wealthy merchants, who used self-portraits as a way of announcing their arrival on the social scene. As form and content changed in the twentieth century, the art of certain artists became investment instruments for the wealthy. It was acquired as much for its marketability and presumed "financial" value as it was for any visual splendor. Top artists are a fraction of the total number of artists worldwide, but they are the producers of a luxury good that is affordable by a select group of individuals (and sometimes institutions). The market for investment grade art exploded by the late twentieth century, driven by a global set of super-rich individuals, institutions such as auction houses and galleries that market the hype, and key artists who have capitalized upon this more overt commercial trend. Contemporary art for some is the must have item, not to be viewed or even donated but to be locked away in hermetically sealed storage to be sold at a profit in future years.

Fine Wine

The third area in our story of luxury markets is that of fine wine. A beverage of choice for many millennia, it has been transformed in the past century into a commodity that has become global in scope with production and consumption increasing in the New World although declining somewhat in southern European countries in the last decade. As with most products it comes in different price ranges with varying degrees of quality. Of interest to us are wines that occupy the upper echelons – those with pedigree, excellent quality, high price and limited availability that are sought after by a small segment of the population. Such wines are typically bought by aficionados who both appreciate high quality and have the financial means to purchase them. They are also being bought by individuals for whom possession of fine wine and a trophy cellar is a mark of distinction. Together, both of these groups are driving the growth of ultra-premium wine purchasing.

It is to monks that one can trace wine's growth in medieval Europe, particularly the Benedictines for upgrading the quality and the Cistercians (founded in 1098) that turned viticulture into a commercial venture.[35] Monks needed wine for three purposes: for the Eucharist at masses, as a complement to meals and as a beverage in their food and drink hospitality obligations. Arguably their early commitment to high quality was because of wine's high symbolic value in masses – only the best should be served. Added to all of this was the lack of reliable potable drinking water; therefore it is not surprising that wine became such a central part of life in European countries. But even back in Roman times wine had acquired a luxury status, the best wine being served at banquets.

Since then certain regions such as Bordeaux and Burgundy in France and Tuscany in Italy have become synonymous with fine wine. And in recent decades some wines from the new world such as Napa Valley California have risen to iconic status. In each case wineries emphasize the uniqueness of location (the mysterious *terroir*), their tradition and reputation, high scores from experts and/or a particular varietal blend as a source of differentiation.

What exactly is a truly exceptional wine that renders it in the category of a luxury good? How does one recognize quality in a product that is susceptible to individual palate and taste variation? In 1855 the French developed a classification system to rank wines from the Bordeaux region. Wine industry brokers ranked the wines according to the chateau's reputation and trading price since this was the informally accepted indication of quality. This classification, with a few recent additions, remains the benchmark for quality in the region and the basis for continuing to charge very high prices. In recent decades, as wine consumption increased in the United States, expert oenophiles developed a numerical scoring system to signify quality to a public that was insecure in their knowledge of wine. Whilst the scores often accompanied more detailed descriptions of body and flavor profiles, the numbers are the key marker of excellence that are used by many to make a purchase decision.

The more familiar one becomes with wine the more a wine's provenance is important since where it is produced (the *terroir*) influences the characteristics that partly define its quality. That and the techniques that go into actual viticulture and winemaking are the crucial components. However, once a geographic area is noted for having the right conditions for making an excellent-quality wine, it acquires an increasingly reverential status in the minds of connoisseurs. When this is achieved other factors contribute to some wines' luxury status by enhancing and emphasizing its distinctiveness. They are typically high price, small scale production, limited availability (wine sold on allocation to select lists of customers), and consistently high scores by experts. Together these evoke a unique and rare product, the quality of which has been endorsed by official taste arbiters. Finally, the overall specificity of a particular wine relies upon a series of related stories and symbolic meanings associated with its owner, winemaker and general aesthetic that further substantiate its distinctive character. Together, each of these contribute to the development of a brand and this can be seen in the recent growth to cult status of certain wines in Napa Valley, California.[36]

It is important to note that wine is an everyday beverage in many regions of the world even though some still might think it constitutes an extravagance. Despite such an image of indulgence it is generally an affordable drink that complements food. However, in recent years there has been significant growth in the premium and ultra-premium segment as customers apparently trade up in their preferences. Having become more knowledgeable about wine, many consumers are becoming more discerning buyers willing to pay more for wine. Quality/price ratios are important determinants in consumer behavior and it is not surprising that wine consumers behave accordingly. What is notable, however has been some of the fastest growth in demand for very high-end wines. Such wines are very expensive and difficult to obtain and represent the pinnacle of recognized oeonological excellence. In recent years much of this growth has come from Asian buyers but that has merely consolidated continued demand from western consumers with more established taste preferences and in the case of the United States a newly found knowledge of fine wines.[37] Asian buyers are more likely to buy recognized brands (particularly wines from first-growth Bordeaux chateaux) whereas American buyers show a wider preference that includes cult Napa wines.

As noted earlier, customers for the most expensive wines generally fall into two categories: those who are wine connoisseurs, and those who enjoy wine but also use it as a status marker. Sometimes the latter are referred to as "aspirers" inasmuch as their purchasing habits are motivated by their external effect on other people – owning fine wine is a demonstration of one's social and economic status.[38] For such individuals high price and high scores for wines are the important indicators of quality. Once purchased such individuals frequently build lavish cellars to display their wine and use such a setting to display and thus consolidate their status.

Wine is an important indicator of status since it confers an aura of sophistication and worldliness. Expensive wines suggest a knowledge and understanding of a product that in many respects remain the domain of the expert. It has become a positional good, a luxury product available to connoisseurs but also aspirational consumers for whom price is an important determinant of prestige and quality.[39] Wines of iconic status (first growth Bordeaux, certain Burgundies, cult wines from Napa Valley, California and Italian wines such as Barolos and Super Tuscans) are at the apex of such lists. Being able to buy such wines of extremely limited availability requires financial resources. Many such individuals however, make such purchases when they deem it advantageous to their social standing.[40] In doing so they are responding to wine producers who continue to build the credibility of their brand through the emphasis upon its inherent luxury status. Such producers have crafted a unique image for a product using basic marketing techniques as well as making themselves distinct from industrial scale production that marks high volume wine companies.[41] Above all their emphasis upon authenticity enables them to command high prices and define the competitive landscape in terms of being specialist organizations in an otherwise broad field of generalists.[42] This form of resource positioning by such firms is part of their success in manufacturing an image of distinctiveness in an industry otherwise dominated by high volume and inexpensive producers – an apparent disavowal of commercialism and rational production in favor of artisanal sincerity. As such, these wines can enter the pantheon of greatness and display the experiential, functional and symbolic value that attracts those seeking luxury goods.[43]

Individuals, Organizations and Globalization

In each of the three areas briefly discussed, there is a common theme as wealthy individuals acquire expensive products that satisfy their desire to possess as well as communicate their status to others. This is certainly consistent with what Veblen argued regarding conspicuous consumption, as well as Bourdieu's work on distinction. Inequality continues to be a principal driver in the process of luxury consumption inasmuch as it enables a select group of individuals in a society to afford unique and expensive products. But the process is more fluid than before, and it resonates with greater cultural vitality than in previous centuries. Unlike much of the past when luxury was seen in a more negative light, today it is a pervasive part of the consumer society. Pre-ordained hierarchies provided a normative rationale for divisions in traditional societies, even if overt and enthusiastic display of such possessions were typically frowned upon. Nowadays such goods are eagerly sought to further confer status and provide visual markers of one's position in society. How might we explain such a transformation of the role of luxury in society?

The advent of industrialization, more social mobility and fluid social structures have rendered status more ambiguous and less proscribed. It has also created greater wealth for a larger segment of the population. Increased buying power by such groups has led to a proliferation of objects and lifestyles that are indicative of elevated status. Moreover, luxury has become much more central to everyday life than before, celebrated in the press and enthusiastically aspired towards by many. The dynamic of consumer culture has eroded many of the sumptuary restrictions that plagued earlier societies and resulted in negative connotations. Today, luxury is omnipresent, generally accepted as means whereby the wealthy can express themselves. It has become more widely accepted partly because its perceived accessibility has increased. That and the fact that there are more and more "entry level" luxury goods available for those who aspire to a luxury lifestyle but lack the financial means to fully realize it. According to some, luxury has been democratized through more affordable entry level products.[44] For others, such accessibility means it has lost its allure.[45] In either case we can see the power that a hitherto elusive concept has been able to exercise in contemporary society. It is what Featherstone refers to as the transformational aspects of glamour: the illusionary and fetish power of objects that are designed to allure.[46]

Twentieth-century consumer culture was made possible by technological changes in manufacturing, notably the growth of mass production and mass distribution of relatively inexpensive goods. But in recent decades there has been a dramatic increase in high priced products in limited supply and supposedly of exquisite quality. In other words a luxury goods production industry emerged, simultaneously supplying an increased demand for status goods as well as stoking the desire in the first place.

As a result of these trends a number of issues merit discussion. Firstly, what type of goods are being sold and how are the firms/industries that sell them organized? Secondly, do the new rich constitute a different type of consumer to their counterparts in the past? If so how might one explain such a difference? This addresses variations in the individual behavioral aspects that relate to the final issue, notably how have globalization and various institutional forces shaped the nature of markets for these products?

In terms of globalization, overall growth (and profitability) of luxury firms and the consumption of luxury goods continues to rise despite a brief slowdown following the 2008 financial crisis.[47] The United States and Europe combined remain the largest market for luxury goods as well as being the site of the major producers of luxury goods. Japan, despite a slowdown in consumer spending in recent years, follows close behind as a major market for luxury goods purchases. However, the rise of new markets in the Asia Pacific region, particularly China, accounts for much of the disproportionate growth during the past decade. High rates of economic growth in China accompanied by increased inequality and dramatic concentrations of wealth (after the United States, China has the largest number of billionaires) have stimulated consumption on an unparalleled scale. Even the newly minted upper middle class in that country appears obsessed with luxury goods albeit through selective purchase of key items.

The global market for luxury goods continues to grow and yet questions abound as to whether such mass marketing of luxury goods dilute the exclusivity of the products that drove demand in the past. Can luxury goods be simultaneously widely available and "rare" – the latter perhaps one of the defining features that separates luxury from "commodities?" Is the consumption of luxury part of the "trading up" phenomenon that occurs as economic growth generates a broader upper middle class but which can quickly fall out of favor when economic conditions sour? Answers to these questions are a crucial part of this book's focus.

In the next chapter I discuss luxury in a broader historical context, examining the role that it traditionally played as a signifier of wealth and status for a small elite and how that wealth was used to mitigate any moral (or spiritual) opprobrium that accompanied it. We note how the function of luxury goods has changed from earlier societies when it was associated with avarice and sumptuary laws regulated many aspects of its display to contemporary consumer materialism where its intended purpose is almost the opposite of earlier manifestations. While remaining a status good, luxury is gradually being redefined as a commodity associated with aspirational lifestyles associated with an upwardly mobile middle class as well as the material means for the "new rich" to substantiate their heightened status. In emerging economies this group seeks the validation of their newfound wealth in traditional markers; in wealthy nations an expanding consumer economy confers purchasing privileges on individuals whose financial gains have encouraged them to embrace conspicuous displays of such wealth.

Part of this discussion inevitably involves understanding the growth of consumer culture in the west following industrialization, mass production and mass consumption. Coinciding with, and a product of economic changes that bestowed more discretionary income for larger groups of the population, consumer culture became an important tool in the process of more fluid identity creation. Increasingly people have the means to express themselves more visibly through their possessions and attire. In promoting an ideology of consumption ("false needs"), capitalist societies facilitated identity construction through consumption – a shift from fixed status groups to more mobile identities in part constructed through dynamic patterns of consumption. Fashion became an important tool in this process because it enabled individuals to visually demarcate themselves from others in ways that others could not afford to replicate. Understanding how these changes in consumerism are linked with fluid lifestyles is the subject of Chapters 3 and 4. How has the growth of more sophisticated notions of "lifestyles," easily manipulated and altered through changing patterns of consumption, shaped changes in the production process of luxury goods? Relatedly, technological transformations have dramatically improved segmented marketing targeting key groups of consumers provide sophisticated levels of consumer seduction.

We are also witnessing a divergence in the luxury market, between the more widely available and extensively marketed affordable luxury goods and those that remain exclusive, rare and extremely expensive. Both segments have shown resilience and are similar (status desire) and yet different in that they constitute different types of products that actually serve different markets. While luxury has never been associated with value, it continues to confer status in ways that are valuable. Status competition appears to be alive and well and this continues to drive luxury sales.

With steady growth in the demand for luxury goods, what organizational changes have occurred on the production side? In the next three chapters I examine luxury fashion, the market for art and fine wine. Examples from each of these areas will enable us to explore the link between individual status seeking behavior, firm responses as they shape and satisfy these compulsions, and the broader institutional environment and global normative framework that sustains such activity. I also discuss how this increased demand inevitably poses problems since it potentially undermines the scarcity value of such goods in the first place. How can one simultaneously satisfy a growing market for such products without undermining the essential criteria of exclusivity? Responses to this conundrum vary. For fashion houses, an increasing emphasis upon the brand and its aura of exclusivity conceals the inevitable rationalization of production that is necessary to meet this burgeoning market. Distinct brand identity ensures a global reputation and facilitates sales to newly prosperous generations in emerging economies alongside traditional western markets in Europe and North America. Much of this has involved industry consolidation as key firms play an important role in defining what luxury is and having the global reach to penetrate diverse markets. Heritage of craftsmanship, premium quality, unique and innovative products go hand in hand with tightly controlled distribution, manufacturing synergies and premium pricing.

In the areas of fine wine and contemporary art, new luxury products are introduced and legitimized by official arbiters of taste (wine critics and galleries/auction houses) to endorse the quality and rarity of such products. Of key importance here is the way in which such goods have been purposefully created or manipulated to satisfy a perceived demand. Stripped of any religious significance or moral suasion art becomes yet another component in a secular material culture where value is assigned via market mechanisms and the actors who coordinate this exchange. Similarly fine wine becomes a collectible commodity that denotes an aura of sophistication for an owner with a visually impressive and architecturally profound cellar. The high costs and subsequent value of art and fine wine can defy the normal logic of depreciation and become assets that can increase in value. Such products are sought out for their intrinsic value as status goods but also as part of an investment portfolio for further wealth creation. This consumption strategy gives us an additional twist on luxury's function – simultaneously a commodity that confers envy and enables differentiation but also one that can now further the very inequality that has endowed luxury with its current vitality.

Understanding the manufacturing of luxury is crucial since it allows us to comprehend how new consumers are urged to use such products as part of their re-imaged lifestyles. It also relates back to the standpoint of the consumer. For as Berry argues, "luxury is an inducement to consumption" thus it must provoke sufficient desire that transcends basic needs.[48] The urge to differentiate oneself appears to be somewhat universal in modern society and consumption is very much related to that in late capitalism, *ipso facto* there is an element of luxury goods consumption that is universal and an element that is more particular (based on having the means to consume). All indications suggests that the desire for and the financial ability to attain, luxury products will continue to be part of a modern society that experiences growth and continued inequality. Moreover, no matter how much criticism is heaped upon an elite that does little to hide its conspicuous consumption, there are sufficient numbers of consumers who enthusiastically embrace opportunities to emulate at least some of that lifestyle.

Notes

1 https://www.vinfolio.com/producer/drc.
2 Wine Advocate.
3 Vinous/Antonio Galloni.
4 Smith, A. *The Theory of Moral Sentiments*, 1984.
5 Montgomery, S.L. and Chirot, D. *The Shape of the New*, Princeton: Princeton University Press, 2015, p. 40.

6 Sombart, W. *Luxury and Capitalism*, Ann Arbor: University of Michigan Press, 1967.

7 Snyder, C.R. "Product scarcity by need for uniqueness interaction: A consumer catch-22 carousel?," in *Basic and Applied Social Psychology*, January 13, 1992, pp. 9–24.

8 Kapferer, J.-N. "Abundant rarity: The key to luxury growth," in *Business Horizons*, 2012, 55, pp. 453–62.

9 Solca, L. "The rich don't drive the luxury sector," *Business of Fashion*, August 23, 2016, p. 1.

10 Quoted in Rachman, G. "Trump and Brexit feed off the same anger," in *The Financial Times*, August 1, 2016.

11 Cotterill, J. "Blue-chip bosses" £5.5m pay packets bolster UK premier's crackdown calls," *The Financial Times*, August 8, 2016, p. 1.

12 Coates, D. *Capitalism, A Brief Introduction*, 2016.

13 Kay, J. *Other People's Money*, New York: Public Affairs, 2015, p. 51.

14 Ibid, p. 51.

15 Bain and Company, *Bain Survey of Chinese Luxury Goods Consumers*, 2013. http://www.bain.com 2013.

16 Wu, K. "Luxury ride-hailing service gains speed," in *Wall Street Journal*, August 5, 2016. B6.

17 Feasherstone, M. "Luxury, consumer culture and sumptuary dynamics," in *Luxury: History, Consumption and Culture*, January 1, 2014, p. 50.

18 Okonkwo, U. *Luxury Fashion Branding*, New York: Palgrave Macmillan, 2007, p. 3.

19 Yurchisin, J. and K.P. Johnson, *Fashion and the Consumer*, Oxford: Berg, 2010, p. 1.

20 Kawamura, Y. *Fashion-ology*, Oxford: Berg, 2005, p. 4.

21 See Davis, F. *Fashion, Culture and Identity*, Chicago: University of Chicago Press, 1992; Edwards, T. *Fashion in Focus*, London: Routledge, 2011.

22 Lurie, A. *The Language of Clothes*, New York: Vintage Books, 1981. p. 27.

23 Kawamura, op. cit.

24 Dirix, E. *Dressing the Decades*, New Haven: Yale University Press, 2016.

25 Ibid., p. 007.

26 For example, VW owns Bentley, Rolls Royce is a wholly owned subsidiary of BMW and Fiat owns Ferrari.

27 Karpik, L. and Scott, N. *Valuing the Unique*, Princeton: Princeton University Press, 2010.

28 Chada, R. and Husband, P. *The Cult of the Luxury Brand*, London: Nicholas Breeley, 2006, p. 27.

29 Deloitte, "Global power of luxury goods" 2014.

30 Jardine, L. *Worldly Goods. A New History of the Renaissance*, New York: WW Norton, 1996.

31 Hughes, R. *The Shock of the New*, New York: Knopf, 1981.

32 Quoted in J. Rothenberg, *Sociology Looks at the Arts*, New York: Routledge, 2014, pp. 213–14.

33 Adam, G. *Big Bucks: The Explosion of the Art Market in the Twenty-First Century*, London: Lund Humphries, 2014.

34 Zaniol, G. "Brand art sensation", in *Cultural Politics*, January 12, 2016, p. 49.

35 Chapuis, C. and Charters, S. "The world of wine" in Charters, S. and Gallo, J. (Eds.) *Wine Business Management*, Paris, Pearson France, 2014.

36 Taplin, Ian M. "Crafting an iconic wine: The rise of "cult" Napa," in *International Journal of Wine Business Research*, February 28, 2016, pp. 105–19.

37 Evans, S. "Treasury Wine's $800 million pot of gold in luxury wines as Asia booms," in *Sydney Morning Herald*, August 16, 2016.

38 Heine, K., Atwal, G. and Ates, Z. "Luxury wine marketing," in Charters and Gallo, op. cit., p. 239.

39 Beverland, M. "Uncovering 'theories-in-use': Building luxury wine brands," in *European Journal of Marketing*, 2004, 38, 3/4, p. 450.

40 Beverland, ibid., p. 451.

41 Beverland, M. "Crafting brand authenticity: The case of luxury wines," in *Journal of Management Studies*, 2005, 42/5, p. 1004.

42 See Carroll, G. and Swaminathan, A. "Why the micro-brewery movement? Organizational dynamics of resource positioning in the U.S. brewing industry," in *American Journal of Sociology*, 2000, 3, pp. 715–62.

43 Berthon, P., Pitt, L., Parent, M. and Berthon, J.-P "Aesthetics and ephemarility: Observing and preserving the luxury brand," in *California Management Review*, 2009, 52/1, p. 49.

44 Faiers, J. "Editorial introduction," in *Luxury: History, Consumption and Culture*, January 1, 2014, pp. 5–13; Featherstone, M. op. cit.

45 Thomas, D. *DELUXE: How Luxury Lost its Lustre*, London: Penguin Books, 2007.

46 Featherstone, op. cit., p. 52.

47 Deloitte, *Global Power of Luxury Goods*, 2014.

48 Berry, Christopher, *The Idea of Luxury*, Cambridge: Cambridge University Press, 1994, p. 5.

2

LUXURY IN HISTORICAL CONTEXT

The city creates luxury, from which avarice inevitably springs, while from avarice audacity breaks forth, the source of all crimes and misdeeds

Cicero, *Pro Sexto Roscio Amerino*

O foule lusts of luxurie

Chaucer, *Man of law tale*

Sumptuary laws represent the highest impertinence and presumption on the part of kings and ministers in their effort to watch over the economy of private people
    The desire of bettering our conditions is a desire which comes with us from the womb and never leaves us till we go to the grave

Smith, *The Wealth of Nations*

A vice or a virtue? Throughout history attitudes towards luxury have encompassed all points on the moral and intellectual spectrum depending on the institutional framework and the socio-cultural context. Rooted in the basic response to the conundrum of what constitutes a need (food, drink, clothing and shelter) versus a desire (non-essential and superfluous), societies have often sought to normatively prescribe behavior and consumption habits as part of overall attempts to regulate morality. Sometimes this entailed the invocation of religious concerns and prescripts (against avarice); in others secular attitudes towards the preservation of community stability were emphasized. By heaping opprobrium on the idea of luxury, Cato the Elder followed by Plato reinforced the ancients' condemnation of luxury by variously equating it with extravagance, licentiousness and even effeminacy.[1] Such behavior was seen as fundamentally destructive of social cohesion since it undermined the cooperative interdependence of the *polis* by encouraging people to pursue more than their basic needs.[2] But far from dissipating luxury pursuits, it often redirected and obfuscated such actions, cloaking material excess under a panoply of quasi-religious fervor or as a demonstration of civic virtue. The former suggested vindication by the gods, the latter a self-serving way of subtly cementing a positional marker.

In today's western society our conceptions and acceptance of luxury are remarkably different. It is thought of as something exclusive, rare and undoubtedly very expensive – the privilege of the few – but not in such censorious terms as before. No matter how much the accumulation of such goods or lifestyles might elicit disparaging remarks by some, most neither question the legitimacy of such excess or that it might entail some form of moral depravity that is disruptive to society. The fact that this is a marked departure from earlier positions suggests a dramatic reversal of broader societal norms and a fundamentally different way of viewing human instrumentality. Luxury is now seen as an intrinsic by-product of inequality which *mutatis mutandis* reflects broader institutional parameters that frame and legitimize social interaction. The pursuit of luxury is accepted as normal, notwithstanding a groundswell of critique and contempt of the bankrupt (morally not financially) elite following the crash of 2008. If our attitudes towards, and even our definition of, luxury differs from previous times in part it is because we view inequality in a very different light and our societies lack the universal moral narrative that disciplined and sanctioned errant behavior. We might despair of the gap between the rich and the poor and view the flaunting of wealth in a pejorative light, but we also recognize that the manifestations of inequality are no longer a matter of divine providence or pervasive ascriptive traditions. No matter how divisive inequality is in contemporary times, it lacks the moral certainty by which past hierarchies were culturally prescribed, normatively sanctioned and materially decisive. Even if mobility today is viewed as a self-serving platitude that reinforces the aura of material well-being for the majority, it is nonetheless accepted *ex cathedra* as the legitimating force behind social structuring. It is both servile and possibly pernicious whilst at the same time enshrined in a laudable testament to material progress.

Over the past century, many societies in the west have promoted social mobility and encouraged greater income equality by various fiscal, educational and welfare policies. They sought to abandon the fixed hierarchies that firmly stratified pre-industrial societies and produced rigid status positions. In doing so, individuals were encouraged to pursue their own agendas, to maximize their self interest in ways that would presumably lead to a greater good for the many. This paean to initiative was the cornerstone of twentieth-century materialism whereby individual success could be measured by the accumulation of goods. The resulting consumer society was in many respects the triumph of mass production, organizationally destined to cement an overall improvement in the standard of living that would assuage the class struggles associated with early industrialism. It also reflects an implicit belief in the inevitability of progress. But this is very different epistemologically from earlier, pre-Enlightenment sentiments.

Pre-industrial societies were far from egalitarian and were institutionally contingent upon rigid hierarchies. The pervasive sentiment was one whereby recognition of inequality was normative yet based upon appropriate displays of wealth by those deemed legitimate to possess it. In other words, excess was conditional culturally upon it not being overly excessive since that could easily be disruptive for society and the fixed order of things. By excessive one means an unbridled enthusiasm in the pursuit of desires since the latter was seen as ultimately harmful for society. Such an association between desire and luxury was seen as pernicious since it undermined the very fabric of socio-cultural stability and thus resulted in a morally censorious attitude towards luxury that was pervasive.[3] In the next section I will examine the rationale behind such condemnations of luxury examining examples of how such critiques gathered potency.

Luxury as a Vice

It is amongst the writings of the Ancient Greeks and Romans that one finds the early articulations against luxury. For the former, ostentation (conspicuous and non-legitimate to some) was permissible nigh encouraged if its purpose was for public splendor and not private indulgence. Quoting Aristotle, the historian of luxury David Clouthier noted that if one's house was to be conceived as a public ornament, this justified spending on lavish furniture and beautiful things; otherwise it would be a mark of vulgarity or "tasteless showiness."[4] In other words owning wealth was not the problem; showing it off inappropriately was. The Greeks reified the simple life, thus extravagance inevitably posed risks if its expression and display marked a person out from his fellows. It suggested contrarian behavior and a willful disregard for the norms that cemented society. In that sense it could be construed as a character fault on the part of the offending individual, possibly subject to sanction. It was a mark of pretentiousness, not dissimilar to many who embrace luxury products today for the sake of pure indulgence, but here it was seen as the first dangerous steps on the path towards decadence which ultimately was corrosive for the whole community. Ironically though, despite this stance, it was acknowledged that such action was a reflection of basic human desire, in many respects a natural tendency. If left to their own devices perhaps most people would succumb to such temptations with the resulting unexpected surprises and sufferings.[5] It was this unpredictability that haunted the Greeks and gave resonance to their perennial obsession with tragedy.

Given the extensive expositions on the topic of greed and desire in classical writings, one cannot help but assume that such behavior was quite commonplace. Admittedly the lack of reliable empirical data to suggest that this was the case renders such an assertion speculative. Yet the constant fulminations against vice and greed is indicative that it conceivably was a problem. In current parlance, constant vocal concerns regarding the suppression of crime logically suggest that crime is a problem in that society. Luxury probably generated the same disdain and concern amongst the ancients. Perhaps the broader question to ask in this regard is why the ancients viewed what even they recognized as part of human character in such a negative light. Why was seeking to fulfill desires seen as potentially destructive? Might it be that the realization of such desires was more readily attainable by a small group in society? In pursuing desires this group could easily differentiate themselves from the majority, inviting invidious comparisons between the haves and the have nots. Such actions, possibly viewed as merely insufferable behavior on the part of the wealthy, nonetheless magnified whatever inequality existed and thus exposed other human frailties such as envy and jealousy by the less fortunate. It also undermined the co-operative interdependence that Plato argued was necessary for the common good especially since no individual was deemed self-sufficient.[6] Since the *"polis"* is structured around the fulfillment of basic needs, anything that transcended such needs could ultimately lead to social conflict and societal dissolution. But Plato also recognized that it was almost inevitable that as societies became more complex, they became more "luxurious."[7] This necessitated territorial expansion to secure the necessary goods which ultimately led to warfare and the need for a military state.

This is an important caveat as it suggests all individuals, *ceteris paribus*, will seek out luxuries if they can afford to materially do so. Perhaps the essence of the ancients' rules were therefore designed to suppress any excessive form of expressive individuality; to not do so would lead to the unraveling of the very fabric of community life. This was more than an expostulatory view of greed, vice and avarice; it went to the very heart of social order and a latent fear of leaving human desires unrestrained. For as Christopher Berry argued in his historical analysis of luxury's various iterations, "unlike needs, luxury is boundless or insatiable," and if left unchecked would ruin both society and its citizens.[8] This is a rather curious condition to note, recognizing as it does that a natural human action (desire) needs to be controlled because of the potentially destructive consequences of its dynamism. But it is equally pertinent to understand the *prima facie* role that community solidarity played in a society where contemporary notions of individualism were conspicuously absent. This renders any significant displays of differentiation potentially problematic because it erodes the fabric of community life and well-being.

Similar sentiments towards luxury continued with the Romans. Their concerns also focused upon community solidarity and the need to suppress excessive individual materialism especially when motivated by the wrong reasons. Scrolling through the writings from Cicero to the fourth-century Prudentius, who integrated classical and biblical thought on the topic, one gets a sense of how luxury (*luxuria*) alongside and perhaps a manifestation of greed (*avaritia*) increasingly was viewed as a vice.[9] Left unchecked, especially in times of scarcity, such behavior could lead to social conflict. Yet Cato saw avarice and luxury as inevitable consequences of city growth even though it led in the past to the destruction of empires[10]; a reading of history that fully castigated those who equivocated on how much material excess might be tolerated. Despite such rhetoric of despair wealth was nonetheless permissible (and probably inevitable) so its strictures often had to be massaged to accommodate a more nuanced view of its deleterious consequences. Since it appeared difficult to fully suppress what were seen as natural human tendencies, how might one reconcile the inevitable with the undesirable? The solution was to justify luxury if its owner embraced public magnificence but not private largesse.[11] You could still lead the Roman "good" life; you merely had to show that all could participate in your venture in some often vicarious way. This apparent munificence not only justified the pursuit of wealth, it rendered it a virtuous activity if visibly subordinated to the promotion of public/community welfare.

Not all activity was afforded virtuous for the Romans in their embrace of luxury. It was also viewed in a more nuanced negative light by castigating those who pursued material riches for what amounted to a way of hiding moral weakness.[12] Or they saw it as a manifestation of effeminacy which would ultimately lead to a dangerous weakness in times of war. For a Republic that was predicated on military superiority this was a grave concern. As Berry notes, luxury corrupts and produces bad cowardly soldiers.[13] Luxury is not just a moral question of greed, its enthusiastic pursuit signifies a weakening of human character and a lapse in the sensibilities that were necessary for maintaining a strong society. Fundamentally then it was a security issue. Not surprisingly perhaps, for a society that was supremely self-confident and outward looking, such vices were seen as external products rather than a function of idiosyncratic behavior amongst the local population. The danger of moral contagion from outside the Empire could easily de-stabilize society if left unchecked – especially if such errant behavior might actually prove desirable to those "less enlightened" segments of the population.

Notwithstanding such a "defense of the realm," perspective, it was obvious that Romans were far from willing to eschew the rituals of banquets and feasts that were an integral part of electoral life. The prevailing political culture encouraged and even demanded displays of magnificence and splendor in public projects. These included the construction of forums and other places for public gatherings. Whilst such rituals were *de rigueur* for even aspiring politicians, tantamount to what we might characterize today as influence peddling, they nevertheless secured a position in the social pecking order. The ensuing accolades might substantiate the status position of elites but they were also a mechanism that secured the political structure.[14] Nonetheless, such "public" indulgences allowed participants to avoid the stigmas of self-indulgence, greed and ambition that provoked condemnation and led to sumptuary laws. The latter was invoked because private luxury was seen as corrupting public service. Whomever ruled was presumed to do so in the best interest of the many whereas if too much freedom to express privilege was conceded to this group, it had the potential to devolve into oligarchic rule of the rich few concerned only with their own interest.[15] Wealth can corrupt; absolute wealth corrupts absolutely!

Constraints on luxury, both legal and normative, were designed to suppress behaviors that might accentuate the visible manifestations of inequality. The latter was seen as natural and inevitable given fixed hierarchies and limited social mobility. It was an accepted integral part of social fabric provided it did not unleash an overly enthusiastic embrace of superfluity. Prevailing norms countenanced the rule of the privileged few since it was seen as being publically virtuous and luxury was somehow displayed as a public good. If however, such luxury was motivated by less altruistic goals it was symptomatic of more distasteful tendencies such as greed and misplaced ambition and thus subject to sanctions. This was cloaked in a morality of self-control from consumption to prevent corruption which as Adams argues "would subvert our ability to aspire to higher things."[16]

Christianity and Luxury

The link between religion and luxury acquired an ambiguous and at times contradictory stance with the evolution of medieval Christianity. On the one hand biblical edicts about giving to the poor, the difficulty of a rich man's camel entering ancient city walls (the proverbial "eye of the needle"), and the "first shall be last" all suggest a rather negative view of wealth. But since wealth did not *per se* mean luxury, the moral dilemma was how the wealthy were to behave and display their wealth? Whereas the ancients were clear about the moral depravity of riches, the early Christian church equivocated somewhat. According to Mark's gospel, the rich would encounter severe difficulties entering the kingdom of heaven. However, most were spared a divestiture of their assets if they could demonstrate that in their soul they remained committed to a virtuous Christian life and display of such wealth did not encourage envy by others.[17] Determining whether or not such lustful behavior occurred was presumably left somewhat ambiguous and as much the fault of the envious person's lack of moral certitude as the one who incited such invidious comparisons. If you could be secure in the self-knowledge that you were not a slave to your riches, this sublimation could ease your way into the kingdom of Heaven.

What is notable about this stance in regulating morality is that responsibility increasingly shifts to the individual. Edicts by the ancients that regulated morality were replaced by internalized moral codes. Material excess is subtly sanctioned providing the owner is able to secure a redemptive peace through good works – the beginnings of "*caritas*." Greed remains problematic but luxury gradually loses its connection with lust and a vice as long as the accumulation of temporal things is a natural thing and does not involve manipulation of money (usury).[18]

The gradual institutionalization of the Roman Catholic Church throughout early medieval Europe was contingent upon definitions of spirituality that embraced luxury providing it could be diverted to service the needs and aims of the church, in essence the glorification of God. By orchestrating the route to salvation, the church's growing presence could remonstrate with those who did not participate in the ritual, confession and appropriate conduct necessary for salvation. Tithing traditionally supported the resources of the Church; now the wealthy could be encouraged to part with more of their money through contributions to "good causes." The Church was suggesting supplementary ways of avoiding penance by facilitating a subtle form of religiously sanctioned income redistribution.

In assessing the church's growing wealth and its ability to administer luxury for its own ends, Adams succinctly states

> The ordained imperial hierarchy was fixed for centuries. Breathtaking extravagance in church architecture, church theater of rituals, and in the splendid costumes and stage props of the principal actors, rivaling any Eastern court, was not seen as sinful, decadent, or worldly. It was a physical manifestation and celebration of God's visible supremacy on earth.[19]

Luxury now acquired a sacred explanation and justification. Whereas the ancients exhorted the wealthy to demonstrate the utilitarian value of their riches through public splendor, medieval Christianity instituted a sacred version of this attitude. The wealthy were encouraged to view their wealth as a gift from God and its true spiritual expression was made manifest by furthering the beauty and magnificence of worship in public edifices. The Church notionally sought to demonstrate its own significance and awe inspiring grandeur through its architecture and art. But somebody had to be convinced to pay for all of this. Since luxury continued to be cast in a negative light (sinful), *ipso facto* those with the financial means to subsidize ecclesiastical excess had to be given a way out of their spiritual (and material) dilemma. The answer was twofold. First, giving to the church was a way to secure the favors necessary for salvation since that institution was the ultimate intermediary between you and God. Whilst certainty was never secure, to not make material intercessions would significantly elevate ones chance of rendering day to day life fraught with uncertainty. Second, wealth suggested that one was possibly viewed favorably by God, by virtue of being the recipient of his earthly largesse. Secure in this knowledge, one could subsidize the magnificence of God's arbiters on earth. Beauty and splendor, especially when provided for the Church, were no longer an aberration but indicative of God's spiritual power.[20] And you could also justifiably retain some of that wealth, splendor and opulence for your own personal enjoyment.

This twin approach provided the necessary room to maneuver to simultaneously acknowledge luxury without viewing it as a vice and then affirm its relevance as an indication of virtuous activities. As with the Romans, luxury per se was not the problem; it was whether it was used appropriately. However, instead of invoking the potential for social disorder, luxury now was invested with a spiritual dimension that could condemn or condone its manifestation. It continued to be seen as the root of greed and thus pre-eminent in the hierarchy of vices, and medieval religion accordingly reinforced an ethic of frugality for most people. Somewhat ironically luxury for the majority was inseparable from lust which complemented decadence as a vice that was clearly not to be tolerated. For the rich its benefits were not subversive because they contributed to the splendor of the medieval church. This *status quo ante* remained acceptable within existing hierarchies until new groups aspired to elite status. It was precisely the arrival of new groups of wealthy merchants in the late medieval period that destabilized this sacred compromise.

The growth of trade and urban centers in much of Europe had resulted in an increase in material well-being for merchants and those who controlled incipient market activity. As Gregory argues,

> Christians high and low were buying, selling, trading, lending, borrowing, and financing in a European economy more profit-seeking than ever, one marked by innovative credit mechanisms, new banking institutions, and time-tested accounting procedures.[21]

Many of the new wealthy avoided criticism for such behavior by bestowing this largess on the poor, using it to serve others and promote the common good by giving to the Church. The latter included activities that harkened back to the ideas of magnificence discussed earlier. Masses were endowed, charities for the poor established, religious orders were the recipients of sizable donations and attendance at confessions increased.[22] This was not necessarily inconsistent with the pursuit of moral virtue that was widespread during this time period in which religion permeated most aspects of life, public and private. But the cynic might also suggest that this was the means whereby people continued to seek ways of improving the odds of their salvation by doing good works and demonstrating spirituality. And presumably there were many who were steeped in the conviction of helping ones neighbor in a simple altruistic way.

What did stand out as quite remarkable was the increase in patronage for religious art and architecture. I deal with this more extensively in Chapter 6 and here merely suggest some of the key themes. Whilst some of this investment went into adornment of public spaces (churches and monuments), much found its way into private chapels designed for private devotion.[23] This was truly a magnificent aesthetic endeavor, dramatically beautifying buildings and presenting us with many of the artistic splendors we revere today. Yet it was also a way of appropriating moral gestures and supposed virtuous activity for private contemplation. This allowed a subtle negotiation between overt displays of earthly goods and a reverence for the sacred – secular self interest in the service of faith. Or as Cosimo de' Medici stated when referring to his support of public projects, (it affords) "the greatest satisfaction and the greatest pleasure, because it serves the glory of God, the honour of Florence, and my own memory."[24] Effectively, the pursuit of wealth was becoming privatized; its earlier moral provenance subordinated to the dissimulation that frequently surrounds status ambiguity.

While the new wealthy sought to emulate the elite, not surprisingly the latter saw such encroachment upon their lifestyle in far less enthusiastic terms. The response to this structural change was twofold. Theologians lent their weight to the old elite's status by invoking tradition as the means whereby the ruling class used magnificence in divine worship. As Kavesi argues, citing the work of Peter Howard, "*magnificentia*" became a potent Christian virtue at the service of the ruling class – an admirable and appropriate display of wealth.[25] This contrasted with the usurpers who were guilty of squandering their wealth with unnecessary expenditures on ornamentation and frivolous activities. In other words, the new wealthy were tainted by their pecuniary activity, admonished for their "arriviste" aspirations and were accused of excessive consumption and wasteful squandering.[26] Their behavior was criticized in sermons as avarice when they were apparently too enthusiastic about their display of wealth. They clearly were not to be accepted as the rightful purveyors of this quasi spiritual magnificence. For the old elite, the newcomers lacked taste and were probably seen as vulgar; they were easily dismissed because they were conspicuously lacking in their grasp of the purported moral virtues that should accompany wealth. And, not insignificantly, they were challenging the old order even though their goals were one of emulation and aspiration.

Second, to ensure that such aspirational goals for this new group were nipped in the bud, sumptuary laws were passed that regulated and controlled most aspects of consumption.[27] Gradual increases in material well-being were notable in areas such as fashionable clothing and ritualized events (weddings, banquets, etc.) and whereas these activities were considered legitimate for the old elite, they were deemed unacceptable for new groups. These sumptuary laws became a feature of thirteenth to sixteenth-century Europe, casting a legal opprobrium on behavior by restricting expenditure on goods and regulating many of the rituals that were a feature of those times. Specifically they established rules as to what different groups in society were entitled to consume, with any excessive displays by all but the old "official" elite viewed as superfluous.[28] Whilst the latter were naturally exempt from such strictures – the usual adumbrations regarding the moral attributes of status were invoked – the pursuit of wealth by others was criticized for its apparent lack of spiritual significance. Such pernicious excessive consumption stimulated vanity and thus rendered illegitimate the very possession of such wealth.[29] But this clearly was not intended to apply to the old elite since their wealth was subsumed under the cloak of tradition and purposive spiritual intentions. Sumptuary laws were first introduced in the thirteenth century throughout much of Europe but especially Italy where new goods and trade were developing. They were not just about the appropriate use of wealth as in the past; they were now designed to regulate precisely who could display that wealth and how. They were certainly not atypical of the highly regulated Renaissance societies where most people recognized and acknowledged their place and role. But these societies were also unleashing material changes that stoked consumerism in ways that threatened the status quo.

England enacted its first sumptuary law in 1336 prohibiting men and women from wearing imported clothing.[30] No more exotic fabrics from overseas for the merchants who had a form of privileged access to such goods. In France the laws extended beyond clothing (what colors or fabric could or could not be worn) to food, jewelry and transportation. They were designed to reinforce the status of the old elite since visible markers of position reinforced the sense of privilege, aura and mystique. How successful these laws were in suppressing ostentatious displays of wealth by others is questionable. Perhaps the levels of growing prosperity was so great, attempts to harness its display were always going to be doomed. Recognizing, as the ancients did, that human desires are irrepressible, growing individualism would need more than moral rectitude and legal mandates to contain human excesses.

The late medieval tensions between old wealth and new money are not surprising since the latter was challenging the social position of the former. It played itself out in the cultural wars of the period in which the church's role in regulating the legitimacy of wealth enforced a *de facto* moral code of financial obligations in the cause of spirituality. In the period between 1500 and 1800 much of this would alter. The changes included increased material prosperity associated with a further growth in trade and markets, incipient industrialization and the progressive acceptance of freedom of thought and expression (including religious practice) that were part of the classical liberal thinking that emerged alongside the Reformation. The latter proved revolutionary since it tore apart previous traditional justifications for hierarchy and inequality that unwelcomed the new rich. In its place it legitimized the new inequalities that represented the triumph of achievement and effort plus it sought to denigrate the old aristocracy. It also reinforced the idea that the natural world could be understood by observation, experiment and mathematical explanation rather than through revealed religious texts.[31] This undermined the credibility of the Church as the principal arbiter of knowledge. Science was elevated to a privileged position of pre-eminence since it offered an objective means for evaluating mankind's progress and betterment. This would be the lasting legacy of Bacon and Newton, cultural entrepreneurs who according to cultural historian Joel Mokyr set in place the institutionalization of science and the belief in technological solutions to social problems.[32] Finally, the Reformation revealed much of the hypocrisy of the late medieval Catholic hierarchy that failed to live up to the biblical commandments. In doing so it presented a wider range of options as to how Christianity could be lived in practice, in particular a new emphasis upon individual motivation.[33] This was not secularization but it did affirm the link between salvation and individual enrichment, even if the latter ignored community obligations. By casting the pursuit of wealth in quasi righteous terms, it re-shaped the links between luxury, virtue and commerce.

Money, Markets and Morality

In his book on the changing conceptions of luxury, Christopher Berry eloquently argues that there is a distinctive shift in attitudes between the pre-modern period and the growth of the Enlightenment.[34] In the former luxury is seen in morally censorious terms as a vice whereas the latter is witness to what he calls the "de-moralization" of luxury. The modern view of luxury is as a by-product of wealth that lacks the moral opprobrium of earlier thinking. It represents a radical rethinking of societal conceptions of the social order, the institutional framework that governs morality, and casts doubt on those who view virtuous activity as mediated by external civic or sacred deeds. Instead the new social order embraces individual initiative and a less ascriptive view of social hierarchy. It eulogizes the rewards that come from hard work and sees them as an insuppressible outcome of human desires. Much of this was made possible by increased trade, heightened market activity and the growth of a powerful merchant class that imbued commerce with a virtuous dimension that had been conspicuously absent in the past. Well-being and prosperity assumed normative salience since increasingly the wealthy were viewed as having a productive role to play. The foremost exposition on this new role came from Adam Smith.

In spite of the many interpretations and exegeses on Adam Smith, most recognize two essential principles that were the cornerstone to his ideas on how nations become wealthy. The first was the famous "propensity to truck, barter and exchange one thing for another" that he saw as the driving force behind much of human initiative. This behavior is neither a moral imperative nor a socialized trait. Instead it is viewed as an integral part of the human psyche, best realized when conditions to facilitate its expression are in place. Second, is the innate desire to better ourselves that arises when we enter into relations with others. These basic precepts are inter-related and, according to Smith, constitute the *modus operandi* of human interaction.

For modern man according to Smith, desire is now seen as natural; a manifestation of one's instinct to better one's condition. To thwart desire is tantamount to stifling human creativity. Seeking fulfillment of such desires leads eventually to a commercial society; the ultimate expression of human instincts. If provided with the freedom to engage in what are essentially market activities and guaranteed the rights and contractual responsibilities that underlie such behavior, purposeful human action can result in aggregate as well as individual material improvement. Impersonal forces (the famous invisible hand of the market), Smith argued, are what structure economic transactions.

In this framework, every man thus becomes a merchant. Such networking interdependence leads to a society where specialized production engenders overall greater efficiency and improved societal wealth ("a civilized and thriving country" to use Smith's words).[35] A society where individuals are left free to pursue their own interests will be one that inevitably becomes even wealthier. Each person will naturally seek to optimize the value that they create and whilst this is solely to satisfy their own gain, the cumulative consequences are beneficial for the collective good.[36] This viewpoint suggested that wealth would be an inevitable by-product of human effort and its pursuit mutually beneficial to the individual and society. Luxury therefore no longer needs to be sublimated to civic or sacred mandates since commercial activity is now virtuous.

For Smith concentration of wealth in a few hands, particularly land held by the feudal aristocracy, prolonged economic stagnation and impeded economic growth. For change to occur, individual freedom was imperative because only when individuals are free to pursue their own self-interests could aggregate material progress be achieved. The rigid hierarchies needed to be dismantled, replaced by a society where personal liberty, personal industry and ultimately personal reward would all work together. Freedom of exchange and guaranteed rights, especially those related to property, were imperative if individuals were to prosper. But for this to work, an institutional framework and the rule of law was necessary and whilst Smith saw this as primarily the responsibility of the King, gradually this obligation was assumed by the state as infrastructural projects, increased education and clear rules regarding market transactions were implemented. The guiding force of aristocrats and kings as arbiters of material progress thus diminishes in importance when compared with the explosive potential unleashed by rampant individualism, unfettered by constraints of status and ascriptive ties.

We sometimes forget that for Smith economics and morality were inseparable. His vision of an efficient society was also that of a just one. In exploring what this meant for civil society Adam Smith wondered whether "moral sentiments" would continue to play an important underlying role. In this respect he lent credence to the abject moral opprobrium that had cast wealth as the personification of dilettantism. He was dismissive of wealth that was not used creatively, inequality being problematic insofar as it stymied opportunism. However, should individual initiative be given free reign, any resulting accumulation of wealth and thus inequality was perfectly legitimate. He acknowledged that wealth was inevitable in such a system but cast it in a more positive light than before, providing inequality did not become excessive. Smith recognized the need for self-esteem as a crucial part of our sensibilities and the basis for ambition. When he states that "the chief part of human happiness arises from the consciousness of being beloved,"[37] he is postulating more than a cynical view of envy. He recognized that we want to be wealthy because others will admire and envy us; in the same way that we think about others who are wealthy.[38]

He viewed work as a purposive activity that endowed human existence with meaning. In fulfilling this mandate, one would be tacitly accepting behavioral codes that were nonetheless rooted in a basic moral framework. Implicit belief in the efficacy of such a system was an affirmation in the moral essentialism that underlies one's activity. What had been more explicit and overt moral codes that governed behavior in the past were now replaced by the virtues of individual initiative – a new form of morality but one that nonetheless was integral to maintaining social harmony.

Berry notes that in his lectures Smith purportedly stated that "opulence and freedom are the two greatest blessings men can possess."[39] In other words, it left free men to naturally pursue material goods because doing so confers the self-confidence and respect we all crave. If we are simultaneously acquisitive individuals and revere those who are wealthy, *ipso facto* we should be perfectly justified in succumbing to our own desires in pursuing the material goods life. By removing the heavy handed discipline of the Church, we could be free to accumulate goods without guilt. Not only that, such pursuit of self-interest and desires promoted the collective good because it proved to be an efficacious ways of managing resources.

Unlike Berry's "de-moralization," a new morality provided conditional support for the cumulative effect of such desires. It recognized the collective material benefits that were transforming society through abundance and variety by endorsing a subjective individual morality.[40] This conferred rights and responsibilities on individuals as part of new institutional structures but also gave them greater metaphysical agency than in the past. *A priori* it permitted individuals to embrace material well-being as a justification of their hard work. In the century that followed his writings, the Industrial Revolution provided precisely the requisite framework for many of his ideas as restructured class systems enabled new groups to capitalize upon the material gains from innovative market forces.

Much has been written on the Reformation and the Enlightenment and how it was an evolving market for ideas that would eventually lead to modern economic growth and industrialization.[41] Marshall has argued that it was not really just about religion or even politics, but represented a wider social schism that engendered polarization but also intense discussion on the nature of social order.[42] Culturally, it restructured beliefs that pertain to how knowledge is assessed and developed and economically provided an institutional structure and political framework that legitimated rule making by the state. The appropriateness of new Protestant religions to entrepreneurial behavior, sustained commercialism and social class in general is complex and has been extensively debated elsewhere.[43] What does seem apparent for our purposes is that whilst individuals were still fraught with anxiety about salvation, many nonetheless found experimental science and technological development economically beneficial; their dilemma was how to reconcile the two. Sometimes this worked quite easily as the Puritans and then Unitarians discovered in their embrace of productively using one's abilities to enhance the glory of God and be materially successful.[44] God was presumed to be rational and enlightened, thus clearly wanting people to be successfully economically. This sanctioned individual happiness and material well-being as benign self-interest that would ultimately lead to greater societal prosperity.[45] If everyone believes in the efficacy of such activity, it fosters interdependence and social cohesion and a *de facto* morality based on material incentives. As Mokyr, partly summarizing Jacob and McCloskey, argues "...religion stressed stability and harmony, but also the assurance that prosperity and material rewards for hard work and ingenuity were perfectly virtuous and moral...it pictured a progressive society as the realization of God's will."[46] The Gordian knot that had privileged the sacred over the secular had finally begun to unravel.

The Advent of Capitalism

The Enlightenment is now recognized as the period when the cult of the heroic individual assumed a distinctly materialist dimension. Doing well for oneself was condoned and material success seen as evidence of effort, ability and determination – each of which could still be cast in quasi-religious terms as the demonstration of God's favor. Religious leaders even emphasized the virtuousness of economic activity especially if it reflected individual capabilities. But many laymen now saw societal progress as natural; that there was no reason to subscribe to the medieval notion of a better world at the end of history or in the afterlife. It was attainable here and now, on earth and was a reward for those who were willing to embrace it fully. Give this new juncture, it would be inevitable that some might prosper more than others; such was the natural basis of a different type of inequality that was emerging. It also put the urban-mercantile class in the forefront since they were precisely the ones to benefit most from urbanization and increased commerce and the ones who gained access through this wealth to the ranks of the upper class.[47]

What emerged from this sustained economic progress was a fundamentally different view of social order; no longer viewing religion or virtue as the underlying structure but instead individuals pursuing their own interests. Hirschman attempted to conceptualize this change when he termed the latter as part of the new rational order whereas "passions" (often contained within religious viewpoints) were detrimental to society and needed to be tamed.[48] Religion was seen as more likely to inflame such "passions" whilst commercial activity associated with the desire for gain ("interests") would be beneficial politically and economically. The pursuit of material interests was thus no longer viewed pejoratively as avarice but now as a means to control the destructive passions of men. Not only would such interests legitimate the underlying beliefs of an emergent commercialism, they provided the new framework for subsequent rapid economic growth.

This constitutes a fundamental restructuring of social thought, how human behavior should be interpreted and evaluated, as well as how social (and political) order is maintained. Science and technology were embraced as ways of analyzing the world and implementing procedures that were consonant with notions of practical improvement. Unsurprisingly, the application of the scientific method did lead to challenges of extant religious thought. No matter how flexible Christianity became in the eighteenth century to accommodate the new work ethic, its adherence to the logic of "faith" would prove increasingly incompatible with a methodological and empirical cause and effect rigor. Technological innovation enabled increased output, improved economic performance and improvements in the overall standard of living; all of which were indicative of new ways of thinking and problem solving based on amoral rational paradigms. Knowledge, as Gregory argues, had become secularized, specialized and segmented and was increasingly distinct from morality.[49] By segmented he refers to the way in which knowledge is universal and objective, not tied to any individual morality or metaphysical beliefs. Specialized captures the increasing relevance of research institutions (such as universities) dedicated to problem solving using rigorous methods of objective science. And secularized represented the break from "divine inspiration" as a tool of analysis. Together these lay the epistemological ground work for an emerging capitalist organization of production and a conditional acceptance of new structures of inequality.

Discussions on the origins of capitalism are numerous but most in one way or another focus upon the commercialization of agriculture, the monetarization of employer-employee relationships and the extent to which old elites either embraced or resisted change.[50] Market institutions have a long history of providing the framework for trade and capital accumulation and were certainly not new to the eighteenth century. What was unique about incipient capitalism was that it infused markets with an unparalleled vigor. Theoretically markets performed a self-regulating mechanism, as Adam Smith argued, but they were also a means of social integration. Ingham argues that this helps explain how private vices could become public benefits and the source of public virtue when he states

Exchange cemented society in networks of mutually advantageous inter-dependence, and it could also be seen as resolving the eternal ethical question of the relationship between individual conduct and the general collective welfare.[51]

This solved the perennial problem of sustaining an appropriate moral code to maintain social order. If the efficacy of the market is predicated on indi-viduals trading and spending money rather than hoarding it, *ipso facto* markets thus become the source of social integration and ultimately societal stability. And the more capitalism evolved in the context of emerging nation states, the more it cemented social relationships in ways that furthered economic progress, especially for the new merchants and entrepreneurs.

An embryonic merchant class that had gained control over an emerging money economy in the eighteenth century was able to organize economic activi-ties through the production and sale of a vastly increased number of commodities. Such activities were sanctioned by the legal security of the nation-state which helped institutionalize banking systems, regulate property and trade, and main-tain law and order.[52] The result was an increasingly secular and liberal culture that embraced economic progress and promoted the accumulation of capital. In countries such as England, the old elite often became willing partners in these endeavors and underwrote many of the changes; other countries' aristocratic elites (Russia and to some extent France) were often less forthcoming and change was slower and politically disruptive.[53] This new economic order inevitably disrupted old class and status positions but to the extent that aristocrats in some countries saw opportunities to underwrite their dominance through new economic means, when this occurred it removed some of the stigmas of commercialism that were redolent of the old class order. Whilst the old elite conceded to the material encroachment on their hitherto privileged position, the exclusionary practices of luxury consumption and adornment that had been upheld through sumptuary laws were loosened as new elites sought to indulge in precisely the same lifestyle markers as their aristocratic predecessors.

At the opposite end of the economic ladder, the average worker became a wage laborer with a small discretionary spending power. As Fulcher has argued, "industrial capitalism not only created work; it also created 'leisure' in the mod-ern sense of the term."[54] The rise of wage labor in the nineteenth-century fac-tories structured working hours but also created non-work time which whilst nominally regulated in some cases nonetheless meant workers were given free time to pursue their own interests. Liberated from the omnipresent constraints of agricultural labor and provided with a "wage," such workers found them-selves as material consumers in a world increasingly full of saleable commodi-ties. Whilst their incomes were far from generous this was a dramatic departure from the preindustrial world marked by scarcity, poverty and insecurity. It was the beginnings of consumer capitalism that we are familiar with today.

The implications of the above structural and ideological changes were extensive. A new capitalist class throughout the nineteenth century was able to consolidate their wealth and social position in society. Even though this new group might continue to be marginalized politically, they were forceful in establishing their social credentials in the status hierarchy by material emulation of the old upper class. This they did through the purchase of expensive goods such as clothing, fine jewelry, grand country estates and lavish entertainment. Luxury had always been a marker that separated the aristocracy from the rest in society; now, as McNeill and Riello argue, it took on new forms and was used to communicate cultural meaning.[55] In the past luxury possession was the *modus operandi* of the aristocratic elite – an obligation that accompanied one's rank in society. By the eighteenth century, it referred to products that were more widely available and used to signify one's new found position.

The new rich copied the old elite but did so with a consumer enthusiasm that would have been abhorrent to the old order. It was a material flaunting of the arrivistes' arrival and a way for them to manifestly enjoy possessing something that was unique, expensive but above all new. Further adding to this consumer omniscience and new found material status was a change in the role of women and the values associated with love and sex – both topics that were perennially lurking beneath the surface of society but hitherto deemed dangerously symptomatic of moral degeneracy. Werner Sombart argued that women played a decisive role in the secularization of sex and love that began in the Renaissance and continued apace in the late eighteenth century.[56] Manifestly objectified in paintings from Titian onwards, women were increasingly seen decoratively in their role in the courts of Europe. They exemplified the luxurious in their attire and cultivated tastes and what started as a fashion trend amongst courtesans soon spread to the wives of bankers, landowners and merchants. Rather than seeking ways to repress carnal desires, societies now conceded valedictory urgency to its expression as a legitimate vehicle for material splendor. Sombart went on to forcefully argue that sensuous pleasure is the root of desire and its ultimate expression is in luxury goods that become more widespread with the growth of capitalism. Or to quote Sombart in Adams' discussion of his central ideas

> ...we find luxury in the ascendant wherever wealth begins to accumulate and the sexuality of a nation freely expressed. On the other hand, wherever sex is denied expression, wealth begins to be hoarded instead of being spent; thus goods are accumulated, especially such abstract forms as precious metals, as in more recent periods.[57]

Rarely has there been such a succinct argument about the link between libidinal excess, sexual pleasure and material well-being and development! Nonetheless it does focus upon how the spread of capitalism further encouraged female display, herself and her accessories, as a mode of stylistic denouement. This was how luxury was playing itself out amongst the wealthy and is a dramatic departure from the moral rhetoric of understated elegance that the ancients condemned, unless part of a civic project.

We have effectively come full circle, from viewing the destructive and destabilizing potential of material excess unless sublimated to the public good, to its essential role in promoting collective welfare when a product of unencumbered individual initiative. Stripped of its ancient and medieval moral opprobrium, the longing for material excess became the *sine qua non* of an ideology that increasingly saw self-restraint as detrimental to human welfare. Wealth was no longer viewed as morally corrosive and luxury condoned when solely the preserve of public benefit or in the cause of sacred munificence. Even in China luxury became simultaneously a form of display and confirmation of status. It was intricately linked with Confucian beliefs that material wealth enhanced moral life.[58] Such displays were always contingent on a "superior" man understanding what was right and not just a vehicle to display the benefits of trade; his behavior was an expression of his soul rather than merely his property. The eventual "cult of the gentleman" infused wealth with a moral aestheticism that structured the norms associated with manners, rites and ceremonies.

In the west, luxury had now become "privatized" – seen as the natural and inevitable expression of human initiative in the pursuit of self-interest. In the aggregate such behaviors were seen to promote societal cohesion and improve the collective good. Desire for wealth was now putatively morally acceptable and increasingly normative – bettering oneself no longer coming at the expense of society. In fact it is quite the opposite – it actually improves social integration and stability. At least that is what Enlightenment thinkers wanted us to believe.

Notes

1 Berry, C. *The Idea of Luxury*, Cambridge: Cambridge University Press, 1999, p. 45.
2 Plato, *Politeia*, ed. J. Burnett (1902), Oxford: Clarendon Press, 1968.
3 Berry, p. 5.
4 Clouthier, D. *The Vice of Luxury*, Washington, DC: Georgetown University Press, 2015, p. 28.
5 Adams, W.H. *On Luxury*, Washington, DC: Potomac Books, 2012, p. 20.
6 Berry, p. 46.
7 Adams, p. 27.
8 Berry, p. 62.
9 Clouthier, pp. 30–31.
10 Ibid.,
11 Ibid., p. 29.
12 McNeill, P and Riello, G. *Luxury: A Rich History*. Oxford: Oxford University Press, 2016.
13 Berry, p. 67.
14 Kovesi, C. "What is luxury?: The rebirth of a concept in the early modern world," *Luxury: History, Culture and Consumption*, 2015, 2/1, p. 30.

15 Ibid., p. 85.
16 Adams, p. 16.
17 Ibid., p. 91.
18 Clouthier, pp. 36–7.
19 Adams, pp. 96–7.
20 McNeill and Riello, p. 47.
21 Gregory, B.S. *The Unintended Reformation*, Cambridge, MA: Belknap Press/Harvard University. 2012, p. 257.
22 Gregory, p. 257.
23 Goldthwaite, R.A. *Wealth and the Demand for Art in Italy, 1300–1600*, Baltimore: Johns Hopkins University Press, 1993.
24 Quoted in Jardine, L. *Wordly Goods: A New History of the Renaissance*, New York: WW Norton, 1996, p. 126.
25 Kovesi, p. 32.
26 Kovesi, p. 33.
27 See Kovesi Killerby, C. *Sumptuary Law in Italy, 1200–1500*, Oxford: Oxford University Press, 2002.
28 McNeill and Riello, p. 52.
29 Berry, p. 103.
30 McNeill and Riello, p. 53.
31 Montgomery, S. and Chirot, D. *The Shape of the New*, Princeton: Princeton University Press, 2015, pp. 14–5.
32 Mokyr, J. *A Culture of Growth*, Princeton: Princeton University Press, 2017, p. 98.
33 Gregory, p. 257.
34 Berry.
35 Quoted in Berry, p. 154.
36 Montgomery and Chirot, p. 47.
37 Smith, A. Raphael, D.D. and Macfie, A.L. (Eds.), *The Theory of Moral Sentiments*, Indianapolis: Liberty Fund, 1984, p. 84.
38 Montgomery and Chirot, p. 40.
39 Quoted in Berry, p. 152.
40 Gregory, see Chapter 4.
41 See Mokyr for extensive discussion on the rise of culture in economic growth and the birth of industrialism.
42 Marshall, P. *Heretics and Believers: A History of the English Reformation*, New Haven: Yale University Press, 2017.
43 For a succinct summary of the social class perspective see Schwadel, P. "Social class" in Yamane, D. (Ed.) *Handbook of Religion and Society*, Switzerland, 2016, pp. 345–71.
44 Merton, R.K. *The Sociology of Science*, Chicago: University of Chicago Press, 1973, p. 232.
45 Gregory, p. 374.
46 Mokyr, p. 246.
47 Ibid, p. 266.
48 Hirschman, A.O. *The Passions and the Interests*, Princeton: Princeton University Press, 1977.
49 Gregory, p. 303.
50 See Coates, D. *Capitalism*, Abingdon: Routledge, 2016 for a summary discussion. Also Allen, R.C. *The British Industrial Revolution in Global Perspective*, Cambridge: Cambridge University Press, 2009; Marks, R.B. *The Origins of the Modern World* (3rd Ed.), New York: Rowman and Littlefield, 2015.
51 Ingham, G. *Capitalism*, Cambridge: Polity, 2008, p. 10.

52 Coates, p. 12.
53 Cf. Barrington Moore, *Social Origins of Dictatorship and Democracy*, Boston: Beacon Press, 1966.
54 Fulcher, J. *Capitalism, A Very Short Introduction*, Oxford: Oxford University Press, 2004, p. 8.
55 McNeill and Riello, p. 100.
56 Sombart, W. *Luxury and Capitalism*, translated by W.R. Ditmar, Ann Arbor: University of Michigan Press, 1967.
57 See Adams, p. 117.
58 Duncan, H. "The role of the Confucian gentleman," in *Symbols and Society*, Oxford: Oxford University Press, 1969, p. 21.

3

INDUSTRIALISM, MATERIALISM AND THE BIRTH OF A CONSUMER SOCIETY

If one wishes to examine the effects of the transition from a pre-industrial to industrial society, whether it be ideological, material or social structural, Britain provides an excellent example since it was the first nation to undergo such changes. Other nations soon followed, sometimes at a faster rate but all generally following the same pattern with similar sets of structural changes. This chapter therefore has a specific focus on Britain inasmuch as many of the changes in consumer behavior and attitudes towards wealth and luxury are embodied in events occurring in that country. It is here that a new industrial class became wealthy, working class material prosperity emerged, and the position of old elites was challenged. The Industrial Revolution that started in the late eighteenth century restructured traditional hierarchies and created a new class of wealthy people whose material gains derived from greatly expanded commercial activities and technological innovation. Britain was the first nation to experience the production efficiencies and increased specialization associated with technological innovation that drove work from the home to the factory.[1] Not only was work transformed, incomes for many increased whilst the old elite's landowning estates increasingly became uneconomic. With an old way of life under threat, attitudes towards wealth were changing. Yet many of the landed elite were astute enough to recognize the economic potential of their property via the selling of coal rights or investments in railways. The bourgeois arrivistes were moving up and the old elite adjusted their behavior accordingly.

A new morality of consumption was emerging that would reposition both the supply and demand for luxury. Justifications for wealth, as we saw in the last chapter, had already undergone ideological transformations. A desire to consume, and the financial means to do so, had supplanted the frugality of previous centuries. Material gains were less likely to be maligned and the wealthy were increasingly exonerated from the multiplicity of resentful accusations that questioned their functional relevance. Meanwhile, an increasingly self-conscious modern consumer was emerging whose self-identity was fungible and ultimately open to manipulation. Understanding these changes is crucial for an analysis of how attitudes towards luxury as well as the consumption of luxury were being altered.

To fully comprehend such developments we need to revisit the cultural changes that had occurred in the previous two centuries. As Joel Mokyr argues, the drivers of technological change were new attitudes towards understanding the natural world and using that knowledge to increase productivity and ultimately living standards.[2] Such cultural changes endorsed accumulation and legitimized the institutional frameworks that encouraged market growth. This proved to be the genesis of a broader consumer society since the dramatic increase in the production of goods at accessible price points enabled a wider segment of the population to become consumers of finished products. More people were buying more products and this fueled economic expansion as well as increasing the wealth for a new merchant/industrial class whose workshops supplied these goods. Whereas the consumer boom of the Middle-Ages and Renaissance was mainly but not exclusively restricted to the wealthy, the proliferation of manufactured goods associated with industrialism widened the access to such goods and transformed market structures.[3] For example, the expansion of the railways and telegraph plus steamships dramatically increased the expansion of markets. The cultural changes that encouraged the maximization of self-interest, together with structural changes that facilitated increased socio-economic mobility, resulted in new classes of consumers. The new consumer was not necessarily a wealthy landowner/aristocrat who craved luxury goods as a mark of status and rightful possession but an ordinary person in search of basic necessities that were now financially more accessible. It was also a newly minted wealthy merchant who was undoubtedly one of the chief beneficiaries of this material and economic progress. Such individuals had accumulated resources following technological change and were often seeking to establish their new found identity through status markers. Such activity typically involved the procurement of luxury goods as they imitated the behavior of previous elites.

In this chapter I examine the rise of consumption and new classes of consumers following the Industrial Revolution. I analyze how new wealthy consumers rationalized their behavior, whether seeing it as a way to reinforce their class and status position or as an acceptable manifestation of their successful work ethic. An ideology of material rewards as an inevitable outcome of a basic desire for self-betterment led to greater material prosperity for those willing to put in the effort. Consumption became legitimate because wealth (and inequality) was a morally acceptable outcome of normal human striving and the maximization of self-interest.

Another group of consumers came from the broader population whose material gains were far more limited. They too were able to gradually indulge in the ethos of materialism. Structural changes and increased opportunities for waged labor enabled them to avail themselves of goods hitherto unimaginable. For this group consumption was initially more about meeting basic needs than satisfying esoteric desires. Initially this was consumption for existence although it eventually morphed into consumption for display, revealing the increased relevance of status groups as prosperity increased. Consumption drove the profits for the firms who provided their jobs, thus further enhancing the wealth of the owners. As living standards gradually rose, eventually they too would embrace consumption as a ritual that would become pervasive and institutionalized by the twentieth century.

By examining both groups of consumers one can gain a sense of the reorientation of attitudes towards material possessions that framed both rich and poor alike. Consumption increasingly became a way of life for many in society, leading inexorably and ritualistically, according to Victor Liebow, to ego satisfaction in commodities.[4] It is amongst the new rich that we find an embrace of luxury products that revitalized and subsequently transformed the production of such goods into an industry itself. Such cultural changes reconstituted the demand for luxury goods since their acquisition could now be seen as a legitimate reward for individual effort and thus less morally suspect. The material products might be the same (paintings, furnishings, dwellings) but their possession was no longer rationalized by "divine right" or ennobled ancestry.

Whilst the pursuit of luxury had become somewhat democratized with structural changes in society following industrialization, what constituted luxury remained for the time being the same. Many moral dilemmas as to its possession, however, were revoked. Opportunities for the realization of luxury were now becoming embedded in ideologies that associated inequality as an inevitable expression of the new industrial societies. This recast the pursuit of luxury less as a *sui generis* expression of elite entitlement and more as an attainable goal for the upwardly mobile. Consumption could be justified as a natural reward for hard work; conspicuous consumption became a measure of success that privileged a new elite who nonetheless aped the behavior of the old.

Culture of Consumption

By the eighteenth century, acquisition of goods by increased numbers of the population marked the beginning of the consumer revolution.[5] Manufactured goods became more commonplace, markets more formally structured and underwritten by institutional rules that guaranteed greater transparency in transactions. Economists began to define the identity of a typical new "consumer" and market-based purchases came to be associated with purported rational behavior on their part.[6] The pricing of goods was seen as determined by market transactions, shaped and disciplined by the fluctuation of consumer desires. Such supply and demand relationships had always existed with the acquisition of luxury goods, albeit in tacit and often opaque fashion. Now, with the systematic widening of consumption and a dramatic increase in the number of consumers, they were becoming formalized and institutionalized.

In the past the attributes of consumer rationality were latent if not non-existent since consumer motivation was seen to be rooted in complex socio-cultural and status contexts. Increasingly markets were seen as institutions for governing economic activity, mechanisms that permit individuals to satisfy their desires through the purchase of products/services.[7] How consistently rational consumers were in their purchasing behavior is, however, difficult to determine. A number of authors argue that non-rational and social influences shaped consumption patterns by new consumer groups just as they had in the past.[8] If consumption is seen as part of managing self-identity, then how individuals behave on a day to day basis continued to be framed by their socio-economic and cultural context.[9] It can, however, be fraught with new sets of insecurities and uncertainty associated with more fluid class and status positions. It might also be wrapped up in a broader understanding of rights and political struggles associated with industrialism that varied from society to society. Being a consumer in Britain was associated with the rights to inexpensive goods that came with free trade; in Germany and China more patriotic overtones that encouraged buying local were the norm.[10]

It is easy to see in the discourse on the rise of the consumer an elegiac testimony to the material advantages of capitalism. A wider segment of society had gained access to commodities even if they were not necessarily expensive goods. They were able to do this since such goods became more widely available and at lower price points than in the past. Whether or not succumbing to these acquisitive tendencies represents hedonistic status competition is not easy to ascertain. The procurement of goods deemed essential to one's existence signify cultural shifts as well as practical necessities. However, production and exchange were being transformed in ways that were associated with a qualitative shift in behaviors and attitudes linked to consumption.[11]

Recognizing the growth of consumption not only encouraged theorizing about the consumer but also the legitimizing rationale for such behavior in the first place.[12] As noted in the previous chapter, elites had always consumed luxury goods (such as silks, spices, chocolate and even coffee) and new wealthy groups appeared willing to indulge in similar activities. The difference now was that material consumption became more widespread as a broader segment of society engaged in market transactions for lower priced commodities. Consumption became more pervasive and was no longer restricted to a small minority. Did the poor buy goods for the same reasons as those of the wealthy? Or did industrialism and capitalism unleash a new *deus ex machina* that saw consumption and consumer behavior as positively beneficial to society as whole rather than satisfying the whims of the wealthy via their luxury purchases? Could the new rich justify their material excess by invoking the secular benefits of their religious calling?

In a way God was replacing tradition as the arbiter of success; the new rich gaining their wealth through self-initiative that was enveloped in the cloak of religious sanction and affirmation. The old rich had often sought to placate God through their generous works and patronage; the new rich saw their wealth as an expression of God's favor towards them. Max Weber wrote about this as the Protestant Work Ethic in action as new ideas and habits underlay the growth of capitalism.[13] But the newly rich were not just working harder; they were consuming more. For them, the asceticism of Calvinism gave way to the new enthusiasm for material consumption that Campbell argues increasingly became the foundation for hedonistic pleasure seeking in consumption.[14]

For the poor meanwhile, opportunities for success were in their own hands if they were willing to expend the effort. They too could now participate in material progress that was associated with the new prevailing ideology providing they had the right mind set. Whilst circumscribed in their available achievements, their position in more fluid hierarchies did provide the allure of success if not always its eventual realization. They were bit part players in the new attitudes and aptitudes that were driving changes but they were eventually to become central to the consumer revolution of the twentieth century.

As we saw in the previous chapter, Adam Smith was the principal interlocutor in this emerging consumer mind set. Max Weber and Karl Marx also offered rigorous commentaries and analyses of capitalism, but it was Smith who simply laid out the essentialism of human effort when freed of traditional constraints. He firmly established a universalism for human behavior that endowed market transactions with a purposefulness that satisfied individual desires and collective economic progress. Maximizing self-interest was for him an intrinsic human trait. If provided with the freedom to engage in what are essentially market activities and guaranteed the rights and contractual responsibilities that underlie such behavior, human action can result in aggregate as well as individual material improvement.

"Self-interest" and "the invisible hand" became cornerstones of Enlightenment thinking inasmuch as they redefined the human condition and gave greater agency to individuals.[15] This proved to be an ideological disruption that delegitimized many of the traditional hierarchies. The sanctification of status through formal rankings was eroding as new wealthy individuals gained power and position. However, whilst the ensuing embrace of market liberalism rejected inherited inequalities it nonetheless legitimized new inequalities.[16] In other words wealth per se was not bad; it was merely how it was attained. Wealth was now seen as a product of human initiative, realizable when the conditions for individual expression and action were institutionalized. This would occur when "good laws" were in place and every member of society has a role to play.[17]

We have seen in previous chapters how consumption is rooted as much in an individual's relations with others; what Trentman refers to as "part of a social positioning system that tells people where they stand...goods simultaneously signal that an individual belongs to one group and keeps others at a distance."[18] Such a need for differentiation goes back centuries and is as much a part of human nature as Adam Smith's enlightened self-betterment. As Weber and Polanyi argued, humans are motivated by social goals more than material ones. In other words we need to see consumer behavior as not just the satisfaction of subsistence but instead as part of a broader set of values that are rooted in distinctive cultures.[19] Market cultures are thus a product of distinctive sets of institutional arrangements that reflect ideological pre-dispositions towards commerce and human agency. Greater material progress is coincidental with increased consumerism. But an expanded culture of consumption continues to embody social traits associated with status differentiation as well as a recon-figured notion establishing one's self identity in a more fluid social structure. Industrialism would be the catalyst that presaged such changes.

Industrialism

North Western Europe was the area where a dynamic and innovative cul-ture of consumption developed in the seventeenth and eighteenth centuries.[20] However, it was England that emerged in the forefront of such trends by the latter part of that period. The English had become more "worldly" (the prover-bial "nation of shopkeepers") in the sense that they realized there were oppor-tunities for creating a better life in this world rather than the world to come. Effectively this refocused attitudes towards work and material enjoyment with an emphasis upon the earthly present rather than an anticipated and hoped for heavenly future. It did not necessarily diminish sacred fervor and the perva-sive desire to anticipate an afterlife; it merely removed some of the heavenly uncertainty for those whose work efforts were yielding considerable material rewards. In fact Weber argued that wealth and status were increasingly seen as a sign of salvation, a tangible material reward and spiritual reassurance for those who were foot-soldiers of capitalism.

In England and eventually in other European countries and the United States, material acquisitiveness ceased to be sinful but was viewed as benign self-interest, what historian Brad Gregory claims as the "providentially sanc-tioned path to individual happiness, societal prosperity, and national strength."[21] In the past, people might have prayed to improve their lot; now they could be more calculating in determining what might be possible.[22] This new found pragmatism did not relegate religion to a second class status but it did pre-cipitate a more nuanced view of evaluating material success as infused with spiritual significance. It removed much of the uncertainty that had plagued earlier generations that had caused them to unleash a flurry of luxuries upon the church as a way of mitigating the possibility of non-salvation. Wealth was now providential as an earthly benefit as well as a heavenly sign. Where religion did suffer was in the area of scientific explanations and the growth of rationality. Mathematical laws provided a rigorous set of procedures for evaluating a wide range of issues that in the past had been seen merely as God's will. Predictability and rational consistency created a framework for problem solving that put humans more firmly in charge of their own destinies. This new found confidence can be seen in the technological innovations that started in the late eighteenth century and increased in place during the nineteenth. Such innovations can be seen in the context of cultural and ideological interactions with other basic socio-economic changes that were occurring at this time. Culture was becoming more secular and people were becoming more preoccupied with economic success. But that success was still viewed as somewhat conditional upon a sacred blessing even as the circumstances that pervaded daily life were changing.

Economic historian Robert Allen argues that three crucial developments, originating in previous centuries, underlie the transformative significance of England's industrial revolution.[23] Together they became constituent parts of the cultural revolution that had driven earlier changes. First, literacy and numeracy had increased dramatically with 53 percent of the population in England able to sign their name by 1800 (from 6 percent in 1500).[24] Both were associated with urbanism and commercial development that required different skill sets to that of agriculture and both led to significant changes in knowledge and outlook. Improved commercial prosperity increased the ability of people to pay for education and mass printing lowered the price of books and other educational materials. This further stimulated an inquisitive as well as acquisitive mindset.

Secondly, the proliferation of new consumer goods (locally manufactured products as well as increasingly imports such as sugar, tobacco, porcelain, tea and coffee associated with increased trade) encouraged people to work harder to earn higher incomes. To buy more goods required a higher income, and the provisions for this lie in the structural changes that were occurring in the transition from an agricultural society. New jobs associated with new industries (textile manufacturing, canals, iron and coal mining for example) and the growth of urban areas were transforming labor markets. The new jobs paid wages that were a more predictable income source than previous occupations and the benefits, however modest, were tangible. Such certainty was in marked opposition to the vagaries of agricultural labor and it helped reconfigure orientations to work. Opportunities for people to improve their material well-being infused work with a calculative dimension. Despairing as they might be of their subordinate position, they could nevertheless envisage a possible respite with hard work. Not surprisingly this stimulated an increase in the intensity of work; what de Vries termed the "industrious revolution."[25] While real wages rose by 4 percent between 1760 and 1820, hours worked greatly increased and the addition of women and children working for pay contributed to 25 percent of household disposable income.[26] Because English wages were already high, the crucial component here is an increase in the hours of work. Real wages did increase significantly by the mid-nineteenth century associated with further technological innovations and increased worker skill levels. But even before then growing aspirations amongst the average worker fueled consumption no matter how dire work and sanitary conditions in the growing urban areas were. This new culture of consumption did not entirely explain economic growth but it did further the urge to acquire that was concomitant with it.

Finally, variations in marriage patterns help explain different levels of prosperity in Europe; north western regions witnessed the postponement of marriage amongst women until their twenties and a lower overall likelihood of marriage. Other regions in east and southern Europe saw women likely to marry in their teens and with a high probability of all women marrying. Later age of marriage resulted in lower fertility rates, smaller families and thus more generally greater family wealth and a higher standard of living. Under such circumstances, more money was available for both consumption and investment, thus driving economic growth and increased commercial activities.

Together these three changes accounted for rising income levels in much of North West Europe during this time period. It was in England, however, that a further constellation of trends help us understand the subsequent industrial innovation. High wages and cheap energy encouraged profitable capital investments in labor-saving technology. High wages encouraged firms to seek ways of substituting capital for labor but they were not the obstacle to growth that they were elsewhere. Firms sought to economize on their use of labor and were able to increase labor output and overall worker productivity whilst still paying high wages. Plentiful supplies of coal reduced energy costs but also meant that firms could still pay high wages and remain competitive; other North West European countries (such as the Netherlands) lacked that basic energy resource and thus faced a significant cost barrier to further commercial activity.[27] This process of transition, from what many referred to as an "organic" economy to a mineral one that relied less on "muscle" power than technology, was crucial for England's sustained growth during this time period.[28]

England's unique wage and price structure and its increasing importance in the global economy are key features behind the industrial Revolution. High wages and longer working hours meant worker disposable incomes were increasing. Efficient commercial production resulted in a wide range of goods with prices low enough for mass consumption. Finally, rationalized production (cheap energy, technological innovation and labor efficiency) translated into higher profits for firm owners. The growing material wealth of the latter and their consolidation of economic power in the transformation from an agricultural to and industrial society, portends subsequent structural changes that would gradually disseminate to other industrializing societies. It was in England however, that this new class of merchants and industrialists, many with modest backgrounds, came to the forefront.

One could plausibly argue that despite high wages, the living standards for the average worker might not signify much progress given the crowded urban conditions and unsanitary dwellings especially in the industrial north where most lived. Marx more than adumbrated on this in his analysis of exploitative work relations in emerging capitalism. For the factory owners and technology innovators, the financial gains however, were significant. Statistical evidence indicates that the number of wealthy had increased significantly following the growth of commercial and industrial production.[29] What started with transformations in the textile industry soon spread to metals, machinery, railways, steam, chemicals and ceramics. Many of these new industries made fortunes for their proprietors; other wealthy individuals were the beneficiaries of speculative activity associated with increased trade and finance. Most had little schooling and learned technical skills via apprenticeships, adult education and experimentation.[30] These were self-made men on a mission and productivity increases as the century unfolded further added to their wealth.

The above trends help us understand the spending boom that occurred in England during the late eighteenth and early nineteenth century, initially amongst the wealthy classes but eventually and much later, following product proliferation, amongst a broad section of society. This consumer revolution meant the wealthy were buying a wider range of luxury goods than in the past, including locally manufactured goods as well as numerous imported products that included foodstuffs as well as textiles. A new class of wealthy merchants now existed alongside the old landowning aristocratic elite and increasingly imitated their behavior whenever possible or practical. For the most part they did not supplant them, instead they sought to complement them and their lifestyle.

The new elite, as with the old, pursued distinction through consumption, accumulating the sorts of goods that would enable them to be identified in ways appropriate to their new status. Fashion proved to be one of the most important signifiers of status so not surprisingly the new wealthy emulated the styles of the old elites.[31] Beautiful materials, rare and expensive garments, unique furnishings, country estates and artist patronage became the *sine qua non* for this group. Their dramatically increased income permitted material indulgences hitherto restricted to a small percentage of the population. Aristocrats set the trends, but they were easily aped by wealthy merchants who were investing in lifestyle markers that would unambiguously communicate and reinforce their new found material status. One of the foremost markers of status was the country estate, traditionally the rural base for the landowning aristocracy but also acquired by those whose improved fortunes provide access to this genteel lifestyle. Such properties, and the lifestyle that accompanied them, allow us to trace how status markers were relished but undergoing change as new ideologies of luxury consumption were evolving.

Home as Domestic Refuge and Emblem of Excess

As more and more people left their home to go to work following the rise of industrialism, the nature and function of houses changed. For the ordinary worker, the home would eventually become a place where one could accumulate material goods to ease domestic drudgery as well as well as place of entertainment with the newest gadgets. They were designed for comfort as well as for show, even if the latter was pursued with subtlety and modesty. For as historian Frank Trentmann argues,

> Mass-manufactured goods brought standardized comfort to the common man. Gas and electricity were filling the home with machines. The radio and gramophone opened it up to a new world of entertainment and sound. And the home itself became a prized possession.[32]

The accumulation of goods by the average worker is one of the quintessential aspects of twentieth-century consumer capitalism. It is the very apotheosis of a century of material growth coincidental with the rise of mass production.

Standards of living for the working and middle classes had risen by the end of the nineteenth century across much of the industrializing world, wages had improved and significant innovations had transformed daily life for many.[33] Worker productivity associated with Fordist work systems eventually enabled firms to produce large quantities, albeit of standardized goods, at appreciably lower prices. Items that might have been construed as somewhat luxurious became affordable and accessible for many. By the early twentieth century, mass production, mass distribution and mass consumption were key features of the new industrial landscape, especially in the United States that was in the forefront of production systems that augmented and often replaced skilled craft workers. Urban and industrial areas saw significant population growth (often through immigration) which further stimulated demand for products.

Whether rented or owned, homes became the place of refuge from the grind of daily work for factory laborers; for the emerging middle class they became an opportunity to embellish their position with the accoutrements of modernity. They were nonetheless a dramatic improvement in efficiency as more and more domestic chores were given a technological makeover. Homes for many provided a domestic and relatively private space for family life. As a product of artificial desires or merely the satisfaction of, and reward for, hard work, Trentmann captured their essence when he stated, "the home emerged as a temple to the self across Europe."[34]

This rampant consumerism as it pervaded daily life is discussed later in this chapter when I examine how such attitudes morphed into an even broader embrace of goods as status signifiers for a wider segment of the population. For the wealthy, the home provided a significant indication of one's position in society. Historically, it had always been more than a place to rest one's head for this class. Aristocrats and the wealthy in many countries had always built imposing residences as monuments to their power and status. As such, houses (and obviously palaces) were a place to entertain with established normative expectations as to style and lavishness. As the new merchant and industrial class of the late eighteenth and nineteenth centuries took their place alongside the old elite, they too embraced residences as way to mark their arrival and establish their full credentials as the new arbiters of style. One of the principal ways of doing this was through the acquisition of a country estate – the ultimate symbol of a *bona fide* "man of position."

Country houses and their surrounding estates were, as architectural historian Mark Girouard argues, "power houses – the houses of the ruling class."[35] There was no ambiguity about their role as they were designed to impress and evoke awe, residences that befit local magnates. They were the visible manifestation of elite status, designed to reinforce the perpetuity of position. They conferred dignity, class and the superiority of all that was upper class. If there was any doubt about such a position, many owners had self-portraits painted that underscored their grandeur.

One notable example of this status display can be found in Gainsborough's 1750 painting of *Mr. and Mrs. Andrews*, on display in London's National Gallery. It depicts the couple, members of the landed gentry whose money came from rents and the family's role as a landlord, in a splendid pastoral setting with rolling hills of the estate in the background). At Mr. Andrews' feet is a loyal and obedient dog gazing forlornly at his owner. Mrs. Andrews is bedecked in beautiful clothes and appears the submissive wife alongside her husband's gun as yet another possession. It was intended to demonstrate the subjects' position as owners of a country estate, the *sine qua non* of aristocratic refinement even if they lacked that historical background. It revealed the wealth and status of possessions as signifiers of appropriate standing in the new, more fluid hierarchies. This was the proverbial new money seeking to behave like the old.

Many of these country houses were castle-like as befits their medieval origins and the need for security. In most cases however, the house itself was a minor part of the arrangement. Admittedly it was where dignitaries could entertain in a lavish style, and when they and their guests ate breakfast on the terrace they could gaze across a vast expanse of land that receded into the horizon. But all of this was not merely the pursuit of Arcadian pleasure. The house was *de rigueur*; the land was the ultimate cachet or what we might refer to today as the "cash cow." It was ownership of land that provided the ultimate basis of this power since it underscored the economic wherewithal to maintain such a lavish lifestyle. Whether feudal serfs who much earlier owed an obligation to fight for the lord to later tenant farmers who did the mundane agricultural work (and could be presumed to vote for him), such was the traditional *modus operandi* of rural power. Increasingly estate owners could rely upon a steady stream of cash from their extensive rural holdings and they frequently used their political position to retain laws that upheld high agricultural prices. Such income was crucial to their financial stability and agricultural innovations over the centuries further enhanced their position. Their political power, whilst not entirely omniscient, was resilient enough for them to retain and perpetuate their privileged position.

One such example of this power was the Enclosure movement that was particularly prevalent in the late eighteenth and early nineteenth centuries. Despite England's lack of a peasantry that was found elsewhere in Europe, many rural folk relied upon land adjacent to villages to graze their few animals. Enclosures involved the appropriation of this "common" land by wealthy landowners who saw it as a way to further their estate efficiency. Land that had traditionally been available to all in the community for grazing, etc., was now fenced (enclosed); sometimes bought and deeded to the new owner or merely acquired through Parliamentary acts (the *Inclosure Acts*[36]) that licensed such seizures. The result was more efficient farming methods, increased crop yields and enhanced productivity. Commodity production had been associated earlier with the wool trade; this merely accentuated such trends and further improved profitability for the landowners.

Marxist historians have long argued that this was a classic example of landowners using their political power to consolidate their material well-being at the expense of the bulk of the rural population who were forced off the land.[37] It also set in place the forced migration from the countryside to the growing industrial areas by displaced small farmers, thus providing the embryonic labor force for the new mills and factories. This agricultural revolution thus became intertwined with the industrial revolution. Crucially though it reinforced the importance of productive land as an important source of income. Given the expenses of running such large houses, without such a revenue stream, the houses themselves became more of a financial liability.

Until the nineteenth century wealth and power resided in the countryside around such estates. Although established wealthy families could and did pass on their estates to subsequent generations, nevertheless there were opportunities for newcomers. In England, those that acquired prominence via other means such as incipient commerce had frequently been able to parley that newfound position by buying country estates. For example, minor Norfolk gentry such as the Walpole family were able to capitalize upon political success and good connections of Robert Walpole and assiduously climb the status ladder when he bought land and built Houghton House in 1721 – "incontrovertible evidence of his power, his wealth, his discrimination."[38] This semblance of class fluidity is an important reminder of the English aristocracy's ability to absorb a certain number of newcomers whom eventually might gain acceptance into the mores of country life. By leaving the proverbial gates open such action replenished those properties that had fallen upon hard times, particularly those who had overspent in an attempt to challenge more established landowners or simple lacked the requisite appropriate heirs. This was social mobility with a vengeance! But it was also testimony to the veracity of landownership as the *sine qua non* of status.

Perhaps, it is no surprise that industrial magnates and those whose wealth derived from technological innovation in the nineteenth century would follow the time honored pattern of buying land and building large houses to demonstrate their conspicuous consumption. They appeared eager to join the landed upper classes because this conferred the power and prestige that their material wealth now subsidized. Such estates were the perfect outlet for their cash. By the late Victorian period, imbued with the possibility of social climbing from their new fortunes, many newly rich saw a multitude of benefits to landownership. These included a periodic respite from arduous urban work or even the possibility of political office. Agents as well as beneficiaries of social mobility, the new industrial and commercial wealthy saw this as a material and symbolic investment in their future legacy. But it was also a way to further leverage their assertiveness in the volatile political environment of the nineteenth century and ensure that their voice (and interests) were heard above the din of more traditional interest squabbles. For others the idea of a country house signified the embrace of a new lifestyle of dignified hedonism. As Mark Girouard argued, it "represented to them peace, tradition, beauty and dignity. They were in love with the idea of being a country gentleman, strolling with gun under arm round their own acres."[39] This was personification of the synthesis between traditional status and new money.

If one examines many of the houses that were built in the first part of the nineteenth century, they were substantial, serious and evocative of a vision of an English gentleman obsessed with medieval grandeur.[40] They were expensive to build and maintain and perhaps unsurprisingly Classical or Renaissance styles were prevalent since this was "the international language of wealth and authority."[41] As architectural historian Simon Thurley states, "Men who had made new fortunes wanted to buy into this vision as much as those who had been substantial landowners for generations."[42] This same pattern can be seen in the rise of gentleman's clubs in London, replete with Grecian and Italianate influences since these were styles befitting the new semi-leisure class.

Ultimately, this was more than a superficial urge to acquire; it was a purposeful attempt to gain access to a deserving way of life that they perceived as a corollary to their material wealth. The more industrialization transformed the urban landscape, the more appealing the Edenic virtues of country life resonated amongst this group. Yet it is with some irony that the very forces of change that were transforming England from a rural to an urban industrial society were the responsibility of precisely this new industrial class whose wealth came from such changes and yet who were desirous of a country idyll. It was this group that in some respects resuscitated the landed upper class through a

large injection of capital and the enthusiastic embrace of all things sophisticated and rural. Like their aristocratic counterparts they too believed what their
contemporary Gilbert Scott saw as the providential nature of their possessions
whereby they "had been placed in a position of authority and dignity" as seen
in the character of their house.[43]

Industrialization did bring some benefits to the countryside. The use of
chemicals for fertilizers, restructuring field layout for improved mechanized efficiency and the introduction of steam technology led to productivity increases.
This met the growing demand for food from urban areas and a growing national
population. Again, quoting Simon Thurley, "Until 1870 England was still a
good place to be a landowner."[44] However, in subsequent decades falling agricultural prices, partly due to cheap U.S. wheat and imports from other countries,
dramatically reduced farm incomes. The costs of agricultural labor was also
increasing with more people drawn to jobs in urban and industrial areas putting further strain on estate budgets. Importing wealthy brides from the United
States for estate heirs somewhat offset the impending financial crisis, but it was
investments from the new moneyed class that provided a lifeline for what was
becoming a more tenuous way of life.

Like some of their fortunate non-aristocratic predecessors the industrialists
continued to invest in country estates and certainly found more opportunities to
do so given the financial plight of some existing owners who were forced to sell.
But they also brought a new twist to their visions of a rural Utopia. Land could
and would be a guaranteed revenue stream but for some newcomers it also might
provide opportunities for ethereal visual splendor that transcended mere farming.
If money was no longer the primary rationale behind agriculture, why clutter the
rural landscape with the visible accoutrements of commerce? Perfectly landscaped
gardens could replace crops; roaming herds of deer could replace cattle. In other
words, the very essence of a country estate was beginning to change for some of
the new owners. It was now as much about display as it was a pace of residence.

Some who had bought into this lifestyle, even back in the eighteenth century,
had nurtured dreams of a pastoral landscape that would surpass agriculture to
include a more manicured, planned garden. Formal gardens, interspersed with
buildings and monuments, had become popular amongst the wealthiest landowners in the early 1700s. Drawing heavily on garden designs in Renaissance
Italy, this style was designed to project an idealized version of nature and allow
the eye to wander in a restful tranquility. An early example of this was Stowe
landscape gardens in Buckinghamshire, built by a military officer, Viscount
Cobham upon his return to England in 1713 after the war with France.[45] With
many of the buildings designed by architect William Kent, as the name evokes,
the "Elysian fields" section surrounding two lakes on the extensive property
suggested a visual splendor that gradually evolves as one strolls through the
estate. This was a fastidiously planned landscape far removed from the intrusion
of agricultural commodity production.

In another example, when the 2nd Earl de la Warr sold his Sheffield estate in Sussex because of money problems in 1769, the new owner John Baker Holroyd, immediately "set about transforming the already extensive plea-sure grounds around the house" and hired the fashionable landscape expert Capability Brown to design the re-envisioned estate.[46] Another famous land-scape architect, Humphry Repton, expanded the park area further in sub-sequent decades. Eschewing the normal income streams from agriculture, Holroyd could afford the extravagance of a formal garden landscape because he had inherited money from his father, who owned land in Ireland and was part of the minor gentry there. For him and his ancestors (until the property was eventually deeded to the National Trust, its current owners, in the twentieth century) the visual splendor of the landscape and formal gardens took prece-dence over income generating agricultural activities. This was pre-industrial Arcadian splendor at its finest.

Such landscape gardens became even more popular during the nineteenth century as new estate owners were captivated by an allegorical appeal to pre-industrial life. By then secular society was less likely to associate gardens with Eden-like temptations; instead they could be envisaged as redolent of an Arcadian past. These were the manifest cultural reactions to industrial-ization that were evident amongst others opposed to the visual degradation of urban and factory life. For example, the Romanticism that was central to nineteenth-century literature and found a vigorous interpretation in painting with the Pre-Raphaelite movement was the quintessential rejection of indus-trialism and urbanism. Interestingly, many new landowners subscribed to this image of a pre-industrial bucolic past. They found solace in an idealized past age of rural tranquility, free from the ravages of industrialism. In construct-ing extensively landscaped and formal gardens, the new landowners sought to actually implement a tangible version of such a society. For those whose wealth came from such a society that they were seeking to escape, it was an ironic statement on changing elite sensibilities. They were not just buying into the status markers of the old landowners; they were carving out another version of rural life that accentuated their wealth by dismissing the normal financial means whereby estates were sustained. Not only were such ventures expensive to implement, especially when drawing upon the services of the best landscape architects, their new owners were also foregoing traditional forms of agricul-tural income, even though prices were diminishing. The latter, a product of increasing grain imports from the Americas, undermined the financial position of many in the landowning aristocracy and sometimes forced them to sell their estates to raise funds for their still lavish styles. However, such events proved of minimal concern to many of the new group of resource rich owners. They were not dependent upon their rural estates as income sources, therefore they could eschew the financial predicament of more traditional owners. The fact that the new wealthy could create rural idylls that defied economic logic furthered their position as bastions of privilege. Increasingly they could be seen as the lavish demonstrations of "conspicuous consumption" that Veblen was writing about at this time.

One of the best examples of someone who eschewed agricultural revenue can be found again in Sussex at Nymans – a large estate about 40 miles south of London. Nymans' founder, Ludwig Messel, was born in Germany but became a prosperous stockbroker in London and in 1890 he purchased 600 acres in the Sussex Weald. He built a house for his family but his real joy appeared to be the creation of an extensive garden and wooded areas designed to evoke a romantic landscape. It was a landscape that contained formal gardens surrounding the house and beyond that rolling hills of meadows and wooded enclaves. It was purposefully designed to soothe the senses with an Eden like vista. As was increasingly the case, he used money that he had made in another occupation (banking) to fund a rural retreat and burnish his status credentials. His was a vision of rural England that even a foreigner could buy into, providing he had the financial resources (he evidently did), embellish and nurture, and subsequently pass onto his descendants as fully fledged Englishmen.

The creation of rural utopias occurred in other industrialized countries. For example a similar pattern of aggrandizement by the new wealthy occurred in the United States in what has now been referred to as the Guilded Age. This refers to the period during the latter part of the nineteenth century when merchants had made extensive profits from new industries, particularly the railways and iron and steel, lavished that wealth on expensive properties and quasi regal lifestyles. Railway mogul Cornelius Vanderbilt was one such individual who was the personification of this new industrial entrepreneur. He made a fortune buying and selling steamships and trading routes in the 1830s and 1840s and then partnered with several new railway companies, rescuing several from bankruptcy before going on to make a further fortune from this new industry.[47] His grandson, George Vanderbilt, eschewing the life of a free market entrepreneur (including questionable practices such as stock market manipulation, collusion and price fixing) decided to use his inherited wealth to build what was to become, and remains, the largest private residence in the United States. Vanderbilt's 250 room, French chateau style *Biltmore House*, situated near Asheville, NC in the Appalachian Mountains, was completed in 1895. Set on almost 95,000 acres it was an imposing edifice with extensively manicured grounds plus numerous working farms that unambiguously communicated power and status. Even after 87,000 acres were sold to the United States Forest Service in 1914 following the death of George, the estate's remaining 8000 acres still provide uninterrupted mountain vistas. Whilst currently open to the public, the house and estate remain privately owned in the family of George's descendants.

The Dawn of Mass Consumption

Earlier I referred to structural changes that unleashed greater consumption by the majority of the population as they wielded increased buying power. This "wealth effect" meant household consumption increased as people felt wealthier. Purchasing power also increased following improvements in the banking industry during the late nineteenth century as organized credit markets facilitated the improved circulation of money.[48] Concomitantly, technological innovation and mass production lowered the price of goods and provided a much wider range of products. The average worker had more discretionary income and there were more goods available at cheaper prices. By the end of the nineteenth century global markets were becoming more integrated, liberalized trade and new transportation technologies lowered the price of many commodities, and increased labor productivity in Europe and North America led to improved worker wages.[49] The latter was particularly noticeable in England where workers had doubled their spending power between 1850 and 1899. In the United States workers continued to enjoy the benefits of higher wages than in other industrialized and industrializing countries, leading to increases in consumer spending. Consumers and consumption were terms that were increasingly entering the normal vocabulary and with that cam questions regarding the underlying utility and ultimate purpose of such behavior.

If people across all sections of society were now buying more, how did they know what to buy? The new rich had clear benchmarks of precisely the requisite goods that would demonstrate their new position and aspired for status. This was most evident as we have seen in their acquisition of country estates together with furnishings, clothing and general lifestyle pursuits designed to denote sophistication (and, let us not forget, the opportunity to enjoy the fruits of new-found wealth). Displaying the appropriate style and fashion were crucial indicators of both class and status. One could argue that this was merely the satisfaction of a higher order of needs that necessarily accompanied material wealth. For the average worker, with considerably more modest income, choosing what to spend that money on was less self-evident. Necessities such as more food and furnishings were unambiguous decisions, as were the purchase of household goods that improved domestic efficiency and relieved some of the arduous tasks that women had consistently faced. But it was also clear that what people wanted appeared to be increasing in volume.

Economist Alfred Marshall posited that historically wants and desires were limited and easily satisfied, but as society progressed and became more civilized, increased efforts were devoted to satisfying an expanding variety of products. Or as Trentmann argues in summarizing Marshall,

> Material satisfaction was guided, or ennobled, to use a Victorian term, by a natural urge for self-improvement....Consuming was like climbing a ladder of ever higher taste and faculties, with each activity releasing new energy to move up to the next rung.[50]

What made such increases in consumption possible was the dramatic growth of goods associated with distribution and retailing innovations. Two developments significantly transformed the landscape of consumption: the railways and the department store. Both revolutionized access to goods and both presage the growth of twentieth-century mass consumption. And both were given a further potency following the increased circulation of newspapers and the rise of advertising. The railways, following the earlier development of canals, provided an infrastructure for the cost effective shipment of goods. The department store emerged in major cities in the industrial world, providing an emporium of goods that could titillate, amuse, entertain but above all stimulate consumers. Possibly, for the first time in history the supply of products actually exceeded what was needed for a minimal existence.[51]

Improved railway transportation, especially in the growing U.S. market, brought rural areas into closer contact with cities, in essence shrinking time and distance. The introduction of mail order catalogues capitalized upon this transportation revolution and gave the rural population access to cheaper prices and mass produced goods.[52] The well-known pioneer in this was Richard Sears, who in the 1880s was employed as a station agent in Minnesota. After buying an unclaimed consignment of watches and selling them up and down the railway line where he worked, he partnered with a watchmaker (Alvah Roebuck) in 1887 and started a mail order catalogue company that specialized in watches and jewelry.[53] To capture a broader market for these and many other products he put together a 532 page catalogue (*Sears Roebuck Catalogue*) that sold everything from stoves to guns to agricultural implements at prices that were less expensive than local retailers. His main rival, the *Montgomery Ward* catalogue, followed a similar mass market strategy, often selling goods at such low prices that small town merchants cried foul and accused the company of fraud. Both were based out of the mid-west which gave them easy access via rail routes to much of the country. Their sales boomed and they were a crucial part of improvements in standards of living for many rural and small town populations who hitherto had been at the mercy of high priced local merchants.

The alternative to buying goods via a catalogue necessitated visiting a store. This prevailing type of retail was practiced nearly everywhere, according to Bhu Srinivasan, and "was a pragmatic, transactional affair. Goods were stocked at general stores behind the counter. Clerks, usually male, brought our merchandise for the customer to review, and negotiation ensued. Prices were based on the customer's savvy."[54] In other words it was a haphazard affair that varied tremendously from town to town. In the United States A.T. Stewart set about changing this when he built America a five story department store, *Stewart's Cast Iron Palace* on Tenth Street and Broadway in New York in 1862. It sold a wide range goods, organized into different departments on each of the five floors on the building, all displayed in an opulent setting designed to reveal the full extent of material life available to American households. Other department stores soon followed in major east coast cities, Wanamakers in Philadelphia in 1876 and Filenes in Boston in 1881, and on the west coast, Emporium in San Francisco, 1896. Their format was generally the same with a wide range of goods designed to appeal to the growing urban population with more discretionary income.

Multi-product retail emporiums had existed earlier, one of the first being *Harding, Howell & Co.'s Grand Fashionable Magazine* at 89 Pall Mall in St James's, London that opened in 1796. It catered to affluent middle-class women selling the latest fashions in such items as furs, fans, jewelry and clocks, and millinery. Because its appeal was to the newly wealthy, the quality was good but the prices expensive. The newer department stores of the nineteenth century, however, had much better price-quality ratios prices and were accessible to a broader segment of consumers. In Paris, Bon Marché had opened in 1852 with an assortment of arcades that Walter Benjamin said captivated the imaginations of many upper-class Parisians.[55] And back in London, American retail magnate Harry Gordon Selfridge, who had risen to be a partner in Marshall Fields in Chicago, opened his eponymous store in 1909 and transformed the retail environment in that city by offering a wide range of fashionable items at appealing price points.[56] Selfridges marketed to the wealthy and middle classes but particularly to those who aspired to sartorial grandeur. Similar to counterparts in other countries, the store also captured the imagination of a new class of consumers for whom shopping became a tool in identity construction and individual authenticity.[57] Self-esteem could be purposefully manufactured through material consumption and clothes often became an integral part of this process. As urbanization and industrialization increased, other countries embraced this retail revolution and similar grand emporiums opened.

For many in these burgeoning cities, department stores were a spectacle to behold, with their vast array of goods tastefully presented in serene settings and staffed by polite, almost obsequious personnel. Part of their allure lie in their creation of an imaginary world for consumers who could viscerally experience the retail revolution if not actually being part of it. For those who did buy, the stores were appealing to the growing sense of individual identities that industrialism was nurturing. The "wealth effect" and the nominal increase in demand meant people could transcend traditional social roles and identities and fashion their own sense of self.[58] It is axiomatic that rising incomes would result in purchasing behavior that surpasses basic necessities and embraces broader indulgences. What is less evident is the rationale for what they bought and why they bought it.

There is evidence that the working class purchased cheap imitations of goods bought by the wealthy.[59] If they had insufficient cash for this then credit plans were available to soothe the immediate financial pain. Again, the rise of retail banking played an important role here. But whereas industrialists had actually bought into the elite lifestyle, working class emulation of middle class material- ism would always be limited. This was watered down consumer democratiza- tion even if it merely provided a glimpse of a better life amidst a daily reality of long hours and often arduous toil. The acquisition of prestige and beauty remained firmly in the grasp of the new wealthy who set about with vigor to supplant the old elite. It is they who drove luxury sales in the nineteenth cen- tury and would continue to do so in the twentieth. Mass production and mass consumption increasingly brought the ideal of material transformation for the working classes but for most the reality was more circumscribed. It wasn't until the twentieth century when income levels further increased and heightened global trade plus production efficiencies transformed the supply of goods that a consumer revolution moved into its next phase. By then brands had become the *sine qua non* of retailing by providing quality and status reassurance for consumers. And by this time a luxury goods industry was emerging as artisanal producers of customized items were being subsumed under global brands that appealed directly to the wealthy as inequality persisted.

Conclusion: Reconciling Old and New

The above examples show how many industrialists bought into the landowning lifestyle but also modified its underlying ethos by accentuating the non-income generating aspects of it. This is indicative of discretionary expenditure pat- terns of the wealthy in the late nineteenth and early twentieth centuries that others have documented.[60] Moreover, it suggests a resolute determination of the newly rich to position themselves as justifiably part of the elite and whose indulgences in luxury products were deemed apropos given their hard work.

Once individual economic ambitions were freed from the constraints of moral opprobrium, luxury consumption and increased commercial enterprise went hand in hand. This is what David Hume had argued when he posited the ben- eficial consequences of such trends in an increasingly urban industrial society.[61] This point is further reinforced by Adams when he states, "the age old tension between wealth and virtue had finally been settled."[62] Wealth was now seen as the logical consequence of individual effort when freed from the fetters of tra- ditional hierarchies. What one did with that wealth was no longer constrained by importunate religious overtures or secular moral fervor. Luxury, *ipso facto*, was therefore no longer a sin, it was a civilizing force since it was increasingly likely to be seen in the most progressive and economically advanced societies.[63]

Earlier, European aristocrats had abandoned their attempts to regulate non elite spending via sumptuary laws, thus opening opportunities for the new wealthy to embrace consumption of so-called luxury products. If excessive expenditures by the wealthy meant embracing the refinements associated with the life of a country gentleman, this merely lent credence to the continuity of norms regarding civilized behavior that one continued to assume appropriate for the upper class – even in republican United States by the end of the nineteenth century.[64]

What civilized behavior actually meant for the arbiters of style and status was constantly evolving even as it continued to be the ethos that implicitly governed attitudes towards material acquisitions. Essentially it is how elite culture resonates with a sense of entitlement, assumed to be innate to a certain class, and how that mindset governs patterns of consumption. The presumption amongst such a group is that certain attitudes and values denote civilized sophistication. But can those sensibilities be learned by the newly rich, enabling them to take their rightful seat at the table of material opulence? As we have seen in the previous chapter, cultural frameworks evolved as societies changed, sometimes undermining and at other times reinforcing cultural entitlements. New material wealth was now empowering embryonic groups in society not necessarily to challenge the *status quo ante* but to attempt to join it. But in doing so they had to absorb the accoutrements of what was seen to be the personification of a civilized person.

Sociologist Norbert Elias wrote extensively about the link between long term structural development and changes in people's behavior and habitus when seen as part of a gradual civilizing process.[65] The concept of habitus, as developed by French cultural theorist Pierre Bourdieu,[66] encapsulates the institutionalization of habits that eventually become second nature ("habitualized") and provide informal guidance as to appropriate behavior. This was especially important for an elite who determinedly invoked informal norms to distance themselves from the masses and to restrict entry to their inner sanctum. Such an intended restricted culture, however, proved more fungible than the elite had hoped when economic conditions changed. In other words, old elite entitlements were progressively on shaky ground. As societies evolved so too did the impermeability of the overarching culture because of challenges from below and outside. For Elias cultural changes from the late Middle Ages to the Victorian era capture the essence of how the newly wealthy sought to successfully imitate the defining characteristics of upper-class sensibility and in doing so purposefully sustained this imperious mindset. This included not just what products to purchase but how to successfully integrate them into a mindset that conveyed the appropriate level of grandeur and arrogance. This was attitudinal change that went hand in hand with material progress, a form of cultural disentanglement and normative repositioning.

Post Enlightenment, the new wealthy ingratiated themselves into the status hierarchy, their enthusiastic presence (and material wealth) lending the requisite gravitas to their enthusiastic acquisition of goods. Furthermore, their presence lent credence to the civilizing mantle since they were demonstrably evidence of socio-economic progress and the embrace of rationalism that constituted a civilized society. Again this legitimized wealth since to be rich and successful was seen as a natural complement to economic progress for society as a whole. Consumption had become institutionalized and rationalized and was dignified by an ideology that sanctioned excess because it was seen as coincidental with overall societal progress. Old wealth was infused with new and elite culture rendered less cohesive but ultimately ideologically more enduring.

Notes

1 Shaw, J. *Shopping: Social and Cultural Perspectives*, Cambridge: Polity, 2010, pp. 27–8.
2 Mokyr, J. *A Culture of Growth*, Princeton: Princeton University Press, 2017, p. 7.
3 Sombart, W. *Luxury and Capitalism*, Ann Arbor: University of Michigan Press, 1967.
4 Liebow, V. Price competition in 1955, *Journal of Retailing*, Spring 1955.
5 Stillerman, J. *The Sociology of Consumption*, Cambridge: Polity Press, 2015, p. 7.
6 Stillerman.
7 Carruthers, B.C. and Babb, S.L. *Economy and Society*, Thousand Oaks: Pine Forge, 2000, p. 3.
8 Slater, D. *Consumer Culture and Modernity*, Cambridge: Polity, 1997; Smart, B. *Consumer Society: Critical Issues and Environmental Consequences*, Sage, 2010.
9 Sassatelli, R. *Consumer Culture: History, Theory, Politics*, Sage, 2007.
10 Trentmann, F. "The modern genealogy of the consumer: Meanings, identities and political synapses," in J. Brewer & F. Trentmann (Eds.), *Consuming Cultures, Global Perspectives: Historical Trajectories, Transnational Exchanges*, Oxford: Berg Publishers, 2006.
11 Stillerman, p. 26.
12 See for example Sassatelli, R. *Consumer Culture*, London: Sage Publication, 2007.
13 Weber, M. *The Protestant Ethic and the Spirit of Capitalism*, New York: Scribners, 1958.
14 Campbell, C. *The Romantic Ethic and the Spirit of Modern Consumerism, Alcuin Academics*, 2005.
15 See Montgomery, S and Chirot, D. *The Shape of the New*, Princeton: Princeton University Press, 2015.
16 Holmes, S. *The Anatomy of Anti-Liberalism*, Cambridge: Harvard University Press, 1993, pp. 3–4.
17 Trentmann, F. *Empire of Things*, New York: HarperCollins, 2016, p. 41.
18 Trentmann, 2016. p. 13.
19 Weber, op. cit.; Polanyi, K. *The Great Transformation. The Political and Economic Origins of Our Time*, Boston: Beacon Press, 1944.
20 Trentmann, 2016, p. 53.
21 Gregory, B. *The Unintended Reformation*, Cambridge: Harvard University Press, 2012, p. 374.
22 Allen, p. 267.
23 Allen, R. *The British Industrial Revolution in Global Perspective*, Cambridge: Cambridge University Press, 2009, p. 11.
24 Allen, op. cit., p. 12.
25 de Vries, J. *The Industrious Revolution: Consumer Behavior and the Household Economy, 1650 to the Present*, Cambridge: Cambridge University Press, 2008.

26 Tombs, R. *The English and their History*, London: Penguin Books, 2014, p. 377.
27 Allen, op. cit., p.15.
28 Tombs, p. 375, Allen, pp. 266–7.
29 Allen, p. 49.
30 Tombs, p. 374–5.
31 See McKendrick, N. "The commercialization of fashion" in McKendrick, N., J. Brewer & J.H. Plumb (Eds.), *The Birth of a Consumer Society*, Bloomington: Indian University Press, 1982, pp. 9–194.
32 Trentmann, 2016, p. 223.
33 See Gordon, R. *The Rise and Fall of American Growth*, Princeton: Princeton University Press, 2016.
34 Trentmann, 2016, p. 226.
35 Girouard, M. *Life in the English Country House*, New Haven: Yale University Press, 1978, p. 2.
36 Between 1604 and 1914, over 5,200 individual enclosure acts were passed.
37 See for example Thompson, E.P. *The Making of the English Working Class*. London: Penguin, 1991.
38 Girouard, p. 4.
39 Op. cit., p. 302.
40 Girouard, M. *The Return to Camelot: Chivalry and the English Gentleman*, New Haven: Yale University Press, 1981.
41 Thurley, S. *The Building of England*, London: William Collins, 2013, p. 428.
42 Thurley, p. 428.
43 Scott, G. *Secular and Domestic Architecture*, London, 1857, p. 142.
44 Thurley, op. cit., p. 428.
45 See National Trust, *Stowe Landscape Gardens*, London: National Trust, 1997.
46 See National Trust, *Sheffield Park Garden*, London: National Trust, 1994, p. 9.
47 Srinivasan, B. *Americana: A 400 Year History of American Capitalism*, New York: Penguin Books, pp. 86–9.
48 See Turner, A. *Between Debt and the Devil: Money, Credit, and Fixing Global Finance*, Princeton: Princeton University Press, 2016, pp. 58–9.
49 Trentmann, 2016, p. 146.
50 Trentmann, p. 14.
51 Trentmann, p. 154.
52 Srinivasan, p. 204.
53 See Micklethwait, J. and Wooldridge, A. *The Company*, New York: The Modern Library, 2003, p. 57.
54 Srinivasan, p. 201.
55 Quoted in Trentmann, p. 191.
56 See Stillerman, p. 35.
57 See Anthony, A. and Taplin, I.M. "Sustaining the retail pilgrimage: Developments of fast fashion and authentic identities," *Fashion, Style and Popular Culture*, January 4, 2017.
58 Anthony and Taplin, pp. 42–4.
59 Stillerman, p. 37.
60 See Trentmann, 2016, Gordon, Tombs.
61 Hume, D. *A Treatise of Human Nature*, 1739.
62 Adams, W.H. *On Luxury*, Dulles, Virginia: Potomac Books, 2012, p. 162.
63 Konrad Kambli, quoted in Trentmann, 2016, p. 118.
64 Adams, p. 161.
65 See Elias, N. *The Civilizing Process*, Oxford: Basil Blackwell, 1994. Also Elias, N. *On Civilization, Power, and Knowledge*, in Mennell, S. and Gouldsblom, J. (Eds.), Chicago: University of Chicago Press, 1998.
66 Bourdieu, P. *Distinction*, London: Routledge, 1984.

4

MASS PRODUCTION, MASS CONSUMPTION AND NEW CONSUMERS OF LUXURY

By the beginning of the twentieth century it was clear that manufacturing was entering a new phase. Electrification, infrastructural networking through sanitation innovations and a constant series of technical solutions to machine production and utilization, were transforming the industrial landscape. Productivity was rising in industries such as steel, chemicals and even household appliances as more and more firms took advantage of the synergies that accompanied technological innovation and diffusion.[1] Worker disposable incomes were increasing and with that the potential for broader sales of possibly more expensive products. To fully capture the benefits of these changes firms needed to find ways to further increase their efficiency and improve their volume and do this whilst simultaneously lowering their prices. The railways had enabled them to realize the potential of mass distribution; now they needed to mechanize production and take full advantage of scale economies. Once mass production of standardized commodities became organizationally proficient, the final problem for firms would be selling the finished products to legions of new consumers who were just beginning to identify themselves as marketplace players.

The growth of an increasingly sophisticated advertising industry provided the means whereby new consumers could be enticed to participate in the materialist dream. Whereas buying and selling in the late nineteenth century was largely done face to face, by the first decades of the twentieth century mass communication transformed this personal relationship and advertising emerged on an industrial scale.[2] For example, in the thirty years between 1880 and 1910 corporate advertising expenditures went from $30 to $600 million a year.[3] The advertising industry worked hand in hand with mass production industries, helping to create consumer desire and satisfy the needs of producers.

It also coincided with the growth of the department stores, which were often glamorous emporiums where prices were fixed and people were free to roam the aisles and examine goods. This was a long way from the haggling over prices that was involved in previous decades where customers waited whilst staff retrieved objects once a price had been agreed.

Mass consumption became one of the defining features of industrial society, driving economic growth and constituting the means by which the majority of the population forged their self-identity. Possession of goods was no longer the preserve of the wealthy or an elite. This democratization of consumption had far-reaching effects since it unleashed material acquisitions amongst a broad segment of the population who had hitherto been weaned on an ideology of frugality. The twentieth century was fast becoming the age of insatiability. As communications researcher Justin Lewis so cogently states, "The desire for a better life became the desire for more things."[4] Lifestyles were defined by possessions and whereas previous generations might have lusted over specific objects (gold, tulips etc.) modern consumerism was becoming inexhaustible.[5] No longer solely the preserve of the wealthy, consumerism had now become a central feature of industrial societies.

For that elite meanwhile, subtle and taken for granted status was now subject to precisely the same forces of advertising manipulation that was seducing the masses. In an attempt to distinguish themselves from the commodities that were widespread in the marketplace, many luxury goods firms were building brands and relying upon their aura of exclusivity to differentiate their product.[6] English firm Burberry, for example, evolved from a purveyor of quality functional outerwear from its founding in 1856, to its current position as a luxury clothing company that still retains its trademark plaid lining in its raincoats as a distinctive design feature. The French House of Chanel, founded in 1909 by Coco Chanel, distinguished itself by offering clothing styles that were a radical departure from the constrictions of Edwardian style. Under her leadership it introduced innovative styles such as the "little black dress" that were popularized by the growing media attention to fashion and celebrities. In each of these cases, the clothing possessed many of the attributes of cutting edge design but was more widely available than custom made clothes of previous generations. But above all it was seen as distinctive and had the quality attributes associated with what wealthy clients desired.

Branding was designed to communicate the essential quality and uniqueness of a product; it was a guarantee of integrity as well as enhancing the emotional bond between the consumer and the product consumed. Such a psychological attachment reassured the wealthy that they were acquitting something very special. In building their brands, firms used price, implied rarity and evocative images of luxury lifestyles. They were also capitalizing upon mass media developments that furthered their reach. And eventually they were able to use their own economies of scale and scope that industry consolidation and growing brand identity was making possible.

Concurrent with the emergence of mass production and eventually mass consumption, the production of high value-added, artisanal products was also changing. In the world of fashion clothing, the department store had begun to democratize and further institutionalize shopping amongst a broader segment of the population. Even the wealthy were now drawn to the elegant retail emporiums such as *Selfridges* in London, *Galeries Lafayette* in Paris, and *Marshall Fields* in Chicago where status and style were conspicuously on display. But that same elite could still draw on the distinctiveness of custom production, albeit one that was increasingly mediated by trends visibly displayed for all to experience. The department store in a way visualized status. It provided displays of styles that were concurrent with those of an elite but did so in ways that also influenced that elite. This was the beginning of the era of fashion designers such as Coco Chanel who were to shape the luxury goods industry in subsequent decades as well as provide inspiration for the aspirational middle classes.

The purveyors of luxury products were undergoing their own changes. More of them had entered the market or like saddle maker *Hermès* diversified to cater to the growing number of now globalized wealthy. Eventually, as Chapter 5 will show, this industry segment would embrace scale efficiencies as it too broadened its appeal to an expanding class of wealthy as well as undergo consolidation. Whilst never mass production of the type associated with standardized commodities, it would nevertheless be a departure from artisanal production modes that characterized its early development. The marketplace for consumer goods would become segmented and structured according to ability to pay, but many of the essential structuring production and marketing principles would coalesce.

Mass Production and Mass Consumption Come of Age

In 1903 Henry Ford, together with eleven other investors, created the Ford Motor Company. After tinkering with cars in the embryonic and increasingly crowded automobile industry in the late 1890s, Ford embarked upon a plan to build cars that would combine quality with customized production. The many small manufacturers geared production to wealthy customers since the machines were so expensive to make. Germany and then France had led the industry in the manufacture of such cars but their domestic markets were rather small. Early on Ford realized that the U.S. provided a larger market even for the large and expensive cars he would start to make. Given his high production costs, the retail price for his first models was high: the Model A, for example, sold for $2000 which was a considerable sum for that time. These were clearly not vehicles intended for a mass market.

Henry Ford increasingly realized that if one could further improve the production efficiencies associated with the organizational and technical innovations that had accompanied the growth of the automobile industry in the first place, he could capture a potentially much larger market for an inexpensive car. To do this necessitated a significant reduction in his overall production costs. Scale efficiencies combined with cheaper workers could enable him to manufacture a larger volume of inexpensive cars. But he needed to find ways of replacing the skilled (and therefore expensive) workers who completed many different labor intensive tasks on what was a stationary product in the factory. Traditional production methods involved workers individually assembling cars using a wide range of tools that were specific to each customized model. Incremental refinements on such processes were inevitable as the industry developed but the overall system still remained costly and unchanged. Output was slow and volume low, although quality was high. Ford was determined to change this and find a way to mechanize production, cut labor costs without sacrificing quality and thus be able to offer a product at an affordable price.[7] By fundamentally rethinking the overall assembly process in ways that would generate production efficiencies and dramatically lower unit costs, he could potentially reach a mass market with an affordable car. In eventually achieving these goals he was inspired by two sets of ideas: Frederick Taylor's Scientific Management theories and production innovations in the meat packing industry. Together, they would provide a dramatic departure from extant manufacturing systems and set the stage for mass production.

Frederick Taylor was an industrial engineer who worked as a consultant for Bethlehem Steel Company in the United States. He was hired in 1899 to find ways of improving production efficiency in various areas of the steel making process. After numerous experiments where he monitored workers on the job, he developed a system whereby workers were given production targets and subjected to structured supervision that specified when and how tasks should be done. If they followed these rules workers could dramatically improve their own performance and thus earn more money (they were paid on a piece rate system). Such workers did not need to be skilled – in fact Taylor explicitly sought out tasks that relied upon unskilled workers to demonstrate that productivity could be improved even with minimal worker skill levels. The workers just needed to be motivated by the potential for higher pay if they would be willing to work harder under routinized supervision. Managers would do the selection and whatever training was necessary and supervisors would dictate the structure and pace of work.

Under these new systems Taylor provided evidence of what he claimed were dramatic productivity gains for individual unskilled workers and thus efficiency benefits for the company. Subsequently referred to as "Scientific Management" this system promised firms the opportunity to reduce waste and cut costs through standardization and regularization of work.[8] By coordinating operations and controlling workers, such a system accelerated work and removed the need for skilled workers. It was a form of bureaucratic governance and technocratic workplace adjudication that was a radically different way of thinking about work organization and worker roles. Costly, skilled and often slow workers were replaced by cheaper, unskilled and more productive ones. Even if these practices were not always fully implemented by firms, the ideology nonetheless presaged the growth of managerial capitalism as the twentieth century unfolded.[9] It provided firms with a rationale for replacing skilled workers with unskilled ones who could do simple repetitive tasks under close managerial supervision. Wage costs could go down whilst productivity and presumably profits increased.[10]

Even before Taylor began his experiments with restructured work settings, pioneering individuals in the meatpacking industry in the American Midwest had experimented with new ways of processing animals for the burgeoning urban markets. Specifically they had introduced a process whereby animals entering a slaughter house could be systematically cut apart. Instead of skilled "butchers" cutting up a purchased animal that had been shipped to their stores in the major urban markets, animals now could be sent to a central location (slaughterhouse) where they were killed and placed on overhead racks that moved through the building as stationary workers cut off various parts of the animal. It was effectively a "dis-assembly" line that enabled less skilled workers to do standardized repetitive cutting tasks, with the actual mechanical conveyor dictating the pace of work. Not only did this remove parts of the animal (typically offal) that were not normally consumed by customers, it also facilitated an increased quantity of the saleable parts being packed together in refrigerated rail cars for shipment to distant markets. This increased the volume of shipped value-added meat parts and dramatically improved the efficiency and revenue stream of the meat packing industry. As Srinivasan notes in his description of the industry's center in the stockyards of Chicago, "In 1905 over 54 million hogs and 13 million cattle – one large animal for every adult American – were slaughtered in the United States, many of them in Chicago."[11]

These two new production systems were conceivably the inspiration for the subsequent manufacturing innovations of the early twentieth century. They suggested that scale efficiencies could be attained using lower skilled and thus less expensive workers, performing routinized tasks with specialized machinery in longer production runs. Relying upon the coordination and central expertise of managers, narrow product lines could produce large quantities of standardized products with dramatically lower unit costs. The latter meant that such products could be sold much less expensively and in larger volumes than in the past. Henry Ford eventually embraced such systems when he built a new car factory at Highland Park, Michigan in 1910 to manufacture his Model T.

The Model T, retailing at $850, was much cheaper than his earlier models and much lighter (1,200 pounds). It was built using an assembly line, similar in basic structure but opposite in function to that found in the slaughter house system. Car parts were moved along a mechanical conveyor to stationary workers who each performed a series of fairly simple and expeditious assembly tasks.

Unlike earlier factories where workers wandered around performing multiple tasks, the work now came to the workers; work tasks hitherto done by a single skilled worker were now subdivided amongst different workers situated along the line, and the line dictated the actual pace of work.[12] Annual output for Ford increased from 18,000 cars in 1908 to nearly 203,000 cars in 1913.[13] But he was not just producing more cars, he was producing them much more efficiently. Car assembly went from thirteen hours per vehicle under the old stationary system to approximately 90 minutes in the new moving assembly line. Such productivity gains translated into even lower prices. The price of the Model T went down to $360 in 1914 and by then Ford had captured forty eight percent of the automobile market (from nine percent in 1908). As efficiency gains increased he added to his labor force to meet the heightened demand for his inexpensive car. More workers, even unskilled ones at lower rate of pay than their skilled counterparts, translated into more potential customers.

Ford's innovative manufacturing systems were eventually replicated by others in the automobile industry, eventually spreading to further industries who similarly gained scale efficiencies. The emerging pattern of mass produced goods at affordable prices was becoming the hallmark of industrial societies. Having solved the problem of cost effective production rationalization, and able to take advantages of distribution efficiencies following the continued spread of railways, manufacturers faced one final problem: how to convince consumers to buy the products. Mass distribution combined with mass production brought a large volume of affordable products to everyone's doorstep. But would people buy them? For centuries working and even middle classes had been cloaked in an ideology of frugality. Discretionary spending was limited. As incomes rose in the late nineteenth century one did see an appreciable rise in material consumption of goods beyond those deemed essential for daily survival.

A dramatic increase in the volume of standardized goods meant consumers had much greater choice. But how would they know what to purchase from the growing array of goods on offer? Since many of the new products were unfamiliar to the new consumers, precisely how might the latter gain the requisite information to make an informed choice? Quality and reliability were generally unknown properties of many new products so consumers might naturally be wary of expending their limited income on a product with which they were unfamiliar. Would they have the income to buy and if they did, why would they choose one product over another?

Two innovations would take the uncertainty out of this decision-making. First Henry Ford introduced his soon-to-be famous "$5 a day" wage. This dramatically increased the buying power of a large segment of the industrial workforce. Second, the growth of the advertising industry introduced mechanisms to reassure the quality and desirability of products for would be customers. This typically involved advertising, product promotion and ultimately brand building. The latter was salient in providing *de facto* guarantees and assurance for a product.

More Money for Workers to Buy Things

Ford's introduction of the $5 a day wage was in many respects almost as important as his production innovations. Labor turnover of around 1,000 percent by 1913, plus high daily absenteeism rates severely disrupted his operations. A predictable supply of workers performing their requisite routine tasks was crucial for the scale efficiencies that the system demanded. When faced with these high rates on his new assembly lines and the obvious worker dissatisfaction with the fundamentally alienating nature of repetitive work tasks, Ford devised a payment scheme designed to retain and motivate his workers. Providing they were never absent from work, such workers could practically double their daily wage to $5. However, any time off, even for routine sickness, would immediately reduce that payment. This higher wage was double prevailing wage rates and thus a very effective financial incentive for his workers. It was also significantly higher than wages in alternative industries at that time.

The effects of this revised wage structure were twofold. Firstly, Ford accomplished his goal of eliminating the disruptive effects of absences on the assembly line. The financial incentive dramatically encouraged workers stay on the job otherwise they would forfeit the extra money. More reliable production systems enabled him to add assembly lines for more cars, thereby using more workers. Secondly, this additional income actually enabled more workers to buy the mass-produced products, including those from his own factories. He was one of the first manufacturers to recognize that the production gains would enable him to pay higher wages without sacrificing too much profit margin and in doing so create a broader class of consumers with incomes that permitted new patterns of consumption.

Admittedly this new wage system was fraught with inconsistencies (part of the wage was actually implemented as a bonus and not all of his workers received it), and it was part of company attempts to extend their control over the worker's domestic sphere (often onerous housing rules and living arrangements were rigidly enforced). And for many it was correctly seen as a deeply paternalistic system that reflected an extension of management control.[14] Nonetheless, it did further the potential for sales since more workers possessed incomes that surpassed that of previous generations.

Ford's innovations were in many respects a crucial benchmark in the growth of industrial capitalism. As Vallas et al succinctly state, "Over the next decade Ford irreversibly changed how work was done, how workers were rewarded, and how Americans lived."[15] The latter proved particularly salient since it signified the rise of modern consumption. Ford was buying worker compliance and attendance at work whilst simultaneously recognizing that those very same workers would now have incomes that would enable them to join an embryonic consumer class. He appeared to have solved the ultimate capitalist dilemma of finding a balance between containing labor costs without sacrificing the buying power of his workers. He did this whilst expanding the size of his workforce, thus adding large numbers of new potential customers. As historian Stuart Ewen succinctly stated, "It became imperative to invest the laborer with a financial power and a psychic desire to consume."[16] However disillusioned with the alienation of work, many workers were thus able to reconcile such frustrations by embracing the chance to become more active consumers.

Selling the Acquisitive Lifestyle

In the late nineteenth century, larger companies had sought ways to differentiate their products from others in expanding markets by building awareness of the quality and utility of such products. Since they were creating an aura of distinctiveness and style, effectively this was the beginning of branding, aided in 1890 by a U.S. court decision that permitted companies to patent trade-marks.[17] Now companies could legally defend their logos as proprietary and advertise their products using such logos. Branded products were crucial for the development of consumption because they provided certain quality assurances for customers. As branding spread, it enabled firms to consolidate their position in markets and clearly differentiate themselves from non-branded more localized products.

The growth of what would become the advertising industry was the inevitable response to the needs of mass industrial capitalism.[18] The market for standardized goods was growing, income levels were slowly rising as workers entered mass production industries, and firms were exploring ways of differentiating different groups of potential consumers in order to sell products to them. Large firms were able to use advertising to persuade consumers that they needed a certain product in the first place and then sell them their branded product. It was institutionalizing the desire to consume but doing it on an unprecedented scale. This was the harbinger of the age of insatiability as commodities became immersed in cultural associations and illusions. But this wasn't the homogenous mass culture of capitalist modernity, the so-called one-dimensional man that the Frankfort school invoked.[19] Instead a wide range of goods were being consumed, some clearly commodified products designed for mass audiences but others serving to differentiate on the basis of consumer taste.

Advertising proved a potent tool in this process, transforming the many aspects of mundane life into exotic, romantic and beautiful activities. Advertising was able to nurture potential consumers and then attempt to control their consumption habits. The subtle ways in which this was done varied but generally relied on the reification of certain values associated with human desires. These included the desire for prestige or status, the search for beauty and self-adornment, and sometimes even just the urge to acquire. In persuading consumers to buy things, as economic historian Frank Trentmann argued, marketers proved successful by reinforcing the idea that, "Wanting stuff was not frivolous. It was about self-fulfillment."[20] Objects ceased to have merely utilitarian functions; they now were defined by their style and value in defining who the consumer wanted to be.

This proved to be a significant milestone in the transformation of what was an evolving culture of consumption that increasingly pervaded most sections of society. Buying things was no longer the preserve of the rich. In fact it was now legitimate and even necessary for most people to participate in material acquisitions that had in the past been shunned. To not do so suggested abject poverty or such a marginal status that one would effectively be relinquishing all rights to be a full participant in society. To be an avid consumer meant indulging in the manifold benefits of mass production. The veritably bounty of available material goods provided ample ways for the average citizen consumer to satisfy whatever needs they were being encouraged to develop. The more they bought, the more mass production industries flourished. Thus was born the notion of the "happy good citizen consumer" who would dominate retailing in the twentieth century. It was as if consumption became the defining mode of integration into society as a culture of materialism became ever more pervasive.

Whilst the mass market society was initially a Western phenomenon, it spread eventually throughout the world. It became the hallmark of modernity, the defining characteristic of civilized essentialism. Advertising became the mechanism that translated desires into achievable gains; it endowed a civilizing component to material goods. As advertising firms were established in the early twentieth century they pioneered demographic analysis of consumers in order to track buying behavior. They examined lifestyle market segments and then related that to product differentiation. By the 1930s they had moved beyond simple demographic analysis to attitudinal surveys, lifestyle activities and intrinsic consumer beliefs.[21] Buying became a way for the average person to partake in a longstanding but constantly evolving concept of the "civilized man" (or woman). If we recall Elias's works on the civilizing process and how it provided a panoply of respectability but also normative constraints on behavior, advertising can thus be seen as the medium for people to fully understand what that behavior now constituted. Mass production begat mass consumption, but the latter was now intricately linked with sign posts and guidelines that denoted the requisite cultural respectability behind such activity. Much of the decision-making ambiguity behind purchasing was removed as brands became the benchmark of respectability, signalizing appropriate consumer choices. Historian Stuart Ewen is perceptively succinct when he comments on this trend,

> In an attempt to implicate men and women within the efficient process of production, advertising built a vision of culture which bound old notions of Civilization to the new realities of civil society. In what was viewed as their instinctual search for traditional ideals, people were offered a vision of civilized man which was transvaluated in terms of the pecuniary

exigencies of society. Within a society that defined real life in terms of the monotonous insecurities of mass production, advertising attempted to create an alternative organization of life which would channel man's desires for self, for social success, for leisure away from himself and his works, and towards a commoditized acceptance of "Civilization."[22]

There remains little ambiguity as to what one should buy and why one should be buying it. Having a better life meant having more things. People were no longer merely satisfying basic needs through the acquisition of material goods. Now such acquisition became an insatiable end in itself as commodities defined lifestyle and ambition.[23] Satisfaction was merely just another product away and we had entered what Justin Lewis claims was the "age of insecurity."[24] Moreover, the essentialism of consumption as a necessary component of mass production systems proved an increasingly inviolable way to confer a semblance of dignity upon the buyer. "I buy therefore I am" as the facetious invocation of existentialist reasoning affirms. But how much did these changing consumption patterns vary between classes? And was mass production the mere commodification of culture? If everybody was now a consumer and self-identity the slave of materialist ideology, what did this mean for the production and consumption of luxury goods? Could the new rich still rely upon their appropriation of taste and the markers of good life to easily differentiate themselves from the majority? If so they needed the requisite knowledge of the social and cultural value of goods as well as being able to use them correctly.

Rethinking Status

Marx, Weber and Veblen laid the groundwork in the nineteenth century for an understanding of how class and status affected life styles and life chances and *ipso facto* implicit attitudes towards consumption. When Max Weber invoked the notion of status or social honor he argued that the upper classes were seeking to maintain their position by necessitating a monopoly over access to luxury goods.[25] Simmel saw similar tendencies as the wealthy adopted fashions that would exclude outsiders.[26] But such formal limitations were no longer sanctioned. Consequently, reconciling expressions of individualism with exclusionary restrictions in a democratic society would almost inevitably devolve into pricing practices – one simply charges a price for a product that dramatically exceeds that which an average person can afford.

Now that shopping had become the preserve of the masses did that erode the distinction between the rich and the rest? If the middle classes were susceptible to the distractions promulgated by advertisers who incessantly pitched images of upper class lifestyles, did it result in the wealthy retreating into their own materialist inner sanctum? In other words, if the masses used referential status markers to motivate their own consumer habits, did elites develop new parameters for success? Did they merely buy more expensive, rare items and thus keep the material distance between themselves and the masses or were they searching for other means to differentiate themselves?

Whereas elites in the past were able to distinguish themselves from the masses by virtue of their ascribed position and rigidly enforced status, industrialization and the concomitant wealth that accompanied it upturned these hierarchies. Access to privileged elite status had become less formally restrictive and the flood gates of consumerism opened following the growth of increasingly sophisticated marketing in the early twentieth century.[27] Growing prosperity, accompanied by an ethic in which material acquisition was viewed as an essential component of an emerging middle class lifestyle, created new markets for products that hitherto had been the preserve of the few. That same prosperity however, had furthered the prosperity of the wealthy and in many cases increased their numbers. Is it possible to differentiate their behavior from that of the majority of consumers, and if so to what can we attribute such differentiation? Was it merely having more money or are there discernable features of high culture that the rich were successfully leveraging?

Pierre Bourdieu's work attempts to answer these questions by invoking the notion of cultural capital as underlying variations in consumer behavior between classes.[28] For him class position connotes economic status, essential values plus cultural attributes that determine how one interacts and thus are perceived by others. These attributes (*habitus*) are acquired through upbringing, education and eventually employment and are consistently revealed through lifestyle behavior. The poorer the individual the more likely he or she would pursue needs-based attitudes towards goods in which quantity surpassed quality. Intellectuals on the other hand emphasize aesthetic or quality considerations in their lifestyle preferences. They are both arbiters of taste and the group who assert their distinctiveness through possessions. Bourdieu placed less emphasis on imitation than Veblen, arguing that each class has greater influence on its members than those from a class above. Looking to others in a similar class position reinforces the sense of self and in doing so reinforce basic inequalities. Different classes possess different and distinctive self-definitions, no matter how aspirational individuals might be. Tastes are rooted in class position but are not necessarily markers for admiration; in fact some upper class tastes can be resoundingly rejected by lower classes.

Since consumption is organized around a variety of spaces, each determined by social class, consumer agency is consequential upon ones position in such a hierarchy; the higher one is the greater the freedom to choose. Whilst mobility is ever-present, it does nonetheless seem that cultural obstacles might impose more rigidity than economic ones. Money might buy the material benefits of elite lifestyles but acquiring the requisite cultural capital might be more challenging.

Bourdieu's work on cultural capital has been extensively criticized for not recognizing other ways in which the upper classes signal status, for instance by their varied tastes in art and music.[29] Cultural consumption becomes a differentiating feature that transcends wealth indicators and is much more expansive in detailing how the wealthy think and behave. In other words notable cultural practices and appreciations indicate a high level of sophistication that is conspicuously absent amongst the masses who tend to be more "univore" in their tastes.[30] Bourdieu's legacy however lies in developing a framework for understanding more of the subtleties of consumer behavior and how it relates to acquired and learned predispositions.[31] For the newly rich it certainly denotes how distinctive values and mindsets are appropriated, but it tends to minimize how such groups might reframe status distinctiveness according to measures more appropriate to their wealth. The new rich seek material lifestyles that are distinctive but are increasingly an amalgam of "old ways" and new patterns. Whilst reverential to traditional manifestations of wealth (opulent houses, expensive jewelry, exclusive forms of travel), this group might be more assertive in their display of such wealth. But in all of this they are aided by the proliferation of brands.

Advertising was predicated upon brand building to provide quality assurances for consumers who lacked discernable product knowledge. The evolving luxury goods industry capitalized upon precisely the same mechanisms to build awareness of its own products. Previously subtle and taken for granted status was now subject to overt messages designed to evoke what material success entailed as well as precisely the products that could satisfy it. It was designed to both appeal to as well as transcend traditional demarcations. Stimulating purposeful behavior amongst the new rich meant providing status signposts to guide appropriate consumption. Acquiring the necessary cultural gravitas could be more challenging but at least there were visual symbols that unambiguously pointed in the right direction. Branding was about lifestyle markers that could unravel the complexities of access; they communicated what appropriate behavior entailed and where money should be directed to secure distinction. In giving agency to the new rich as they sought the evolving meaningful symbols of success, advertising essentially delivered taste via consumption.

The automobile industry provides interesting examples in this area. Mass produced cars were preceded by custom built automobiles that were available only to the rich. However, once mass produced firms were firmly established and a mass market became pervasive, some created niche products that were more customized to meet the needs of the rich. Other longstanding luxury car companies such as Rolls Royce and Bentley eschewed mass production trends and continued focusing upon a limited output of finely crafted and expensive vehicles that were designed to be unambiguously luxurious. In either case brand building was crucial to differentiate these products from the largely utilitarian products of the mass market.

The new wealth generated by industrial and then subsequently post-industrial society enabled a larger group of individuals to indulge in heightened levels of consumerism that dwarfed even that of the new middle class. The rich were palpably richer as the twentieth century unfolded and there were more of them globally. Whatever this group might have lacked in firmly circum-scribed status that distinguished elites of old, they aggressively asserted their buying power to formalize their new position. This gave further credence to Veblen's argument about conspicuous consumption but also recast such vesti-gial behavior as more fungible. The status-fueled rivalry that characterized the rich as they accumulated, displayed and imitated was given greater resonance by newly wealthy individuals whose fortunes came from the mass production industries and progressively more sophisticated manufacturing.

These groups were the new consumers of luxury products and the lifestyles associated with them. They were the driving force behind the growth of a luxury goods industry, specific details of which are discussed in the next chapter. Their wealth differentiated them from the majority in society, as wealth had done in the past. But they were the beneficiaries of an ideology that legitimized it and was more permissive of material acquisition. They could enter the pan-theons of the discerning few and exhibit the lifestyles and predispositions that relished their distinctiveness from the rest of society. As a consequence, luxury has actually become more pervasive, firmly ensconced and legitimated amongst those whose wealth unabashedly permits indulgences that in the past might have been seen as circumspect. Furthermore, its resonance has been fueled by growing inequality which has accentuated the gap between the middle class consumers discussed earlier and the rich.

Whilst the persistence of inequality has been a fundamental feature throughout human history, its current iteration stands in contrast to the perception of social mobility and improved living standards associated with mass consumption. As economic inequality increased, both in developed and emerging economies, there has been a corresponding increase in the demand for luxury goods.

Inequality and Materialism

If inequality has been a fundamental feature throughout human history, how much has it changed in recent decades? In his recent book on global inequality, Branko Milanovic addresses this when he asks "who has gained from globalization?"[32] Part of his answer is that Asian poor and middle classes have been winners since it has elevated many of them from poverty. However, the other clear winners, those whose incomes have risen significantly in recent decades and who are part of the global top 1 percent, are overwhelmingly from the rich economies as well as a few emerging economies. Here the U.S. dominates closely followed by Western Europe, Japan, Oceania and then the BRIC countries. Individuals in these countries who constitute the new rich are responsible for driving the sales of luxury products. Whilst it is difficult to gauge exact income levels in previous centuries and thus the true measure of past material inequality, there is an abundance of information on income and wealth for more recent times. This enables us to better comprehend how current trends in inequality are shaping buying patterns and ultimately luxury goods consumption.

One of the first things of note is that income gaps have grown wider in the developed world in the past few decades, essentially furthering the prosperity of those who were already well off.[33] These are both absolute and relative gains. The rising inequality within countries is due in part because the returns from capital, according to Thomas Picketty were always higher than the rate of economic growth.[34] The really wealthy had the means to further their wealth whilst others, more reliant upon income, saw their wealth remain stagnant.

A clearer perspective on the income gap comes from analysis using the *Gini coefficient*. For example the United States, Census data on family incomes since the 1960s shows that households with incomes in excess of $100,000 have seen increases over this time period whilst those with incomes of less than $44,000 have seen virtually no income growth. The incomes of the top 5 percent went from an average of $154,000 in 1966 to $310,000 in 2010; the top 20 percent from $100,000 to $187,000. The average incomes of the fourth quintile went from $31,000 to $37,000; those in the bottom quintile from $14,000 to $15,000. Put another way, the ratio of the average income for the top 5 percent to the average of those in the bottom 20 percent went from 11 to 21 times.[35] Looking at more recent data from the Federal Reserve, one notes that the top 3 percent received 30.5 percent of total incomes in 2013; the next 7 percent received 16.8 percent. Just over half the remaining income thus went to 90 percent of the population. Furthermore, the top group saw their incomes rise over the previous two decades whilst median family income for the majority of the population, adjusted for inflation, has fallen since 2010. A similar pattern to these disparities can be seen in the UK where the share of the top 1 percent in gross income has more than doubled since 1979.[36] Likewise China, Brazil, India and South Africa have seen notable increases in income and wealth inequality in recent decades following sustained economic growth that has disproportionately favored the few.

Shifting from income measures to wealth, one notes how the United States has the world's largest concentration of billionaire wealth ($2.8 trillion) whilst three quarters of newly minted billionaires came from India and China.[37] Globally the total wealth of billionaires has risen by 17 percent since 2015; Asia (mainly China and India) now has the largest number at 637, the United States has 563 and Europe, 342.[38] Asian billionaires are typically younger than their western counterparts and are more likely to have acquired wealth from entrepreneurial ventures and new technology firms. Looking at this another way, globally, the number of ultra-high net worth individuals (UHNWI) has grown by 60 percent in the last ten years – a growth that reflects increases in asset prices and investment returns following the global financial crisis.[39] The faster rate of growth has largely been in emerging economies and the number of UHNWI is forecast to grow strongly over the next five years.[40]

Inequality takes on a more nuanced dimension when one considers inequality of consumption; specifically who spends what and where? Aside from the inevitable digressions on relative and absolute poverty that are often the focal point on consumer spending – in this instance the tangible impediments – it is worth briefly examining what the wealthy buy with this excess income.

What are People Buying?

Werner Sombart referred to the growth of hedonistic consumption that corresponded with the Renaissance and acted as a stimulus for luxury goods such as expensive celebratory events and the increasing role of courtesans (mistresses) for wealthy men.[41] Experiences were valued as highly as material possessions although courtesans simultaneously provided both. As noted in the previous chapter, material indulgences on fashion, housing and home decor were a feature of eighteenth- and nineteenth-century European societies as newly wealthy groups positioned themselves alongside the old elite, the traditional standard bearers of taste and style.[42] Once industrialization unleashed opportunities for hedonistic instant gratification, the wealthy were forced to reassert their attempt to exclude outsiders from the products and lifestyles that they embraced.[43]

Precisely what sorts of luxury products are being bought? According to consultants Bain & Company, there continues to be steady growth in most luxury segments, led in 2016 by luxury cars, luxury hospitality and personal luxury goods (jewelry, watches and leather goods) which account for approximately 80 percent of the market.[44] Luxury car sales were up 8 percent over the previous year and totaled €438bn; luxury hospitality was up 4 percent (at €183bn); fine wines and spirits (€66bn). Fine art was also a strong performer with 6 percent growth over the previous year; post war and contemporary paintings being most in demand. Whilst there was a slowdown in growth (1 to 2 percent over 3 percent for the previous year) in personal goods some of this slowdown is attributed to currency fluctuations as well as a decrease in buying by Chinese consumers. When compared to market growth of 13 percent in 2011, the slowdown is significant. But given that other economic sectors were still struggling to rebound from the 2008 recession and median incomes were flat in many high income countries, any growth could be considered in the circumstance to be quite robust.

It is also interesting to note a significant growth (5 percent) in luxury experiences (cruises, spa vacations etc.), particularly amongst Chinese consumers who are the biggest spenders globally in this category.[45] Like their counterparts in high income countries, this group contains keen investors in art but they are also showing a distinct inclination towards spending on sports teams where price tags have increased for elite programs.[46] In terms of demographics, rich millennials in China are driving much of the recent growth in luxury goods. *Hermès* for example saw a 12 percent increase in their revenues in Asia (compared with 11.5 percent in the Americas and seven percent in Europe) which they attribute to the growth of that segment of the population and their continued enthusiasm for top luxury brands.[47]

What are the attributes that people consider when buying luxury goods? Considering the high price and limited availability there remains a strong case for arguing that scarcity is one of the key drivers. In an Aston Martin print advertisement some years ago two men were pictured next to a new car outside a house; one man (a neighbor) asked the other (owner) about the car in the driveway. The owner replied by giving the name of the car (Aston Martin DB9) and describing its attributes (hand made by craftsmen and capable of astonishingly high speeds); when the neighbor asked where he could get one the owner simply replied that he probably could not since no more were available (a mere 4500 were made for worldwide sales). The car is the epitome of luxury and with a sticker price of $250,000 – more than the median price of a home in most U.S. cities – clearly beyond the financial means of the average consumer. It is unambiguously a luxury product that can be widely seen but only a few can actually own.

Manufacturing scarcity is a crucial strategy for luxury companies as it uses limited availability to stimulate demand. This is a fundamental component of luxury branding strategy that is opposite to mass market branding designed to increase the volume of sales. Rarity translates into exclusivity, echoing Simmel's argument regarding the behavior of the wealthy and their attempts to prevent others (the proverbial masses) from obtaining the same products. With rarity comes high price. Here one invokes the old adage that if you have to ask how much a desirable object costs then you probably cannot afford it. There's a saying in the French wine world that if a producers starts talking about "la gout de terroir" (the taste of terroir) then get out your wallet! Consumers are thus presented with tangible barriers to purchase that effectively de-commodify the product. Luxury producers universally pursue "premium pricing strategies" since high price (and presumed excellent quality) is an intrinsic characteristic of a luxury branded product.[48]

In evaluating what luxury consumers in the United States regularly state as the attributes they consider when buying luxury goods, quality is uppermost, followed by price and then brand name. In a 2012 U.S. consumer survey by Accenture, 75 percent listed quality as the primary attribute in evaluating/purchasing luxury goods followed by price at 69 percent and brand name at 25 percent. It is important to note that many people equate high price with quality so it is not surprising that the two are so closely inter-related. Furthermore high price is what distinguishes luxury goods from premium goods and whilst the latter often has a simple functional value, the former relies upon scarcity and symbolic value that is invariably associated with a brand.[49] High price, as Kapferer argues, creates the rarity of the product since it makes it less available to the majority of the population.[50] Luxury goods thus have symbolic value that makes them desirable and since they connote financial sacrifice by consumers who purchase them, adds to the perceived value.[51]

Finally luxury remains firmly anchored in the allure of exclusivity. A good example of this can be found in a recent article by Katherine Clarke in the "Mansion" section of the *Wall Street Journal*.[52] In this article she chronicles a trend of "over the top" mansions being built by Los Angeles' developers, each one of the properties the embodiment of exceptional luxury befitting an aristocrat of days past. Priced at $180 million, one mansion is 34,000 square feet with 9 bedrooms, gym, 2000-bottle wine cellar and a floating staircase. The most expensive lists at $500 million, is 100,000 square feet, has 20 bedrooms and includes a nightclub, five elevators, a beauty salon and a jelly fish aquarium. One owner was quoted as saying "my job is to touch every one of your senses. If you're fortunate enough to have that kind of money, your home should be your kingdom."[53] Not surprisingly there are great rivalries amongst the developers and their owners to lay claim to the biggest, most opulent residence. A similar competition is driving the high end of the residential market in other major cities throughout the world. The super-rich have not lost their appetite for residential opulence as they appear to engage in a form of property "one-upmanship." In many respects this is a continuation of past practices surrounding the super-rich and their homes that we chronicled in the previous chapter.

The twentieth century saw the development and sustained growth of mass consumption. Initially made possible by a unique set of technological, scientific and organizational innovations, it was subsequently fueled by the growth of advertising. Advertising gave firms the opportunities to develop their brands and then market them to a population whose disposable incomes had increased. The growth of middle class prosperity, despite setbacks such as the Great Depression, became part of a new culture of consumption that became increasingly pervasive in industrial societies. Material acquisitions became the *sine qua non* of respectability. The consumption of goods became perfectly acceptable for all walks of life for in many ways it was the manifestation of individual success.

For the wealthy elite, whose numbers were increasing, satisfying their own craving for appropriate indicators of their status could have been challenging. Often lacking the requisite cultural credentials that their forebears had inherited, the new wealthy needed to find ways to navigate the often tortuous route to social prestige. As in the past, they were able to use their fortunes to buy access to elite lifestyles. They accomplished this in the time honored fashion of buying the most expensive, exclusive high quality products and lifestyles. But they were also able to capitalize upon the very medium (advertising) that had produced mass consumption to learn the subtleties of *noblesse oblige*. Bombarded with images of the good life, they could be visually socialized into what such life entailed. They might not be fully in possession of the appropriate habitus, but they could acquire enough to gain a foothold from which to leverage further benefits. Finally, they were presented with a wide array of luxury products that themselves had been transformed in the twentieth century with the growth of luxury goods manufacturers. It wasn't mass production of standardized products but it did entail production of larger quantities of expensive items than ever before. What had in the past been artisanal in nature, luxury was now an industry replete with multi-national firms peddling the good life across the globe. Brands had replaced individual craftsmen, and branding secured the reputation of firms that were increasingly becoming consolidated. Luxury had become an acceptable lifestyle providing one had the financial means to attain it. The moral opprobrium associated with it in the past was now replaced with envy even if questions as to how the wealth was attained lurked ominously in the background. As wealth and inequality increase globally, the luxury goods industry has developed strategies to appeal to what is becoming a more homogenous global elite – at least in their tastes.

Notes

1 Gordon, R., *The Rise and Fall of American Growth*, Princeton: Princeton University Press, 2016.
2 Lewis, J. *Beyond Consumer Capitalism*, Cambridge: Polity, 2013, p. 60.
3 Budd, M., Craig, S. and Steinman, C. *Consuming Environments: Television and Commercial Culture* (2nd Ed.), New Jersey: Rutgers University Press, 2004.
4 Lewis, p. 54.
5 See Campbell, C. *The Romantic Ethic and the Spirit of Modern Consumerism*, Oxford: Blackwells, 1989.
6 Okonkwo, U. *Luxury Fashion Branding*, Basingstoke: Palgrave MacMillan, 2007.
7 Smil, V. *The Rise and Retreat of American Manufacturing*, Cambridge: The MIT Press, 2013, p. 54.
8 Guillen, M.F. *The Taylorized Beauty of the Mechanical*, Princeton: Princeton University Press, 2006, p. 19.
9 Waring, S. *Taylorism Transformed*, Chapel Hill, NC: University of North Carolina Press, 1991.
10 Smil, p. 54.
11 Srinivasan, p. 269.
12 Vallas et al., p. 86.
13 Smil, p. 57.
14 Vallas et al., p. 92.
15 Vallas, p. 85.
16 Ewen, S. *Captains of Consciousness*, New York: McGraw-Hill, 1976, p. 25.
17 Strasser, S. *Satisfaction Guaranteed: The Making of the American Mass Market*, Washington, DC: Smithsonian Institution Press, 1989.
18 Ewen, p. 31.
19 Marcuse, H. *One Dimensional Man*, London: Routledge, 1964.
20 Trentmann, p. 316.

21 Wilson B.S. and Levy, J. "A History of the Concept of Branding: Practice and Theory," *Journal of Historical Research in Marketing*, 2012, 4(3), pp. 347–68.
22 Ewen, p. 48.
23 Lewis, J. *Beyond Consumer Capitalism*, Cambridge: Polity Press, 2013, p. 54.
24 Ibid, p. 54.
25 Weber, M. *The Protestant Ethic and the Spirit of Capitalism*. New York: Scribners 1958.
26 Simmel, G. *The Philosophy of Money*. (3rd ed.), London: Routledge Kegan Paul, 2004.
27 English, B. *A Cultural History of Fashion in the 20th and 21st Centuries*, Bloomsbury: London, 2013; Zukin, S. *Point of Purchase*, Routledge: London, 2005.
28 Bourdieu, P. *Distinction*, London: Routledge, 1984.
29 Lamont, M. *Money, Manners and Morals*, Chicago: University of Chicago Press, 1992.
30 Halle, D. *Inside Culture: Art and Class in the American Home, Chicago: University of Chicago Press*, 1993; Peterson, R.A. and Kern, R.M. "Changing highbrow taste: From snob to omnivore," in *American Sociological Review*, 1996, 61, 900–7.
31 Featherstone, M. "Perspectives on consumer culture," *Sociology*, 1990, 24/1, pp. 5–22.
32 Milanovic, B. *Global Inequality*, Cambridge, MA: Belknap Press, 2016, p. 10.
33 OECD, *Perspectives on Global Development*, Paris, 2008, 2011.
34 Picketty, T. *Capital in the Twenty First Century*, Cambridge: Harvard University Press, 2014.
35 Deaton, A. *The Great Escape*, Princeton: Princeton University Press, 2013, p. 189.
36 Atkinson, A.B. *Inequality*, Cambridge: Harvard University Press, 2015, pp. 20–1.
37 UBS, "New value creators gain momentum," *Billionaire Insights*, Zurich, 2017.
38 Ibid.
39 Knight Frank, *The Wealth Report*, London, 2016, p. 22.
40 Wealth-X, *Applied Wealth Intelligence*, London, 2017.
41 Sombart, W. *Luxury and Capitalism*, translated by W.R. Ditmar, University of Michigan Press, Ann Arbor, 1967.
42 McNeill and Riello, *Luxury: A Rich History*. Oxford: Oxford University Press, 2016.
43 Stillerman, J. *The Sociology of Consumption*. Cambridge: Polity Press, 2013.
44 Bain & Company (2016), *Luxury Goods Worldwide Market Study. Fall-Winter 2016*, Bain & Company.
45 Deloitte, *Global Powers of Luxury Goods*, Deloitte, Washington, DC, 2016.
46 Kapferer, J.-N. "Abundant rarity: The key to luxury growth," *Business Horizons*, 2012, p. 454.
47 Smith, R. A., "Hermès wants to hang out," *Wall Street Journal*, 4 April 2019, p. A12.
48 Turunen, L.L.M. *Interpretations of Luxury*, London: Palgrave Macmillan, 2017, p. 36.
49 Kapferer, J-N. and Bastien, V. *The Luxury Strategy: Break the Rules of Marketing*, London: Kogan Page.
50 Ibid.
51 Turunen, L. *Interpretations of Luxury*. London: Palgrave Macmillan, 2017.
52 Clarke, K. "War of the Megamansions!" *Wall Street Journal*, 7th September 2018, M1 & M6–7.
53 Ibid, p. M7.

5

AT HOME IN THE FIELDS OF LUXURY

From Artisan Production to Global Brands

If we are to understand the concurrent growth of luxury goods in the age of mass production and consumption, it is important to examine changes in how luxury goods firms are organized and how they have consolidated their position in an increasingly global market place for luxury products. Key to this discussion is the notion of branding, specifically how firms create an identity that permits consumers to appreciate the inherent value added of their products. In the last chapter we saw how brands were a crucial informational component of new product sales to groups of consumers conspicuously lacking requisite product knowledge. They were communication symbols that gained traction with the rise of consumer-oriented economies.[1] Mass production ushered in what D'Arienzo calls the "product centric" century in which producers possessed power by virtue of the demand for goods exceeded the supply.[2] But a shift in this balance after World War II, when supply exceeded demand, resulted in more assertive marketing campaigns to offset market saturation. This gave rise to lifestyle fashion brands that told stories to take advantage of consumer desires rather than basic needs. Luxury firms were pioneers in capturing the essence of desirability because their narrative appealed to the symbolic consumption that permeated consumer emotions in a stratified society. Wants and needs could be satisfied by an ever-wider array of commodities but luxury brands emphasized the importance of desire as a driver of consumption for a wealthy elite.[3] Seemingly superfluous, luxury products could nonetheless capture the passion endemic amongst the rich as they sought lifestyle differentiation. Furthermore, such goods delivered on a range of emotions and feelings that transcended their simple material acquisition.

In this chapter I argue that in the past few decades brand awareness has been an inextricable part of recent luxury growth, driving global sales from an increasingly pre-eminent group of luxury conglomerates. Furthermore, in the past few decades, industry consolidation has occurred and now provides what are large firms with the organizational and financial wherewithal to develop global reputations built around distinctive brand propositions. In fact brands became the organizing principle behind a new business management model replacing earlier structuring around product categories.[4] Luxury now transcends local specificity and artisanal uniqueness, replaced by a cornucopia of material indulgences that resonate with exclusivity claims but that are nonetheless produced for a wide but restricted market of wealthy consumers globally.

Luxury Branding

Luxury is currently a trillion dollar global market as luxury brands have expanded into international markets using divergent ideological and cultural imaginaries to appeal to new consumers.[5] They explicitly align their strategies around consumer desires amongst the UHNWI since that is a more intense behavioral driver.[6] Their business model, as Kapferer argues, focuses on "the creation of value through rare and unique singularities."[7] Whilst this is not new in terms of the goods produced, the organization of what is now a luxury goods industry signifies a fundamental change from past practices. Production, distribution and sales are structured globally. Brand development has become an essential part of any firm's growth trajectory as well as their fundamental identity. Products that were unique or authentic have been replaced by goods categorized according to their expensiveness, rarity, prestige, and high quality. Such a multiplicity of interconnected features lends a more powerful resonance to marketing since it bestows simultaneously cultural, status and reverential significance to material consumption. Luxury firms remain in the business of selling dreams to aspirational consumers but they are now able to do it with enhanced financial alacrity. As Bernard Arnault (CEO of *LVMH*) summarily stated, "what interests me in luxury is not creativity but the idea of transforming creativity into profitability."[8]

Essential to the growth of luxury firms in the twentieth century have been strategies that focus upon marketing and brand building. Whilst brands have been around for hundreds of years, their current potency lies in the ability to consistently symbolize product credibility.[9] They are the *de facto* guarantee that allows consumers to be drawn to the brand in the first place and then sustain the subsequent attachment. As luxury fashion expert Uche Okonkwo argues,

> Every brand possesses the characteristics of identity, promise, value and differentiation. These are the features that create the relationship between the consumer and the brand...From the consumer perspective it is "the promise and delivery of an experience," while from the business perspective it is "a distinguishable piece of intellectual property and an intangible asset that secures future earnings."[10]

In some respects luxury brands flourish by giving consumers more than what they expect by offering an almost magical quality to the experience, something that is special and is simultaneously timeless and modern. *LVMH's* Arnault sees this as what distinguishes successful luxury brands from those whose sales might be lagging.[11] And he goes on to note in the same article that this is what enables firms such as his to charge a price premium, grow fast and be very profitable. It is the allure of the experience or product that is quintessentially different, something that evokes a feeling of privilege. This is what couturier *Christian Dior* successfully did with his fashion house in the decade after World War II as he successfully tapped into the post war desire for opulence after years of austerity. Sophistication, refinement, elegance and romance were all metaphorically wrapped into his finely crafted women's gowns. He was selling an expensive dream that he knew a small segment of the population could afford because they wanted an escape from the wartime drabness. Now they could indulge without the guilt that might have plagued such behavior in the war years. He was quoted as saying that he desired "to make every woman look and feel like a duchess."[12] Given that 75 percent of Paris's fashion exports in 1950 carried the *Dior* label, it appears he was successful in nurturing that visceral dream.

The above indicates the subtlety that surrounds the message that luxury firms disseminate. Yet this remains part of an increasingly coherent strategy whereby they unambiguously communicate their core elements to consumers: brand strength, differentiation, exclusivity, innovation, craftsmanship and precision, premium pricing and superior quality.[13] Unlike mass-produced goods with an emphasis on cost containment and thus low price, luxury goods embody a broad set of tangible features (quality, durability, etc.) as well as intangibles, particularly hedonic appeals. The latter attempts to capture the emotional self-enhancement that many embrace through their experience of luxury.[14] The former remains a *paean* to status affirmation in its unambiguous display of material wealth and even cultural sophistication. Furthermore, in some cases it can be a synthesis of symbolic meanings and material objects, both an escape and a visible manifestation of affluence. Both are nonetheless integral to the message conveyed by the brands. As Seo and Buchanan-Oliver summarily state,

> In the first instance, luxury brands could be the focal point of an escape, as consumers internalize brand stories and the brand imaginary to perform their escape from daily routines. In the second instance, luxury consumers may use branded products such as bags as materials which are integral in the accomplishing of escapism.[15]

In either case they endeavor to capture consumer desire, albeit in differentiated ways that reflect varied consumer attributes.

Whilst further burnishing their brand image through complementary appeals to individual self-attainment, luxury firms have notably undergone organizational changes that have enhanced their competitive position in a crowded marketplace. Whilst not necessarily embracing mass production, luxury firms have become much larger and consolidated, often by acquiring small family-owned and managed firms. These firms are brought under a broader corporate umbrella, restructured and professionally managed as part of global enterprises. The sheer volume of goods that are now produced therefore transcend that of small-scale artisanal manufacture and imply certain economies of scope if not scale. They have transformed a production system that was rooted in artisanal creativity and embedded in individualistic, craft skills into one that is in some respects almost commodified.

Until the late 1980s most luxury fashion companies were family owned, often run by the founder or his/her successor.[16] But it was during this time that new opportunities in the luxury market were emerging, associated with increasing growth of the wealthy worldwide, together with demographic and cultural changes. In particular the rise of female labor force participation by professional women in western societies, postponement of marriage by such individuals and reconfigured lifestyles around "indulgences" and experience seeking activities all contributed to a demand for luxury products. Partly as a response to such changes the 1990s saw the growth of a new type of luxury firm, one that was larger, better managed and with clear strategic and resource capabilities that enabled them to sell multiple product lines in a global marketplace. Some remained family owned whilst others were publicly listed companies with a professional management team that oversaw a brand portfolio. Both types were focused upon growth strategies that would deliver above average returns by leveraging the synergies of scale and applying rigorous management methods.

Increasingly, many of the smaller family firms found it difficult to implement the requisite innovations. Typically they lacked the managerial professionalism as well as financial and technological resources to respond to this new demand and found it harder and harder to go it alone and compete with the emerging resource-rich conglomerates. Real estate costs for prime urban locations often priced out such small firms; the growth of e-commerce required a large investment and expertise in digital marketing that was beyond their capabilities.[17] *Gucci* (owned by *Kering*), for example, dominated the fashion scene in 2018 by going beyond traditional runway presentations and focused instead upon a massive social media campaign to generate hype and interest in its products.[18] Media analysts argue that this sort of social media investment has fueled *Gucci*'s explosive growth in recent years.[19] Clearly a successful strategy since its revenue doubled over the past three years and reached €6.2 billion in 2017, this nonetheless required significant commitment of resources to new marketing platforms. *Kering* had the skill sets to accomplish this whereas a stand-alone *Gucci* probably would not.

In addition to scaling issues, there are also generational problems as younger family members lack the enthusiasm for taking over the business. Some owners are reaching an advanced age with no heirs apparent. For example, in addition to struggling to attract young Chinese shoppers who are driving sales in luxury footwear, luxury Italian cobbler *Salvatore Ferragamo* has yet to find a successor to the founder's widow who died in October 2018.[20] Some firms such as *Armani* have relied for decades upon their inspirational founder whose personality provides much of the strength behind the brand. Without him it is questionable whether the company can manage the same trajectory and success.

All of these trends are most evident in Italy, long seen as the quintessential site for luxury goods, but now witnessing firms struggling to compete in a transformed marketplace. The flexibility that came with small size and the earlier ability of fashion firms to utilize decentralized networks of specialists (accounting services, legal advice, technology design capabilities, etc.[21]) are no longer sufficient for the new marketing and production pre-requisites. Ironically in some case demand had far outstripped supply capability. This followed a surge in wealthy individuals in emerging economies where demand for western brand luxury products was increasing to consumers. What is demonstrably a success story for the industry as a whole is nonetheless a crisis for smaller producers unable to adapt their business model to the new operational exigencies. Some decided to stay small and serve a limited clientele but in a global marketplace they risk being ignored and relegated to a secondary status as sales deteriorated. As a consequence, many decided to sell to the larger conglomerates.

Conglomerates meanwhile have seen their sales increase. For example, French conglomerate *Kering* saw an 8 percent, 30 percent and 33 percent sales growth in, respectively, 2016, 2017 and thus far in 2018; *LVMH*'s figures for those same years were 6 percent, 12 percent and 12 percent. This contrasts with privately held *Prada* (−10 percent, 0 and now 10 percent) and Tod's (−8 percent and − 7 percent [2018 not reported yet]). For the iconic *Tod's* this follows a five-year trend of declining sales. Despite being well established, many of these latter firms have been built around the personality of their owner. Their vision was generally predicated upon an understanding of a pre-existing marketplace that is now dramatically changing. That marketplace is now more global, differentiated and most importantly more costly to compete in successfully without the benefits of size. Consequently many such firms are struggling to retain the requisite sales growth that will continue to burnish their brand image. Eventually this can lead to their sale, especially if they cherish the firm's legacy and seek to retain a semblance of association with its success. The latest example of such a transaction was the September 2018 sale of privately owned *Versace* to *Michael Kors* for $2.1 billion with every indication that more will soon follow. What is notable is that when a sale does occur, the firm becomes increasingly identifiable as a brand that is distinct from the funding owner. It retains its distinctive image but without the "personality" of the founder. A new management team often replaces the old family, although it might retain the services of a key designer whose own personality and flair might be crucial to the brand identity.

As more small firms have acknowledged the difficulties they face in transformed marketplace, the resulting sales of such firms has transformed the structure of the luxury goods industry, with increasing numbers of acquisitions and eventually consolidation into conglomerate structures. Yet traditionally luxury firms embellished their reputation by emphasizing their smallness and in many case the slowness of production. Paradoxically then, large firms can dilute their image and identity associated with rarity and exclusiveness by appearing to be too large and impersonal. Resolving this dilemma has been a crucial part of brand management and marketing, the cost of which ironically is only possible with the financial benefits of size. To retain the image of uniqueness, conglomerates typically retain the actual name and subsequent brand identity of the acquired company. This provides the value-added legitimacy as consumers continue to associate products with a distinctive heritage. Customers buying *Gucci* products might not be familiar with *Kering* even though the latter's resources have enabled the former brand to retain its exclusive appeal.

Firms construct or "craft" luxury brands by attempting to define the characteristics that they believe their customers want. This can include intrinsic aspects of quality and design. What is also paramount is how firms convey their message in ways that target consumer self-interest.[22] This brings us back to understanding what drives consumer desires for luxury products. Foremost here is how the needs of the buyers of such products reflect changing views of status and entitlement. Prestige, value, distinction and quality remain uppermost in the criteria by which the rich evaluate goods and activities. But as they do so, does this signal any underlying attitudinal changes in values or is it a manifestation of new patterns of inequality that are increasingly pervasive? Do consumers in different continents want different things or can one adduce similar patterns of desire for having, owning or using products? Has status seeking behavior become subsumed under more subtle forms inconspicuous consumption or even the desire for self-transformation and uniqueness for some[23] whilst others continue to glorify the visible manifestations and display of their wealth?

To answer these questions necessitates disentangling the relationship between supply and demand for luxury products. Increased industry consolidation has provided large firms with more sophisticated production and distribution capabilities. Building a coherent brand identity allows them to leverage these assets as they market products to consumers whose tastes are somewhat fungible. They simultaneously appeal to and cultivate luxury sensibilities, but always retaining their emphasis upon desirability through scarcity and rarity.[24] Appeals to history and heritage are often uppermost in such narratives, since this emphasizes authenticity as well as an appropriate aura of cultural gravitas – one has only to examine the success of *Ralph Lauren*'s invocation of Edwardian England at its sartorial finest to realize this. Whilst this is not a feature that is exclusive to luxury goods firm, its centrality to luxury brands renders it as a non-negotiable imperative. Timeless character and exclusivity are central to luxury fashion companies whose brands explicitly focus upon nurturing a culture of rarity and excellence. Their elevation of artisanal craftsmanship belies their multi-product strategies; but limited product offerings in each of these categories cloaks the aura of rarity that sustains the overall brand exclusivity.

Luxury Goods Firms

Throughout history expensive and rare objects have been manufactured, crafted and customized to meet the desires of the rich. The latter could fulfill their wish list of goods by contracting directly with merchants who would then attempt to fulfill the order. Spices, silk and porcelain were well known early exotic luxury goods that were imported from Asia to satisfy the discerning and wealthy in Western Europe. This was followed by an unprecedented quantity and variety that came in the seventeenth and eighteenth centuries courtesy of the European East India companies.[25] Eventually European manufacturers were able to imitate many of these products to simultaneously satisfy what was by the late eighteenth century a surge in demand from the newly prosperous groups[26] and burgeoning mercantilist policies. This demand accelerated in the nineteenth century and one begins to see the emergence of firms actively crafting products that cater to certain activities such as travel or clothing that had been produced locally up to that time. It is the fashion industry that personifies many of these changes since it was one of the first to be transformed from a localized production and sales system to one geared towards national and international markets. As an industry it covers a broad range of products (from watches to jewelry, clothes to accessories such as bags), but its significance lies in the way branding was successfully developed by the new fashion firms. Increasingly brand identity became *de rigueur* for them to survive.

Historically, the wealthy were the arbiters of style and were deemed the most fashionable. Following industrial production and commodity consumption, style permeated most segments of society and fashion became democratized following the growth of affordable clothing. Status subsequently became separated from style as the wealthy sought products that were discernably distinct; fashionable but not in the sense of mass trends. Elite tastes might be influenced by the broader culture but in actively seeking unique products, such individuals were able to differentiate themselves from commodity fashion. As the numbers of rich grew, so too did an industry develop to satisfy their sartorial needs.

The Business of Fashion

Fashion historian Emmanuelle Dirix argues that the business model of fashion was introduced around 1858 by Charles Frederick Worth in Paris when he rationalized what had been a haphazard system of dressmaking.[27] Whilst the elite had always had their clothes made for them, Worth conceived the notion of a collection to stimulate desire and provide a broader aesthetic and cultural framework for products. He sought to develop a systematic client relationship in which customers would be able to regularly update their clothing in accordance with the latest trends. He offered them unique items that were custom made and expensive – "luxurious, innovative and exquisite garments" – all at a price beyond the reach of normal consumers.[28] Craftsmen in Italy were providing similar services but were part of much smaller entrepreneurial ventures that limited their reach outside of what was still a largely regional set of city states.[29] They did nonetheless capitalize upon a pervasive cultural commitment to the aesthetics of style that characterized the wealthy in Italian society.[30] Similar cultural accolades applied to the French who were seen as fashion arbiters by the late eighteenth century thus lending cultural legitimacy to manufacturers that developed there during the next century.

Whilst the fashion industry was artisanal at its inception, it increasingly had to adopt the practices and production systems that characterize industrial capitalism if it was to meet the growing demand for luxury goods amongst the late nineteenth- and especially twentieth-century elites. With the advent of the department store as the emporium for the masses, vast quantities of mass produced inexpensive garments flooded the market. Such goods were eagerly sought by the thriving middle classes who were embracing the more egalitarian access to fashion.

The luxury goods sector meanwhile developed its own trajectory. Firms were selling lifestyles rather than appealing to the more fluid identities of the majority of the population.[31] Company names meanwhile were becoming better known by-words for quality and status. They not only allowed the rich to communicate how they wanted to be seen, they also enabled them to distinguish themselves from the masses. But it all came at a significant price premium. And for the companies themselves, if they were to meet the growing global demand, they had to adopt different production and distribution practices. There proved to be a limit to how artisanal one could be, even if one added workshops and trained more craft workers. Small might be beautiful and connote Arcadian images of pre-industrial craft settings, but increasingly these firms were forced to develop twentieth-century practices if they were to meet the growing global market for luxury goods.

This meant rationalizing supply chains, developing distribution networks and above all managing the "brand." The latter necessitated more sophisticated marketing techniques, greater capital investments and significantly improved organization resources. It also resulted in rethinking management models whereby brands were used to organize the overall business rather than product categories. Brands could more effectively engage with consumers as long as the communication was managed centrally and consistently reinforced a coherent message.

The Frenchman Bernard Arnault, head of *Louis Vuitton*, epitomized the changes that would occur in the industry during the 1980s when he set about designing what he said was the *business* of fashion.[32] He embarked upon an extensive strategy of merger and acquisitions, bringing *Moet and Hennessy* under the newly renamed *LVMH* label and then, often aggressively, sought out and acquired small fashion houses that fit in with the overall multi-sectoral luxury portfolio he was developing. This occurred in several other emerging luxury brands such as *Richemont* and *Kering*. In each case smaller firms, frequently the dominant player in a niche luxury market with significant brand recognition, were acquired, sometimes retaining previous owners in a managerial role as symbolic heads but primarily retaining the original name of the firm. Centralized supply and distribution chains permitted greater efficiency but also more profitability. Professionalized management structures and extensive marketing resources built even greater brand recognition that was crucial as the new conglomerates exploited growing global sales opportunities.

Other luxury firms chose a slower, more organic growth strategy, preferring to develop new lines alongside existing ones but always under the brand umbrella. For example *Hermès* started out as a saddle maker, then a multi-product leather goods company, before moving into clothing, watches and other accessories but always under the distinctive *Hermés* brand. This was a less-aggressive strategy than the one that relied upon acquisitions and certainly one than did not lead to the sales volume of the increasingly larger conglomerates, but nonetheless one that retained control of the high value, integrity and ultimately status of the band. When such firms produced handbags or clothing items, discerning customers knew instinctively that the workmanship and quality surpassed most others.

As a result of merger activity and multi-sectoral, individual firm growth, by the beginning of the twenty-first century one finds a smaller number of firms who account for a larger share of the multi-billion dollar luxury industry. Furthermore, in the past decade not only have sales for luxury goods in general continue to grow, those of the top ten conglomerates has been superior to that of other companies in the sector.[33] Table 5.1 shows the brand value of the top ten luxury brands worldwide; Table 5.2 indicates the sales trends of these companies over the past five years.

TABLE 5.1 Brand value of the top ten luxury brands worldwide

Rank	Brand	Parent	Brand valuation ($ billions)
1	Louis Vuitton	LVMH	29.25
2	Hermès	Hermès International	23.4
3	Gucci	Kering	13.5
4	Chanel	Chanel SA	11
5	Rolex	Montres Rolex S.A.	8
6	Cartier	Cie Fin Richemont	5.85
7	Burberry	Burberry Group	4.29
8	Prada	Prada S.p.A.	3.95
9	Christian Dior	Christian Dior S.A.	2.35
10	Tiffany	Tiffany & Co.	2.3

Source: Millward Brown, Statistica, 2017.

TABLE 5.2 Sales of leading luxury goods companies worldwide in million euros, 2012–2016

Company	2012	2013	2014	2015	2016[a]
LVMH	28,103	29,016	30,638	35,664	37,318
Kering	9,736	9,656	10,038	11,584	12,103
Richemont	10,150	10,649	10,410	11,427	11,933
Luxottica	7,086	7,313	7,652	8,837	9,618
Swatch	6,401	8,111	7,978	7,742	8,250
Chow Tai Fook	5,374	9,293	7,276	6,882	7,044
Ralph Lauren	5,040	6,935	6,691	6,658	6,900
Hermes	3,484	3,755	4,119	4,841	5,245
Michael Kors	1,812	3,082	3,838	4,089	4,288
Coach	3,457	4,724	4,220	3,680	3,900
Tiffany	2,754	3,752	3,732	3,604	3,759
Prada	3,297	3,587	3,552	3,548	3,553
Burberry	2,418	3,222	3,191	3,194	3,314

[a] estimates
Source: Statistica, 2017.

In the next section I briefly outline the genesis of the top three firms, paying attention to their different growth strategies. However, each is indicative of the general trends towards production and marketing scale synergies across product lines that firms are pursuing. The narratives reveal how firms sought to capture the essence of their unique history and tradition whilst the parent conglomerate pursued an integrated, multi-product global strategy. In doing so they have been able to construct a unified identity that transcends the sum of the parts.

LVMH Moët Hennessy Louis Vuitton SE

One of the best known luxury goods companies, *LVMH*, has its origins in the late eighteenth century as purveyors of alcohol to the wealthy. Champagne producers *Moët et Chandon* was created in 1743, and sales grew rapidly through the next century reaching 2.5 million bottles by 1880. It acquired rival champagne houses in the twentieth century, consolidating its position as the dominant producer. *Hennessy* was founded in 1765 by Richard Hennessy, an Irish officer serving in the army of Louis XV. His express aim was to create the world's finest cognac. In 1817 Henry IV of England asked him to create "a very superior old pale cognac" thus giving birth to the initials VSOP (very superior old pale) that many consider the benchmark of quality for cognac. Sales grew throughout the nineteenth century, including the first deliveries to China in 1859 and then in 1870 the creation of "XO (extra old) The Original" designed initially for family and special friends. In 1971 the company merged with *Moët* which allowed both companies to leverage international growth potential. Sales slowed in the 1980s and in 1987 *Moët Hennessy* merged with *Louis Vuitton*, although each company's management and subsidiaries remained intact following the merger.

In 1854 Louis Vuitton Mallatier founded a company in Paris named *Louis Vuitton* that supplied luggage to wealthy French families. His success was predicated upon his ability to capitalize on changing transportation technologies as well as the demand for luggage as railways provided more and easy opportunities for individual mobility. He invented a design for trunks made of lightweight and airtight "trianon" canvas with flat bottoms that permitted stacking. He changed the "trianon" design to beige and brown stripes in 1876 and by the end of the century his trunks were *de rigueur* for wealthy travelers throughout Europe. They were made by hand by craftsmen taking up to 60 hours and stamped with an individual serial number; plus they had solid brass pick-proof locks with one key for all of the luggage.[34]

After opening a store in London in 1885 and then what was the largest travel goods store in the world on the Champs-Elysees in Paris in 1913, the company added others in the next decade in New York, Bombay, Washington, Buenos Aries and Alexandria. With an increase of leather used in products, the company was able to broaden its line of goods to include purses, bags and wallets, capitalizing on its increased brand image as purveyors of luxury products. In 1987 the company merged with *Moët et Chandon* and *Hennessy* to form *LVMH*.

In the 1990s, the company embarked upon a further growth strategy through acquisitions and product diversification; their busiest years were 1996–1997 when they spent more than $3 billion. These included personal beauty lines, the formation of a watch and jewelry division (*Tag Heuer, Zenith, Ebel* and *Charmet*) plus clothing companies (*Thomas Pink*) and *Phillips Auctioneers*.

Their current wine and spirits division is organized around 24 "houses," which include additional champagne producers *Krug, Dom Pérignon* and *Veuve Clicquot*; classified growth Bordeaux wineries such as *Château D'Yquem* and *Château Cheval Blanc*; and Napa, California producers such as *Newton* and the just recently announced 60 percent ownership in the Napa cult winery, *Colgin Cellars*. LVMH revenue has more than doubled between 2008 and 2016, from just over 17,193 million euros to 37,600 million. Currently, as seen in Table 5.2, they are the leading luxury goods company by sales volume. Even with some slow-down in growth after the financial crisis (their sales did in fact drop slightly between 2008 and 2009), they continue to be in the front of an industry that has tripled in size since 1996. They are a major presence in China, which together with millennials has been the growth engine for luxury in the past two years.[35] They have also become veracious acquirers of niche luxury firms.

Hermès

Originally a saddle and harness workshop founded in Paris by Thierry Hermès in 1837, the company catered to a very excusive clientele of aristocrats interested in equestrian affairs. When the founder's son Charles-Emile Hermès took over the company in 1880, he began a focus on increased international retail sales and expanded the market to include other wealthy individuals in Europe, North Africa, Asia and the Americas. Key to the company's strategy was a focus upon artisanal production utilizing craftsmen located in a workshop (not a factory according to the company), and specializing in essentially custom made goods. By the 1900s the firm had expanded to include saddle bags and then leather handbags (1922) that used a patented zipped design. In 1929 the company branched into clothing and introduced its first women's couture collection that was previewed in Paris and in 1937 introduced the famous silk scarf (allegedly one is sold globally every 20 seconds!). This was followed by the *Kelly* bag (named after Grace Kelly who carried a crocodile handbag to conceal her pregnancy) in 1956 and then the leather *Birkin* bag (after actress Jane Birkin) in 1984 – this bag has the longest wait list for any accessory, 6 years. The company hired famous fashion designed Jean-Paul Gaultier in 2003 as the company expanded its ready to wear lines, all of which played to the company's equestrian roots. It added watches and other fine jewelry to its line to provide discerning customers with a full range of branded items.

Hermès revenue has more than tripled from 1624 million euros in 2007 to 5202 million euros in 2016, with the fastest growth occurring since 2010.[36]

Kering

In 1963 Frenchman François Pinault started a company in Brittany that specialized in timber trading. Following various acquisitions (including a distribution company and department store *Printemps*) in the next two decades his company (*Ēstablissments François Pinault*) became a major force in the French retail sector and was renamed *Pinault-Printemps-Redoubt* (PPR) in 1994. In 1999 *PPR* purchased a 42 percent share of *Gucci* (for $3 billion), followed by the acquisition of French high-end jewelry house, *Boucheron* (2000), Italian leather goods maker *Bottega Veneta* (2001) and fashion house *Balenciaga* (2001). These acquisitions were a purposeful attempt to reposition *PPR* as a purveyor of luxury goods, albeit operationally as an umbrella of notable established brands in a wide selection of sectors. In the last decade, the company has gradually sold off its holdings in the mass market retail sector; *Le Printemps* in 2006, multi-media and bookseller, *Fnac* in 2012 and French mail order retailer, *La Redoute* in 2013. It further consolidated its luxury position with the 2004 acquisition of further ownership in *Gucci* (at 99.4 percent), *Sowind Group* (owner of Swiss watch company *Girard-Perregaux*) and Italian bespoke tailor *Brioni* in 2011. Further additions to the luxury watch portfolio were added with the acquisition of *Ulysse Nardin* in 2014. To provide a new identity for their emerging luxury brand collection *PPR* was renamed *Kering* in 2013.

Kering's revenue for the past decade has fluctuated more widely than *LVMH* and *Hermès*. It dropped from 17,207 million euros in 2008 to 9656 million euros in 2013, but it has rebounded somewhat since then to 12,385 million euros in 2016.[37] In some respects this represents acquisition costs and write downs in underperforming areas. If one looks at brand performance, Gucci stands out accounting for just over 50 percent of revenue share followed by 14 percent each for Bottega Veneta and Saint Laurent (other brands in their portfolio account for approximately 20 percent of revenue).

Consolidation and Growth

The previously mentioned three firms exemplify various strategies that luxury goods companies have pursued. *LVMH*, from its origins as an artisanal manufacturer to its eventual mergers and recent acquisitions of notable luxury brands, continues to build upon its history and traditions whilst adding to its broad portfolio. It has now become a multi-sectoral umbrella brand. Whilst the company is well recognized in its own right, its various stand-alone brands are relied upon to drive sales across a wide spectrum of products. *Kering* meanwhile has attempted to build a luxury brand from scratch by acquiring existing brands and like *LVMH* sought scope efficiencies through back room operational restructuring and marketing and distribution rationalization. Finally *Hermès* has pursued an organic growth strategy, developing luxury products in house and leveraging the established brand identity by retaining the name for all of its new products.

Each company has successfully targeted new consumers in emerging markets whilst continuing to build upon an established base in rich countries by offering new product extensions. By extending their range of products (what Kapferer recently described as "sell-all brands"[38]) they are also able to cover the costs of high rent shopping districts that attract the new consumers. But this has also enabled them to move from being simply in the fashion business to offering a "lifestyle" through their numerous brand extensions.

In spite of the above-noted strategic variations, the similarities behind consolidation extend beyond these three firms to encompass a broader industry trend. As noted earlier, until the late 1980s most fashion industry firms were small family-owned enterprises. They catered to a select group of consumers, primarily in Western nations and Japan. With varying degrees of managerial professionalism, they maintained a fairly stable production system that was located in their home countries (Italy and France being the dominant places). In the subsequent decades however, a series of changes have altered the market for luxury and consequently the ways firms structured production. Neoliberalism became more firmly established in the dominant Western economies and stock markets grew, credit became more widely available and consumer confidence increased.[39] Emerging economies, particularly China but also Russia, India and Brazil, saw enhanced economic growth and the emergence of an elite wealthy class with heightened discretionary income. There has been some slowdown in the rate of wealth growth in some of the countries in the past year but the trends are nonetheless impressive. Even though data on global wealth (including property and net financial assets) are somewhat imprecise, a recent Credit Suisse report indicates that the top global 1 percent have more than one half of the world's wealth.[40] It is to this group that luxury firms target their marketing.

The growing demand for luxury goods as a result of these changes corresponded to structural changes within the industry itself. Individuals outside the luxury sector recognized that there were above average earnings potential for this industry and together with some of the more established luxury firms discussed above, began acquiring many of the smaller family run firms. This "corporatization," to use Fabian Csaba's terminology, brought more professionalized management practices and investors injected large amounts of capital.[41] Certain organizational efficiencies were attained but the new corporate structures were much more likely to be subject to pressure for increased sales and stable earnings required by listed firms. This pressured the need for global growth and the search for new markets in emerging economies plus finding additional ways to extend their brand in traditional markets. Attempts at the latter have included reaching out to rich millennials with re-designed stores and innovative products, as well as managing more e-commerce. For example, *Hermès* in their new store in Manhattan's Meatpacking District has moved away from the intimidating formal boutiques to an open, friendly space designed for customers to "hang out."[42] Everything is designed to be informal and fun, with products such as skateboard bags alongside more traditional "hip" bags. Seen as a way to integrate the two retail channels of digital and brick and mortar, this is a concept aimed at new customers hopefully without alienating traditional older ones.

Industry consolidation has allowed firms to pool common resources (especially in centralized distribution and delivery) and realize economies of scope. Products in *LVMH* and *Kering* are typically organized around group structures which yield scale efficiencies in advertising and cost savings through heightened bargaining power. It has also enabled them to protect their brands from excessive exchange rate fluctuations by pooling currency hedging at the corporate level. Multi-brand strategy also optimizes constant growth by offsetting any slack in one or more product lines. Each of these has been part of the rationalization in back office operations that has provide cost savings and furthered the competitive advantage of the larger firms.

As noted earlier, a crucial component of any luxury goods firms is its brand value since this enables it to charge a price premium for its product. The key features of such branding have already been discussed (unique and appealing products; consistent premium quality, tight control over distribution; exclusivity; heritage of craftsmanship; global reputation; emotional appeal; premium pricing; and high visibility) and an extensive literature on luxury branding provides a litany of these core principles and firm practices in action.[43] Firms devote considerable attention to engaging consumers in ways that reinforce the potency of the brand personality and the brand image to consolidate their prestigious identity.[44] To do this necessitates a constant evaluation and monitoring of market conditions, as well as developing psychographic assessments of consumer segments. Of particular use here are segmentation models that enable firms to identify core customer groups according to psycho-sociological dynamics. Under such modeling target customers are classified into one of two categories: high wealth/low need for status (referred to as patricians) and high wealth/high need for status (partisans).[45] Others might have limited wealth or aspire to high status, but they are generally not included in the ultra-high net worth (UHNW) group of the much hyped top 1 percent. It is these two groups that are core to luxury brand strategies since they are the principal drivers of sales.

Another category in such models include "low wealth/high need for status" but their importance for luxury firms is limited even though they often constitute the group seeking aspirational or entry level luxury products such as small purses or bracelets. Such so-called "democratization of luxury"[46] gives resonance to those who seek to "trade up" in their material acquisitions but such behavior is restricted to a few products or experiences and lacks the comprehensiveness of those who are fully committed to the luxury lifestyle. Large luxury firms can nevertheless indulge in such production lines but in doing so they remain cognizant of brand dilution. It remains a fine balance between offering entry level products that are inexpensive and commodifying the luxury brand.

The latter would clearly negate the authenticity and rarity aspect (plus pricing) but big luxury firms appear to have embraced this strategy as a way of weaning future consumers on the brand by providing symbolic emotional brand attachment.[47] By expanding offerings some firms see this as a way to grow – the so- called "new luxury" – but others see it as "trading down," even if it does meet a perceived consumer need.

The problem is that fundamentally the essence of a luxury product is its rarity. Limited availability means only a few people can possess or experience it and scarcity creates value. If it is rare it will probably be very expensive and if it is expensive it should be of very high quality. History and heritage are important components of this overall image because they lend authenticity to the overall aura of privileged possession but an excess of such products undermines this. This brings us back to the early discussions on why people buy such goods and the answer still firmly remains status driven and an expression of one's privileged position. Status seeking consumption via "entry level" products for aspirational buyers might resonate among marketing departments. On my drive to work each day I pass a billboard for a local realtor which exclaims "Selling luxury at **all** price points." Patently absurd as this is, it nonetheless succeeds in appealing to those who expect a high level of quality even at low prices. It dangles the prospect of luxury for those who cannot afford it so in that sense is tapping into the same vein of self-achievement that twentieth-century materialism unleashed. But it is not what we understand to be luxury nor can it be. True luxury products are firmly rooted in an appeal to those at the top of the hierarchy. It is the super-rich who possess the financial means to buy such products and in societies where supposedly meritocratic ideologies are tacitly accepted, this becomes a way to identify oneself. It differentiates those who have much from the majority whose means are more limited. It is fundamentally a *paean* to inequality.

The luxury goods industry has witnessed significant growth in recent decades, despite recessions and other economic downturns. More importantly it continues to be a very profitable sector. As *LVMH* CEO Bernard Arnault claimed, "luxury if the only sector providing luxury margins."[48] Aimed at a small set of the world's population, the industry unambiguously communicates the virtues and privilege of owning a rare product that epitomizes the apotheosis of success and status. Again, citing an *LVMH* executive, "there are four main elements to our business model – product, distribution, communication, and price. Our job is to do such a fantastic job on the first three that people forget about the fourth."[49] It is not necessarily that the wealthy cannot afford it; they are merely seduced by what the product confers rather than equivocating over how much it costs – unless of course they rationalize the high price as a signifier of quality and ultimately status. Firms have successfully fused the tangible objective benefits of material possession with the intangible emotional and experiential aspects (both buying and using). The experience refers not just to the thrill of taking an expensive cruise; it is the way one feels when indulging in a luxury purchase. Perhaps it is a reaffirmation of ones' status in the eyes of others; a form of referential posturing. Or it could be the gratification that comes from selecting a product that you have been convinced is unique, rare and of the highest quality and is tailored (however viscerally) to your needs.

Luxury goods firms, especially those listed in this study, continue to promote the uniqueness and superiority of their product; that it endows class and status but most importantly it is not for everybody. Product placement advertisements prominently reinforce this claim and are pervasive.[50] There is no better summary of this position than *Rolex* in their advertisements referred to earlier which hype the watches' exclusivity to those who are wealthy. Such firms have also significantly improved their ability to reach a global audience and have developed more sophisticated ways of monitoring consumer behavior and consumer preferences. Given the growth in supply of luxury products to meet the heightened demand, especially in Asia, it might portend a decline in perceptions of exclusivity. Can luxury goods face market saturation as in other product lines? One luxury CEO noted this concern but invoked the "Veblen good" theory whereby prices can rise when demand soars.[51] Most luxury consumers are not price sensitive; in fact many still view high price as a sign of quality. This executive merely added significant price increases to the firm's handbags and other accessories and sales continued without abatement.

Globalization has in many ways resulted in a homogenized culture of wealth with key products having the same brand status worldwide. A *Ferrari* is as valued in China as it is in Brazil; a *Hermès* accessory confers the same aura of elitism in Japan as it does in the United States. Luxury firms have recognized and embraced the fact that a new wealthy class in emerging economies has enthusiastically taken to emulating their counterparts in the west. As in the richer countries of the west, inequality has underwritten the surge in consumption of luxury products and delivered consistently high earnings for the major firms that dominate the market. Sustaining this growth depends upon the high level of wealth that this inequality generates.

One of the recent challenges facing luxury goods firms is how they manage their communications in a digital age. They have rationalized their supply chains and spruced up the malls where their flagships stores are outposts of desire. But they can now gather more information on their customers via digital platforms, especially millennials who are often averse to brick and mortar retail therapy. In 2017 only 9 percent of total personal luxury sales occurred online, but that has risen from 1 percent in 2005.[52] In fact two-thirds of millennial's purchases are "digitally influenced" (i.e. they see products online and then make a purchase in a store). Clearly the next generation of luxury consumers expect to be "seduced" online, and firms need to develop channels that will meet these changing parameters. This is especially significant given the growing importance of established online giants like Amazon, Google and Alibaba who could disrupt the luxury market by leveraging their digital expertise. We noted earlier how social media investments have been crucial in the success of several brands. If they are to generate symbolic meanings in what they are selling, they must operationalize radically different communication platforms. There has been some talk, not yet formalized, of *Kering* and *LVMH* pooling their resources to use *Yoox Net-a-Porter*, the Italian/UK luxury e-tailer to gain traction in the e-commerce market.[53] This would be a way to less expensively garner the requisite expertise and stay ahead of digital giants such as Amazon. The key is to be able to retain the exclusivity and sense of specialness, as well as tapping into the emotional dimensions behind luxury sales, and to do it with a new group of consumers for whom symbolic meanings might be at variance with established ones and who react according to constantly evolving patterns of material indulgence.

Notes

1 Arienzo, W.D. *Brand Management Strategies*, London: Bloomsbury, 2016, p. 5.
2 Ibid, p. 6.
3 Belk, R., Ger, G. and Askegaard, S. "Metaphors of consumer desire," *Advances in Consumer Research*, 1996, 23, pp. 369–73.
4 Ibid, p. 19.
5 Ko, E., Costello, J.P. and Taylor, C.R. "What is a luxury brand?" *Journal of Business Research*, 2017, pp. 1–9; Seo, Y. and Buchanan-Oliver, M. "Constructing a typology of luxury brand consumption practices," *Journal of Business Research*, 2017, pp. 1–8.
6 D'Arienzo, op. cit. p. 19.
7 Kapferer, J.-N. *Kapferer on Luxury*, London: Kogan Page, 2015, p. 153.
8 Thomas, D. *De Luxe: How Luxury Lost Its Lustre*, 2007, New York: Penguin Press, p. 13.
9 Okonkwo, U. *Luxury Fashion Branding*, Hampshire, UK: Palgrave, 2007, p. 9.
10 Okonkwo, pp. 9–10.
11 Wetlauf, S. "The perfect paradox of star brands," *Harvard Business Review*, 2001, 79/9, pp. 116–23.
12 Jacobs, L. "Timelessly elegant, yet avant-garde," *Wall Street Journal*, November 28, 2018, p. A18.
13 Som, A. and Blanckaert, C. *The Road to Luxury*, Singapore: John Wiley & Sons, 2015, p. 6. See also Turunen, L. *Interpretation of Luxury*, London: Palgrave, 2018, Chapter 3; Fionda, A. and Moore, C. "The anatomy of the luxury fashion brand," *Journal of Brand Management*, 2009, 16(5), pp. 162–67; and Okonkwo, 2007.
14 Makkar, M. and Yap, S. -F. "Emotional experiences behind the pursuit of inconspicuous luxury," *Journal of Retailing and Consumer Services*, 2018, 44, p. 228.
15 Ibid, p. 5.
16 Som and Blanckaert, p. 17.
17 Ryan, C. "Italy's the 'IT' place for some luxury shopping," *Wall Street Journal*, 2018, November 17, 2018.
18 Dalton, M. "Building buzz off the runway," *Wall Street Journal*, September 27, 2018, p. A14.
19 Ibid, p. 14.
20 Ryan, op. cit.

21 This refers to post war Italy's so-called "flexible specialization" discussed by Piore, M. and Sabel, C. *The Second Industrial Divide*, New York: Basic Books, 1984, and Taplin, S.-F. "Segmentation and the organization of work in the Italian apparel industry," *Social Science Quarterly*, 1989, 70/2, pp. 408–24.

22 Prendergast, G. and Wong, C. "Parental influence on the purchase of luxury brands of infant apparel: An exploratory study in Hong Kong," *Journal of Consumer Marketing*, 2003, 20(2), 157–69; Fionda and Moore, op. cit.

23 Seo and Buchanan-Oliver, p. 7.

24 Turunen, pp. 39–40.

25 McNeill, P. and Riello, G. *Luxury: A Rich History*. Oxford: Oxford University Press, 2016.

26 Csaba.

27 Dirix, 2016, p. 007.

28 Ibid.

29 Crane and Bovone, 2006.

30 Taplin, 1989, p. 418.

31 Anthony, A.K. and Taplin, I.M. "Sustaining the retail pilgrimage: Developments of fast fashion and authentic identities," in *Fashion, Style and Popular Culture*, February 4, 2017, pp. 33–50.

32 Chada and Husband, 2006.

33 Deloitte, 2016.

34 Martin, 1995, p. 750.

35 Sanderson, R. "Europe's leaders in luxury have their designs on smaller groups," *Financial Times*, October 16, 2018, p. 13.

36 Statista.com, 2017.

37 Ibid.

38 Kapferer, 2015, p. 20.

39 Csaba, F.F. "Redefining luxury: A review essay," *Creative Encounters Working Paper #*, November 15, 2008, Copenhagen Business School, pp. 18–19.

40 See *The Economist*, "Picture of wealth," October 27, 2018, p. 69.

41 Csaba, p. 19.

42 Smith, R. "Hermès wants to hang out," *Wall Street Journal*, April 4, 2019, p. A12.

43 See for example Bevolo, M., Gofman, A. and Moskowitz, H. *Premium by Design*, Farnham: Gower, 2011.

44 Okonkwo, p. 110.

45 See Han, Y.J. "Signaling status with luxury goods: The role of brand prominence," *Journal of Marketing*, 2010, 44, pp. 15–30. Also D'Arienzio, pp. 71–4.

46 Silverstein, M.J., Fiske, N. and Butman, J. *Trading Up: Why Consumers Want New Luxury Goods and How Companies Create Them*, New York: Penguin, 2008.

47 Boston Consulting Group (BCG), *Opportunities for Action in Consumer Markets— Trading Up*, Report by Boston Consulting Group, Boston, 2003.

48 Quoted in Kapferer, p. 42.

49 Personal communication.

50 In the September 2017, Men's style magazine supplement to the *Wall Street Journal*, the first pages contained advertisements for LVMH, Cartier, Hermès, Ralph Lauren (Purple Label), Zegna, Dolce & Gabbana, Saint Laurent and Giorgio Armani. On the other side of the Atlantic, the September 9, 2017, Luxx supplement to *The Times* contained the following advertisements in this order: LVMH, Dior, Omega, Cartier, Dom Pérignon and Bulgari.

51 *The Economist*, "Lux in flux," April 1, 2018, p. 53.

52 Ibid, p. 54.

53 Sanderson, p. 13.

6

ART

From Aesthetics to Investment Grade Collateral

Visual representations are as old as civilization and bespeak humans' desire to express themselves visually in ways that confer permanence. Leaving their mark for others to contemplate and puzzle over, our ancestors bestowed these visual narratives for posterity. The early cave paintings presumably told stories about daily life; the struggles and conflicts plus the near constant search for sustenance in an environment unimaginably hostile to today's inhabitants. They continue to evoke wonder and awe and a certain amount of confusion as to their meaning. We infer that they played a role in these early civilizations even if we are not certain exactly what that role was. We can only speculate if certain specialists were assigned the task of painting them or that they were merely sophisticated doodles by bored cave dwellers seeking a distraction from a long, cold night – not that dissimilar from the marks scratched in desks by attention challenged schoolchildren desiring to render their presence in symbolic form for future generations!

As to their function, were the paintings designed for collective enjoyment and reflection or restricted to a select few? If the latter, then we have the beginnings of art as a privileged product, the status of which is immediately enhanced because of limitations on its viewing. Depending upon the demand for such products we can perhaps presume that a degree of scarcity was present. If they were freely available for all to view, however, their function takes on another meaning. Whatever the case, these depictions are the precedent for art as we understand it today.

Art is a tangible product, designed to communicate a self-conscious sentiment by the artist. Once produced it can enter a marketplace of exchange and consumption, as a commissioned product or one conceived in a style that the artist believes is consistent with the prevailing consumer taste. Artists might contradict such a demand-driven production schema, especially those in the past century who have striven to use their art as a protest or visual gesture in opposition to established aesthetic norms. They might argue that their art is a product of psychological, unconscious dimensions of reality that is deserving of aesthetic investigation.[1] Or they could be immersed in self-referential agendas that are at best seeking an alternative reality or at worst a nihilist agenda. Yet despite such oppositional tropes, once they enter the marketplace they are engaging in a social relationship with buyers (plus any intermediaries) within the institutional confines and conventions of the day, whether solely commercial, religious, or perceptual.[2] By creating a physical object that changes hands, their intentionality becomes subsumed under that of the new owner. The latter's motives for the acquisition can be varied, as we briefly discussed in Chapter 2. But through their purchase they are shaping the cultural ideology of the art market, sanctifying the domain of transactions and providing a material value to what had hitherto been an aesthetic expression.

Georg Simmel argued that the value of an object depends upon the demand for it, although he recognized that certain products with time will transcend mere utility value to reveal aesthetic value.[3] In other words when objects have their beauty affirmed, they acquire dignified significance and in essence become objectified. But this raises the question of who determines the initial value of a work of art and how it journeys through the academic halls of art historians who endow it with possible cultural legitimacy that further embellishes that value. For Pierre Bourdieu, the answer to the first part of the question is unambiguously the dealer. It is he who consecrates the value by putting it on the market and establishing a price. He is the authority, the arbiter of transactional value and thus by extension the moderator of style and taste. He endeavors to manipulate demand but is also at the mercy of changing consumer tastes and altered rationales for material acquisition. Renaissance patrons, wealthy merchants and industrialists, and most recently ultra-high net worth individuals, purposively buy art but their reasons for doing so have varied.

Because of their physical location cave paintings take on a unique permanence, not unlike frescos by later generations. Their status as a tradable commodity is lessened and thus their value to later generations remains as an historical artifact. But they continue to be one-of-a-kind objects, thus rendering them somewhat similar to artistic products as we understand them. Their value remains in their uniqueness even though we do not assign a price to them as we do with other works of art and that enter the marketplace.

It is precisely the latter type of art that is the subject of this chapter, specifically how its role and function have evolved over the centuries. Art has always been simultaneously a medium of communication as well as a privileged object. In this chapter I will argue that the latter implies an aura of exclusivity that puts art firmly in the category of a luxury good. Whilst its value is variously a product of market forces, scholarly and professional assessment and religious assignation, in recent decades it has been used by some as an asset that potentially yields financial returns. Rather than merely an (expensive) object that is visually pleasing or one that renders status to its owner, it has become a tradable commodity with an inherent market value. As we shall see later in this chapter, increasingly art is viewed in terms of its financial value which can often replace aesthetic considerations. This more nuanced view of its function is important because it adds a further dimension to the role art plays as a luxury product. Implicit and aesthetic acknowledgment of art's virtuous position as a cultural good is now supplemented by tangible measures of its financial value as seen through the development of institutional frameworks for the sale and purchase of such works. This can reaffirm any status attributes and embellish them with even greater scarcity credentials for potential owners.

In art (and wine, which is the subject of the next chapter) we see products whose initial function has changed over time and in some instances acquired venerable status as luxury products. That is not always surprising since many objects assume different functional status as they age – for example, old tables become collectible antiques after acquiring a certain patina. In a contemporary age of mass production, individual craftsmanship is venerated, hence the presumption that a handmade product is an expression of uniqueness rather than serving a mere utilitarian function. And what might have been an inexpensive item designed for everyday use 100 years ago now becomes a collector's item, even if its function remains the same. The greater the lapse in time, the more intrinsic value is attributed to the object. Similarly, the further the distance from its initial inception, the more unique it can become. Not surprisingly some mass produced objects have attempted to capture the aura of antiquity, designed to evoke an elevated status by simple reference to a past distinguished age. As McNeil and Riello argue, Josiah Wedgwood was the master of using classical vocabulary as he deployed new production techniques to manufacture tea sets and decorative items.[4] By giving them classical names and emphasizing that they were produced in a factory called Etruria, they were designed to suggest a traditional elegance and luxury. In doing this he was the consummate marketing genius of the eighteenth century, providing the "luxury" of antiquity for the rising middle classes, and enabling mass-produced objects to resonate with sophistication that has continued over the centuries. He manufactured a sense of time and historical imagery by invoking the past to endow a product that was designed to be essentially timeless – a product for the ages.

Whilst recognizing that what constitutes luxury varies through time and place as well as being culturally and socio-economically context specific,[5] it is interesting to examine the trajectory that certain goods take as they acquire such esteemed status. How did art acquire status as a commodity when its initial function was rooted in a medium of visual expression; a tool for the communication of sentiments, emotions as well as allegorical narratives steeped in religious significance? What started out as a form of visual storytelling anchored in cultural specificity became a marketable artifact that eventually became an asset class of its own. Art entered the realm of luxury when it was used by the wealthy to enhance their status or possible salvation. It became a valuable cultural artifact when specialists in an evolving marketplace assigned a monetary value that subsequently morphed into aesthetic legitimacy when scholarly experts conferred their academic approval.

Art's Changing Role

I would like to use the Renaissance as the starting point for our discussion of art's changing role, noting that aside from the aesthetic classicism that subsequent generations have lauded, even then art was intricately tied with a market, thus revealing a clear commercial position in society. Art was a consumer product, subject to the ebb and flow of market forces as well as the institutional setting that structured transactions and eventually created specialists who acted as intermediaries and assigned value to the objects. Whatever symbolism, allegorical references and inherent visual beauty resides in paintings and altar pieces of this time, so much of the content was also a visual inventory of consumer goods.[6] Lisa Jardine makes this argument quite forcefully when she reviews Renaissance painters claiming that their reputation often depended upon "their ability to arouse commercial interest in their work rather than in some intrinsic criteria of intellectual worth."[7] By suggesting that consumerism was an integral part of Renaissance art, she highlights the centrality of acquisitiveness as a driving force in an evolving market for art. For example, Carlo Crivelli's (1430–1489) *Annunciation with St Emedius*, painted in 1486 and now hanging in the National Gallery London, is ostensibly a depiction of a patron saint. But is also a visual representation of the many luxury goods that were available in late fifteenth-century Veneto area of northern Italy; in some respects a medieval catalogue of material objects designed to stimulate acquisition.

Markets were evolving around the trade in commodities as saleable items became measured items and price quantified everything. This was part of innovation patterns in Western Europe in the late Middle Ages with monetary currency providing a valuable means of exchange and an increasing ideology of quantification. What Crosby refers to as the "measure of reality" was the shift from a qualitative to a quantitative reasoning made possible by increased commerce and emerging nation states.[8] By bringing buyers and sellers together, market interactions became institutionalized and provided a structure and process that set pricing as well as a degree of accountability. The centrality of the market extended to art where paintings were used to depict images of often exotic material goods that could be purchased (an early paean to the twentieth-century catalogue). More importantly the goods referred to were part of a world wide market in luxury commodities that was thriving during this time period.[9] They were also a means for patrons to advertise their wealth and status, a testament to their self-assurance and undisguised authority but also pre-eminence in a commercially mediated society. As historian Richard Goldthwaite argued, paintings enabled the owner to establish a special identity in society, in particular as a symbol of power.[10]

Since art is inherently a visual medium designed to evoke some response from a viewer, it is easy to concentrate on the stylistic changes that have occurred through history. Seen this way artistic output is embedded in broader socio-cultural features and emerges as an expression of or a reaction to prevailing norms. Artists might not be captives of culture but they often negotiate a tortuous path between convention, conformity and rebellion. Yet whilst we currently revere the artist for his or her originality and uniqueness, it is important to remember that in the Renaissance their role was quite different. According to Lisa Jardine, "the Renaissance artist was a craftsman in the service of the powerful (and) painting was an inexpensive form of luxury decoration."[11] This notion situates the artist in a demand driven marketplace where wealthy clients commissioned (or implicitly encouraged) specific themes that were often contractually enforced.

Take for example the so-called "revolution" of the earliest painters such as Giotto di Bondone (1266/7–1337), who broke from Byzantine traditions by depicting humans in a natural rather than stylized way. Perhaps his best known work (the *Scrovegni Chapel in Padua* [circa 1305]) consists of a series of frescos that depict the life of the Virgin and the life of Christ. They are visual narratives, albeit sometimes in allegorical form, and were commissioned by a local notable, *Enrico degli Scrovegni*, for a chapel to serve as a family worship and burial space. Presumably he felt that a beautifully adorned chapel paid by himself would stand him and his family in good stead as they prepared for the afterlife. Other commissions followed for the Giotto. For example, frescos at *Santa Maria Novella* were commissions for the Dominicans [circa 1290]; in the *Basilica of St Francis at Assisi* [1306–1311] for the Franciscans; and the *Church of Santa Croce in Florence* where he painted chapels for four different Florentine families. His works were illustrations of familiar texts, a new visual language that told stories to a largely illiterate population. Documents from the first decade of the fourteenth century indicate that Giotto was sufficiently famous to be given numerous additional commissions from throughout North Central Italy which resulted in him accumulating large estates.[12] These where artistic works in religious settings, replete with sacred themes often intended to bestow a secular halo of dignity and wealth on the person commissioning them. The Friars that could afford his works embraced its beauty; the Florentine elite wanted a visual memorial to their grandeur.

Other notable artists followed a similar path, either working for commissions or being sustained by stipends from wealthy patrons. These include Michelangelo and Raphael whose fame was based upon Papal advocacy. In the increasingly prosperous city state of Venice, Titian's (Tiziano Vercellio, 1488/1490–1576) famous painting of a reclining nude woman, *Venus of Urbino* (1538) was acquired by the 24-year-old Guidobaldo II della Rovere when he became Duke of Urbino following is father's death. Possibly a commission or a painting that might have aroused his interest when he saw it in the artist's studio, it nonetheless epitomized art's value as a product that could convey multiple levels of meaning – in this case a visual message to his new wife on the importance of sensuality as well as a marker of his new found ducal status. The fact that a young man such as himself could afford a painting by a recognized elite artist was a measure of his elevated material status and self-assuredness and inevitably produced envy by others who saw it in his possession (albeit in his bed chamber where paintings of salacious nudes were frequently located).

Not surprisingly artists had to become attuned to the dictates of the market if they were to be successful. The Venetian artist Tintoretto (1518–1594) was astute in his pricing policies, determining the average market price of his rivals' works and then undercutting them in what he charged. A century later, Giovanni Batista Tiepolo (1696–1774) painted many allegorical biblical scenes because there appeared to be a market for such images, thus assuring him of a steady flow of sales and commissions. At the same time, Giovanni Antonio Canal (Canaletto, 1697–1768) catered to wealthy Europeans whose travels to Venice stimulated a desire for a visual memento. He focused upon this export trade by painting numerous images of Venetian canals, the Rialto bridge and St Mark's Square that were sold to these travelers, possibly as mementos of their travels as well as a sign that they had the requisite aesthetic taste. The British merchant and banker, Joseph Smith, who was appointed British Consul in Venice in 1744, was his major advocate and in addition to acquiring many of his paintings, also acted as a sales intermediary for other customers in England. He encouraged Canaletto to move to London in 1746 where the latter proceeded to paint scenes depicting life in the metropolis and its emerging grand architecture for wealthy English merchants.

In each of these cases, artists were providing a desirable product that had suitable religious resonance, a vestigial morality metaphor or a visual narrative that gave the owner bragging rights and a conversational reference point when surrounded by the great and good in their own residence. For the elite buyer, this was a respectable form of consumerism. Their sustained acquisitiveness sustained a market place for luxury commodities of which art assumed significance. Because an artist's reputation depended upon their ability to arouse commercial interest in their product, they became cognizant of shifts in the marketplace. And since patronage was the *modus operandi* in much of the art world, demand-driven themes assumed salience and structured many market transactions. If we therefore view the Renaissance as the age of mercantilism and acquisitiveness, then not surprisingly art assumes commodity-like status. It was a transactional tool in a culture where the urge to own was elevated to a privileged status; a coveted commodity that endowed the owner with respectability (or salvation).

Ostentatious behavior aside, some owners/patrons saw art as vehicle in the path to salvation. As we saw in Chapter 2, paintings could be commissioned and then given to churches or other religious institutions. They might be a gift to signify the wealth and status of the benevolent donor. Or there could be a more subtle message. Such work might be dispatched to religious institutions as indulgences or even penance for earlier sins. A healthy market in the sale of indulgences continued to be vital to the ongoing wealth of the Papacy, but here the transactions were visual materials that benefited churches as well as the memory of their patrons. The painters and sculptors were willing to oblige by producing images inspired by sacred texts that would encourage reverential contemplation in churches and public spaces. But even in these circumstances, such art had a monetary value inasmuch as the chosen artist was frequently one whose reputation was sufficiently high to be selected in the first place. And such reputations were made in the market place. The patron hopefully felt the higher the price paid, the more likely one's path into the afterlife would be assured.

For all their aesthetic splendors, Renaissance painters had clearly delineated markets for their product and were enthusiastic adherents to a system of clientelism that was unambiguously supply and demand structured. However, as religious orthodoxy was challenged, an increasingly secular culture emerged around the institutions of commerce and capital and a new consumerism was forged.[13] What had hitherto been art produced for a cloistered elite, now became a self-referential vehicle for an ascendant merchant class increasingly confident in their own material acquisitiveness. Thus the church was replaced by wealthy merchants and landowners who wanted depictions of themselves to display their power and wealth.

In trading centers such as Antwerp, merchants whose wealth came from international commerce and export trade, used that money to purchase art that often depicted landscapes and self-portraits. That plus still life and genre paintings replaced religious and mythological subjects. In their search for appropriate paintings they were aided by a small but growing class of dealers. In what was generally a depressed economy in Antwerp in the seventeenth century, a luxury market for art was surprisingly vigorous but depended upon the skill of specialized full-time dealers who could source art and export it to clients overseas.[14] They were able to identify new artists whom they felt would appeal to a new international taste, sometimes creating and supplying demand in new marketplace channels. Their role as sales channel intermediaries diminished the need for patronage (except amongst the best known artists) and they formed and controlled the new markets for art. They became the link between influential artists and the rising wealth in Europe; sourcing a luxury product for wealthy individuals who lacked the time or knowledge to seek out appropriate paintings.

When England's Charles I (1600–1649) indulged his passion for collecting art, he inspired other court dignitaries as well as the aristocracy to behave accordingly.[15] In effect he was legitimizing informal norms of using art to depict status. Italian Renaissance paintings were the preferred object because of their high value and sense of permanence. Such works had entered into the pantheons of aesthetic legitimacy thus rendering any doubts about their commercial value spurious. Together with many of his close associates, Charles amassed a sizeable collection of what came to be known as Old Masters. Following his execution in 1649, a secondary market for paintings emerged as his estate was dispersed. Estimated at over 1760 paintings, the availability of such works spurred interest amongst those who sought the ennobling effect of ownership of paintings with distinctive "royal" provenance.

With growing wealth from its colonies Britain's economic power grew in the eighteenth century and sparked the beginning of a consumer revolution in that country. An increased number of wealthy families with greater disposable income bought art because it was assumed to be the "done thing" for the wealthy. They imitated the aristocracy in their material acquisitions and providing it was the correct type, art assumed the requisite cultural significance. The increased prosperity that accompanied the industrial revolution merely accentuated this trend and a formal marketplace for art was further consolidated. Two notable innovations accompanied these trends: the establishment of auction houses and the rise of official dealers who managed sales transactions. The latter played simultaneous roles of placing appropriate art in the right hands as well as establishing *de facto* aesthetic legitimacy for artists; the former institutionalized the exchange of property by bringing buyers and sellers together as a quasi-formal framework. In essence what was emerging was a system whereby aesthetics and financial value were fused together as these new institutions were providing the structure and basic architecture to frame the market place for art.

Market Intermediaries: Auction Houses and Dealers

Sotheby's (established 1744) and Christie's (established 1766) emerged as English institutions catering to the English aristocracy whose traditional fascination with country pursuits were now being piqued by an interest in art. Paintings were increasingly viewed as conversational pieces, especially when seen in the context of the grand tour that many of the families had made. Vistas of Imperial Rome were more romantic than rural England and enabled the owner of such paintings to position themselves as connoisseurs and sophisticated world travelers. Country estates were the perfect place to display such works and after the secondary market had taken off by the early eighteenth century there was additional interest from new estate owners whose money came from commercial and industrial ventures.

The first truly international dealers were probably the agents of the Medici's who were sent to Antwerp to buy paintings and tapestries to be shipped back to Florence with other commercial products such as wool.[16] Presumably they were entrusted to buy paintings by the foremost artists and were probably given little discretion other than negotiating over price. There were, however, other European merchants who specialized in buying and then exporting paintings for resale in other countries. They formalized what was an embryonic market but were also more speculative in their approach than the Medici agents.

By the seventeenth century, dealers and agents were assuming a more prominent role in arbitraging paintings between countries, using price differences to manipulate markets in different countries. Dealers often worked with artists and so they developed relationships and grasped who was painting what and how good they were. Given the lack of clarity as to what criterion one should use to evaluate contemporary painting, especially since visual narratives were in the same state of flux as the societies themselves, subject matter varied. In some cases dealers themselves encouraged certain subjects such as peasant life and grand evocative landscapes designed to document caricatures and expose the chaotic intensity of the new urban culture. Presumably they were cognizant of what buyers wanted or at least were able to speculate about future trends given their knowledge of buyers. A good example of this shift can be seen in the popularity of the Dutch/ Flemish artist *Pieter Bruegel the Elder* [1525/1530–1569]. His so-called genre paintings were in demand by the Brussels elite such as the banker Nicolaes Jonghelinck who owned sixteen paintings. Their evocation of the quirks associated with the burgeoning towns provided a humorous and almost anecdotal quality to paintings and were certainly conversation pieces in the homes of the wealthy merchants in Antwerp who were also some of *Bruegel's* biggest customers.

As with any product with intangible value, the market was fraught with uncertainty. And yet successful dealers were able to identify certain artists whose work in certain areas proved popular with local elites as well as foreign buyers. The most marketable products thus became "brands" inasmuch as the artist became an acknowledged entity and his/her works deemed of cultural and material significance.[17] With such success came greater wealth for dealers and a growing recognition of their legitimacy and power in shaping the market for art.

By the eighteenth century, the demand for art had increased, especially amongst the newly rich in industrializing England. The role of dealers was crucial inasmuch as they could be the purveyors of cultural and positional credibility for this new class of collectors. Something had to decorate the large walls in the large houses and fine art fulfilled this purpose quite splendidly and was further evidence of the owner's wealth, taste intelligence.[18] As Philip Hook argues, "to form a collection had moral, intellectual and social benefits. It was one of the things you did to announce yourself as a gentleman."[19] Having the requisite degree of taste and an appreciation for beauty, as defined by a growing class of art specialists, suggested connoisseurship, dignity and sophistication. This connoted wealth but also suggested an appreciation of one's ultimate purpose in life and the world to come. Fashion and taste in art inevitably varied and this added a further dimension to the selection process.

It was into this context that Sotheby's and Christie's were established, the latter proving particularly successful at locating foreign consigners. The founder and owner, James Christie, was particularly adept at early marketing techniques by using the media to advertise his sales. His co-ownership of two daily London newspapers enabled him to disseminate information about his sales to those he felt susceptible to the sort of media influence that could stimulate consumerism. Christie's also pioneered certain financial schemes that provided advances to sellers and then subsequently guarantees, essentially changing the auctioneer's role from agent to stakeholder.[20] By the mid-nineteenth century, Sotheby's and Christie's were the dominant auction house in England, outperforming all of their competitors. They had consolidated their reputation as purveyors of fine art, particularly the popular field of Old Masters, and re-defined the operational nexus of auctions.[21]

Auction houses proved increasingly successful in promoting art as a luxury product, in part by their rigorous promotion of provenance when art came from famous estates. Whilst dealers and agents had the inescapable "whiff" of trade about their activities, auction houses stood resplendent as pillars of respectability, staffed by gentlemen who clearly understood the appropriate gravitas in what was nonetheless a market transaction. Their timing was prescient in that they could link new money with old art, but they were also at the cusp of a cultural sea change. Economic progress was seen as relentless but not without questions regarding the fabric of society. Social cohesion was fragmenting as the old hierarchy was implicitly and sometimes explicitly challenged by new forces. Auction houses offered a way to reconcile this impasse. They established themselves as purveyors of "high culture" at a time when industrialization was transforming the countryside and urban growth apparently destroying many of the traditional links with the natural world. The efficiency gains of modern factories and the relentless march of technological progress was seen by nineteenth-century aesthetic warriors such as John Ruskin as detrimental to the fabric of society. Whilst critical of the alienation of modern work, he and others argued for a return to nature and things local. But he was at his most adamant when preaching the need for beauty in everyday life. Yet not everyone could live in his beloved Venice, but if you were rich enough you could at least adorn your country houses with magnificent paintings by Old Masters of that city. Christie's, in particular, made this possible; Sotheby's was not far behind. Ironically they both peddled Arcadian beauty to those whose fortunes came from precisely the activities (coal, iron and clay mining; canal and road building) that were destroying the rural idyll they were seeking to capture in paintings.

In addition to auction houses, the nineteenth century saw a significant increase in the number of dealers, some of whom became household names to the new rich as the "go-to person" to buy art from. Dealers had worked with auction houses, selling and buying paintings for clients who lacked the knowledge to trust their own aesthetic instincts. One of the best known in Victorian England was Ernest Gambart. He thrived by catering to the pictorial needs of the new wealthy mercantile class. Speaking of his clients, the new bourgeoisie, art critic and former auctioneer Philip Hook concisely states, "he was there to comfort and pleasure them, to identify the sort of paintings they liked, and to give them more and more of them at higher and higher prices."[22]

Not for the first time did customers implicitly assume that high price equaled quality, but his strategy further leveraged this tactic by invoking expert opinions on his sale works. This public relations activity involved using influential critics (including at one time John Ruskin) to essentially endorse the works he was selling.[23] He used galleries to host his sales, sometimes even charging admission to the public to view a particular painting. He traveled extensively in Europe, developing important contacts for potential sales including works by artist outsiders to the normal market whom he felt had future potential. Most importantly though he had a clear sense of what his customers wanted but often only after he had discussed the virtues of certain painters with them. He listened carefully to them, discerned their taste and aspirations, and then politely reassured them of how certain works would best meet their goals. His long career is a testament to his success in re-interpreting and shaping his clients' needs in ways that coincided with his own business interests and he did this without them forfeiting their trust in him. This subtle influence enabled him to place works that he could obtain at good prices with customers who trusted his judgment as to the value and status of a panting. He was the consummate dealer and market maker. By securing paintings for wealthy clients he not only embellished his own reputation but also proved instrumental in confirming the aesthetic value of certain artists. This role of tastemaker or taste shaper subsequently led to higher prices and status value for the new owners.

Gambert was also one of the first to realize the importance of the new American market, but it was Joseph Duveen, one of the legendary dealers at the end of the nineteenth century, who capitalized upon it most successfully. It has been calculated that Duveen was responsible for the import of three quarters of the best Italian art into American collections during this time and he supplied 50 percent of Andrew Mellon's collection that was subsequently given to the National Gallery in Washington, DC. His role as *de facto* cultural ambassador to the new world is perhaps best summarized by Philip Hook in his cogent assessment of Duveen.

> On the one side of the Atlantic there existed a bevy of increasingly rich Americans who had everything except class and history, and on the other a slew of European aristocrats, torpid with class and history but increasingly in need of money. How to remedy the situation? What could be satisfactorily transferred between them that would endow class and history to the former? Art, in which "old" Europe was rich, was the perfect commodity.[24]

By the late 1800s, the land rich and increasingly cash poor English aristocrats were eager to unload some of their ancestral cultural legacy. On another continent American industrialists were keen to embellish their material wealth with the appropriate social standing that comes from an art collection, especially one with such vestigial provenance. It is this market that Duveen manipulated for decades, aided by acknowledged experts such as Bernard Berenson whose attributions nurtured the speculative nature of many transactions.[25]

In what was an increasingly entrepreneurial age, dealers such as Duveen and Gambart were the consummate entrepreneurs, profiting financially and also culturally from their transactions. They were perfectly positioned to understand the evolving demand for the cultural capital that the new bourgeoisie so earnestly sought. The latter could seek redemption in art because it offered the refinement that their material success could not easily satisfy. At the same time dealers could shape opinion and taste; they could educate their customers and provide an appropriate rationale for a particular purchase. They were simultaneously cultural ambassadors and commodity salesmen, brokering luxury to those who needed it as an aesthetic affirmation of their material status.

Modern Art and the New Marketplace

By the nineteenth century many artists had started to liberate art from the conventional forms and realistic depictions of nature and in doing so shocked and surprised clients and the establishment. In many cases they were less dependent upon patrons since they were able to exploit the market via dealers who assumed a vital middleman role. Impressionism, Cubism, followed by Dada and Surrealism in the early twentieth century broke with convention, and art became a vehicle for protest, experimentation and the urge to explore the subconscious. The latter was given agency by Sigmund Freud, who provided the rationale for exploring the inner sanctums of the brain in ways that could be subsequently unleashed in painting. At the same time Modernism captured the attention of those who either embraced the mechanistic, technologically transformed society as a paean to progress or rejected the anonymity and stultifying hierarchies and repetitious nature of modern work and life. For the latter, the dystopian future needed serious questioning and possibly rejection. The former meanwhile were happy to flirt with utopian dreams since they had the potential to liberate individuals from any remaining residues of pre-Enlightenment culture.

Although individuals and institutions continued to acquire art, there was greater uncertainty as to its aesthetic status and even its intrinsic value became more circumspect. It was as if artists were freeing themselves from the received aesthetic dictates of the past, casting aside convention and embracing a freedom of form that was a reaction to industrialism as well as its embrace. For collectors who increasingly made up the ranks of patrons, the challenge was self-referential – identifying someone you liked but then justifying that decision on looser aesthetic grounds than in the past.

Into this potential abyss entered a new breed of dealers such as the Frenchman Paul Durand-Rual. Faced with a new aesthetic in Impressionism, he enlisted the help of critics and organized one person shows of artists and provided comprehensive catalogues to explain the subtleties of this new style. He recognized the need to educate the public about such works but also realized that the higher the price he could charge the more legitimate his artists would be perceived. By speculating on artists such as Millet, inflating prices for his paintings, and closely monitoring sales at auctions, he was able to convince a wary public that this new style would in fact become *de rigueur* in the near future. This worked quite well in America where he was instrumental in building Impressionism into a brand. To quote Philip Hook again, "America was a new young country susceptible to new young art."[26]

European art might now be visually challenging but it still came from Europe and was the latest iteration of a painting tradition that stretched back to the Renaissance. The artistic credentials remained impeccable and the dealers such as Duran-Rual reminded clients of that legacy. Despite the difficulty in viewing and understanding contemporary art of that time, he was able to demystify and explain it satisfactorily to his clients. For him to be successful he had to educate his clients if they were to appreciate this new movement. Specifically he extolled the virtues of newness, works that were exciting because they posed a different agenda to that depicted by art in the past. This was art shorn of its classicism; art that was designed to make you think rather than leisurely contemplate. Many of the artists were unknown which also posed a challenge. His big success came with Impressionism and he seized the opportunity to emphasize its inherent strengths (bright colors and bold brushstrokes) as emblematic of a new visual narrative that would supplant earlier dated techniques. His essentialism was "buy it now while you have the chance before others enter the market."

Interestingly, when Impressionist sales took off in America, Europeans reconsidered their own ambivalence to the style. As Duran-Rual's fortunes increased he was able to live a lifestyle that was commensurate in many respects to his clients. Ironically, such opulence on his part merely served to further reassure his wealthy customers who felt comfortable dealing with a person of wealth and substance – he was like one of them. More than any other dealer of this time period, and there were others who successfully built careers in this evolving marketplace, he created a market for a style of art and then amassed a fortune in providing for that market.

More dramatic changes occurred in the art world during the early decades of the twentieth century. Industrialized warfare, technological changes, massive unemployment, and socio-political unrest resulted in an erosion in the earlier confidence of modernization and the presumed socio-economic benefits of industrialization. Artists positioned themselves at the cross roads of this cultural crisis. Some opposed, excoriated and sought to subvert the process; others affirmed its vitality and glorified its implicit rationale. Each in their own way was questioning the function of art and its market. For whom were the paintings or sculptures intended? Was the supreme purpose that of shock, as the Dadaists claimed, with evident disregard for any commercial value to be attributed to art? Or was all of this mere propaganda designed to bring attention to artists so they could sell more in a marketplace where traditional patronage had dissipated and new types of buyers were emerging?

Modernism in particular had attempted to redefine the purpose of art by conceiving it as an overt vehicle for ideological expression and protest (Duchamp's "Urinal" and Picasso's "Guernica" being good examples of this trend). There was confusion about what paintings meant (titles were often as mystifying as the paintings themselves) and the "shock of the new," to use Robert Hughes book title,[27] confounded many who assumed that art should not be visually challenging and of uncertain cultural provenance. What did all of this mean for the value and pricing of art? This growing aesthetic uncertainty confused buyers who were often risk averse when it came to embracing revolutionary styles. In addition if the new art was to assume monetary value rather than merely be an ideological expression of some nihilistic identity, somebody with intellectual status had to endorse and explain its significance. Yet again dealers stepped up, eager to demonstrate the sometimes unsavory and often unique eclecticism of the new genres to their stable of collectors. They were well positioned to frame the art movements as expressive of the changing times. After all they argued, allegorical sacred paintings of the Renaissance were a departure from earlier visual renditions but are now accepted as part of the accepted tradition. The Modernist were merely tapping into that seam of stylistic innovation.

Dealers repeatedly invoked art's one of a kind status which continues to confer a symbolic value. Their goal was to convince enough people willing to take a chance that these new styles were not only aesthetically legitimate, they could also be valuable. Even though some critics decried the intellectual and aesthetic poverty of modernism, others saw it as a legitimate response to the excesses of industrialism and technological change. If dealers could suitably contextualize the art against the background of such transformations and position paintings as a legitimate expression of the pervasive cultural angst, then art's unique visual identity might persuade reluctant buyers of its ultimate worth.[28] And by now dealers had sufficiently sanctified their own legitimacy as cultural ambassadors to the newly wealthy, that their credibility was unquestioned.

The most powerful dealers could brand artists and educate the public about their virtues. They did this by not so subtly reminding consumers that what they were buying was the latest manifestation of a visual expression with a history stretching back to the Renaissance, albeit one forged out of a new movement that castigated the old without denigrating the essentialism of the painted canvas (or object).[29] Since dealers were also in the forefront of chronicling the history of modern art, they could disseminate information that would be vital to their cause. Such information, together with academic studies, provided the critical rationale for acceptance of new art styles. As in the past, many of these new artists were depicted as geniuses and thus collectible. Ultimately, for the wealthy buyer in search of the appropriate visual credentials, this was all that mattered.

Dealers continued to play an important role in sourcing art, especially amongst living artists who were willing to sign exclusive agreements with them. In 1910 Picasso signed a three-year agreement with Daniel-Henry Kahnweiler whose reputation was based on his ability to create an aura of sophistication and aesthetic privilege on the buyer.[30] For the first four decades of the twentieth century he managed to cultivate an atmosphere of genteel intellectualism in his gallery, dispelling concerns clients might have had about the new art forms, such as Cubism, that he was selling. No grubby commercialism here. He was the quintessential cerebral dealer who was able to infuse a sense of gratitude in those who were fortunate enough to be able to buy a painting from him. Other, young dealers in Germany and Switzerland in the early twentieth century were likewise responsible for promoting Modernist art to an audience in that country still coming to terms with the visual revolution of that time. Alfred Flechtheim and Paul Cassirer successfully persuaded wealthy clients in Germany that paintings by George Grosz and Otto Dix had redeemable value despite their sometimes shocking or anti-bourgeoisie subject matter. In Switzerland Ernst Beyeler thrived by building a sense of urgency amongst his clients, always suggesting that other buyers were keenly interested in a particular painting.[31] This inevitably inflated the price but the buyer was satisfied in the knowledge that he had acquired something that somebody else wanted so it must be valuable!

Revitalized Auction Houses and Dealers Become Galleries

After World War II auction houses were undergoing significant change. Because of their improved organization capability they provided not just a marketplace for sales but also became repositories of information through their sales records. They could marshal data on not just types of paintings sold but also who the growing numbers of buyers were, what style they preferred and what price points they gravitated to. Greater transparency about what sold and for how much energized the market and created *de facto* benchmarks for certain styles. This effectively formalized data on art prices, documenting trends as well as evolving types of art that sold best. In doing this they were tacitly giving an unambiguous monetary value to works of art, thus providing another dimension to a painting's worth. A painting's inherent aesthetic value was now complemented by a monetary assessment of its worth. If certain artists sold for high prices it suggested a demand that would result in a further rise in price. Thus art began to take on the mantle of a tradable asset. The wealthy now might buy art as part of an investment strategy, with an eye to reselling in the future for a higher price.

At Sotheby's, the arrival of Peter Wilson as chairman in 1958 transformed the auction house from a trade wholesaler dealing largely in estate liquidations following "death, divorce and debt" to a glamorous emporium where dignified contests over art trophies were conducted in public amongst the genteel classes.[32] He was the consummate salesman in recirculating the art of the elite, from those who perchance did not appreciate its aesthetic credence to those who embraced its financial worth. He sought to position Sotheby's at the apex of art sales by glamorizing the whole process whereby one bought art and making the event a public spectacle. He effectively institutionalized the drama inherent in the actual process of selling luxury. The act of acquisition in the auction room became almost as important as the status that came from the eventual ownership. To cite auction historian Philip Hook again who cogently summarizes Wilson's legacy,

> Everyone went home elevated by contact with the mysteries of great art, but also energized by their proximity to great financial transactions, the drama of those transactions heightened by the climactic moment of the fall of the hammer. The power of the marketing, the glamour of the event, the beauty of the art: All combine to create something definitive about the pricing achieved, and to invest an authority in the ringmaster of those prices, the auctioneer.[33]

Unsurprisingly other major auction houses were soon to follow with this drama, whether it was the English aristocracy who were Christies' clients, or the eminent European and American families whom Sotheby's and then Phillips went after, the latter increasingly invoking their strong involvement with contemporary culture.

Dealers meanwhile continued to assume prominence via their now formalized presence as gallery owners, particularly in New York which was becoming the center for sales of contemporary art. For example, Leo Castelli opened a gallery in his apartment in 1957 and used the space to sell paintings by the Abstract Expressionists. As in the past, his clients were wealthy, often financiers. Whilst these people might have heard of Jaspar Johns or Andy Warhol, it was Castelli who convinced them that owning works by such artists would improve their cultural worth. These artists were hip and this counter-cultural vibrancy apparently resonated with clients whose lives were otherwise a model of decorum and conventionality.

In subsequent decades gallery owners such as Larry Gagosian and David Zwirmer have continued this trend, building artists into brands and then managing sales in a carefully scripted way to maintain an aura of scarcity. With galleries located in the major art market cities of the world, their increased physical size also garners attention. Big and bold, the iconic white cube space that has museum like atmosphere is now the preferred setting to garnish attention for collectors. It confers bragging rights for the gallery owners who compete with each other, as well as convincing customers of the importance of the art contained therein. To quote former Sotheby's former auctioneer Tobias Meyer on the necessity of size,

> "You sell more if you have a bigger space." Artists in the twenty-first century want galleries on the scale of their ambitions, and the vast white cubes deliberately evoke museums, conferring a sort of cultural imprimatur in the visitors' mind.[34]

The past few decades have seen greater acceptance of non-conventional forms and oppositional art, with movements such as Abstract Expressionism, Pop Art and most recently conceptual art such as that by Damien Hirst and Jeff Koons. Restored consumer confidence in contemporary art's marketability also mirrors subtle change in the motivations of buyers as well as continuing changes in the marketplace for art. People buy art for many reasons, perhaps best summarized by the following categories: material possession and accumulation, emotional (learning to appreciate and the fun of ownership), and social (status building but also sharing with other likeminded individuals).[35] Art is a discretionary purchase but one that is steeped in a long history of exclusivity. As has been discussed throughout this chapter, art is a positional good for many collectors, a way of gaining cultural reassurance through affirmation of their taste. And the more expensive the piece, the greater the desire for it amongst the very rich. As art writer and expert on art markets Georgina Adam notes about the current popularity of Jeff Koons' works amongst billionaires, his instantly recognizable works confer status and prestige upon the owner plus demonstrate his financial prowess in gaining such exclusive pieces.[36]

Since the 1990s there has been a significant interest in expensive works of art in emerging economies. Many of the recent high value purchases have come from collectors in China as well as the Middle East. In 2017 the number of global ultra-high net worth individuals (net worth of $30 million or more) rose by 12.9 percent to 255,810 people with the fastest growth in the group coming from Asia where the growth was 27 percent.[37] There is a strong correlation between the performance of the art market and economic growth and the rapid growth of China's economy since the 1990s has fueled the art market there.[38] China now accounts for 26 percent of the world's billionaire population and 17 percent of total global imports of art now come from Asia. Japan, India and China now account for 32 percent of world wealth and whilst the slowdown in the Japanese economy since the late 1990s hurt art sales there, China has stepped up to be a major player.

As with their western counterparts, many there view art at the apex of their needs. This is especially the case with trophy works of art – expensive works by famous painters that provide bragging rights for the new owner because they possess it and others do not.[39] As with their European counterparts of previous centuries, and the Gilded Age Americans who were so eagerly sought by dealers, the motivation to own remains intricately linked with social status. For many, art remains the quintessential positional good. Hence the importance of international brands that possess the requisite cultural authenticity and a universal acknowledgment of their value and status. It also seems that dramatic price increases for key artists in recent years has further fueled buying amongst UHNW individuals there. That and the limited supply preserves the scarcity factor so important for these collectors.

Is Art a Good Investment?

By the late 1970s art began to acquire status as a formal investment tool; a way of diversifying and hedging ones portfolio away from normal financial products.[40] Wealthy people in the past bought art because it spoke to them in visual terms. But they also recognized that its rarity might have a residual monetary value that could increase in time or if nothing else it would hold its price. Now some buyers were specifically looking for a return on their investment by buying famous works, storing rather than displaying them and anticipating their value to increase prior to reselling. This " financialization" of art has influenced art markets, especially auctions were major works that often reappear after 'disappearing for many years'.[41]

It was clear that works by certain artists, especially in the field of contemporary art, have considerable financial value; not merely a decorative piece but potentially a financial asset. If this is the case then art assumes another value dimension as speculators and art funds increased, with groups and individuals being formally advised on buying art for its investment potential.[42] Even institutional investors got in on the act. The British Rail Pension Fund put 6 percent of its money into a wide range of art through the 1970s, securing an overall 4 percent return on their investment by 1980.[43]

Dealers have always proclaimed the unique properties of art works, sometimes even highlighting the residual financial worth of the art work. Now some were arguing that in addition to any intrinsic aesthetic worth, a work of art could possess a monetary value that could increase in time and thus be thought of as an investment. Monetizing the value of a work of art provided a further dimension by which one could evaluate artists. Some wealthy collectors appeared to embrace this new financial logic, buying works and then storing them in secure warehouse settings. Some preferred anonymity, others enjoyed the celebrity status of the purchase but claimed security issues by removing the work from public view. Various financial reports acknowledge the increase in the purchase of tangible assets such as art and fine wine by the wealthy as a way of diversifying their portfolio. Art is a portable product that can be moved from country to country to take advantage of different tax regimes and currency fluctuations. The cost of moving, storage and insurance is not insignificant but still small relative to the price of the work. But as with any investment, there is no certainty that values will increase. The percentage of collectors pursuing such hedging strategies is difficult to determine, although one recent estimate suggests that 80 percent of all the art in the world is in storage at some time.[44]

Much has been written in recent years on this new speculative behavior, but the general conclusion is that with the exception of a few top brand names, monetary gains are limited.[45] Art is illiquid, trends hard to anticipate, and the product difficult to sell unless it comes from one of the top 1 percent of artists. For example, *Artnet* magazine estimates that almost 45 percent of all post war and contemporary art sales came from just twenty-five artists in 2017.[46] This hyper concentration pushes prices up for these artists and encourages bidding wars. For other artists however, the resale prospects are dire, with estimates of 80 percent of art bought at sales or fairs reselling at less than the purchase price.[47] Whether dealers overtly encourage some collectors to think of the investment angle for their purchase, is difficult to ascertain. However, given the high profile results of a few recent sales, it is perhaps not surprising that some collectors might be seduced into seeing a potential profit angle from their purchase.

Despite the trend of art as an asset or asset class, the intrinsic gains are most likely realized in non-financial terms, as a product with intangible cultural value. At the high end of the market, art remains a luxury product, the unique-ness and rarity of which bestows hedonic benefits to the small number of people able to afford it. UHNW collectors can be part of a select and distinguished group whose financial means gain them entry to a rarified world of aesthetic passion and social exclusivity. A unique combination of emotion and hard numbers brings together individuals who use art as a vehicle to participate in a marketplace that synthesizes the essentialism of a rare work, the passion of col-lecting but also the realization of possible monetary gain.

Auction houses, mega galleries and now the burgeoning number of Art Fairs position themselves as *de facto* arbiters of taste by simultaneously commodifying the product as well as restricting its supply. They cater to a select global group of UHNW individuals whose acquisitive drive for art is often top of their needs list – true trophy products because of their uniqueness and rarity.[48] This group and the institutions that cater to them are driving interest in and demand for certain types of art.[49] Such individuals might treat art as an investment grade product but it nonetheless confers the requisite status on their new found wealth. Art markets have thus been transformed with the product itself granted a more ambiguous status (visual icon or illiquid asset that can yield future profit). The people buying great works of art are financially the same; their numbers have merely increased and expanded in geographic scope. They are in wealthy countries and in emerging economies. But if more art is bought as an investment opportunity and then stored away from public view, does this transform art into a commodity, devoid of the visual splendor that marked its earlier function? Possibly. And yet there remain powerful bragging rights to the buyer of an eminent painting, such as the recent high profile record $450 million sale of Da Vinci's *Salvator Mundi* to Saudi prince Bader bin Abdullah bin Farhan al-Saud. The buzz and glamor of the sales room or gallery creates a frenzied atmosphere as does peer emulation as a driver of desire. At the same time many twentieth -century artists have broken with the old formulaic prescriptions that defined their earlier submission to patronage. They, their dealers and auction houses now are closely associated with the global elite and in so doing art continues to be aligned with luxury goods.

Conclusion

Historically art occupied the realm of exclusivity inasmuch as it was in finite supply. It has been a product that the wealthy acquired to keep for themselves or donate to religious institutions to salve their conscience. It became a valuable aesthetic commodity because of this differential demand and its status as luxury good solidified when certain artists proved more popular than others. Increasingly art was used to validate the status of the newly wealthy merchants, who used self-portraits as a way of announcing their arrival on the social scene. As form and content changed in the twentieth century, the art of certain artists became investment instruments for the wealthy. It was acquired as much for its marketability and presumed "financial" value as it was for any visual splendor. Top artists are a fraction of the total number of artists worldwide, but they are the producers of a luxury good that is affordable by a select group of individuals (and sometimes institutions). The market for investment grade art has exploded in the late twentieth century, driven by a global set of super-rich individuals, institutions such as auction houses and galleries that market the hype, and key artists who have capitalized upon this more overt commercial trend. Contemporary art for some is the must have item, not to be viewed or even donated but to be locked away in hermetically sealed storage to be sold at a profit in future years.

These brief narratives provide several stories. One is how markets evolve as consumer tastes change, institutional settings alter and production capabilities are transformed following technological innovation. This is also part of continuing structural changes in society, more pronounced inequality and in the twentieth century more fluid identities. Less-fixed statuses provide individuals with a more constant ability to seek to differentiate themselves not just from others but also from their past. This has provided a surge in materialism and at the top end a dramatic increase in demand for luxury goods.

The second theme traces how commodities function differently in time periods as they meet varied demand imperatives. Art that was infused with religious significance but nonetheless a marketable commodity (as was the artist) has acquired increased status as an investment grade asset. By the twenty-first century certain artists have been able to utilize the changing market place in which art is sold (mega galleries, art fairs, art consultants, etc.) to maximize their own status as well as provide objects that transcend mere visual aesthetics and become prized commodities.

In the brief descriptions offered above, one can trace the purposive creation of markets geared towards manipulating scarcity. But in both instances the final products were more than mere commodities or even material acquisitions. In fact rather than an expression of material wealth, possession of cult wines or contemporary masterpieces conferred a cultural superiority for the owner, thus taking us back to the behavior of class and status groups referred to in earlier chapters. They are an experience good that can be appreciated by connoisseurs because they privilege an aesthetic dimension that is timeless.[50] In Renaissance times they provided spiritual relief from uncertainty for the patron and a revenue stream for the artist. Stripped of aesthetic evaluations, the work of art was embedded in a market designed to bring together those whose status allowed them the luxury of expensive acquisition and donation with cultural and religious imperatives that sanctioned reassurance of a future after life. Perhaps most luxury goods reflect a degree of cultural insecurity amongst its practitioners. Status and wealth can be ephemeral, inequality timeless but also fraught with uncertainty for those currently exercising the material options of their wealth. Those who purchase expensive works of art or fine wines are participating in an evolving marketplace whose values change subtly but nonetheless confer a sense of satisfaction for the owner in knowing that they are part of an exclusive club. How much they seek acknowledgment of such a position varies. But they are occupying a unique space that for centuries has enabled the wealthy to circumscribe their way of life with material acquisitions that provide reassurance and enhanced self-satisfaction.

Notes

1 Bonner, S.E. *Modernism at the Barricades*, New York: Columbia University Press, 2012, p. 37.
2 Baxandall, M. "Conditions of trade," in Baxandall (Ed.), *Painting and Experience in Fifteenth Century Italy*, Oxford: Oxford University Press, 1988, pp. 1–28.
3 Simmel, G. *The Philosophy of Money* (3rd ed.), London: Routledge Kegan Paul, 2004.
4 McNeil, P. and Riello, G. *Luxury: A Rich History*, Oxford: Oxford University Press, 2016.
5 Armitage, J. and Roberts, J. "Critical luxury studies: Defining the field," in Armitage, J. and Roberts, J. (Eds.). *Critical Luxury Studies*, Edinburgh: Edinburgh University Press, 2016, pp. 1–21.
6 See Jardin, L. *Worldly Goods*, NY: Norton, 1996, p. 9.
7 Ibid., p. 12.
8 Crosby, A. *The Measure of Reality*, Cambridge: Cambridge University Press, 1997.

9 Jardin, op. cit., p. 19.
10 Goldthwaite, R.A. *Wealth and the Demand for Art in Italy, 1300–1600*, Baltimore: Johns Hopkins Press, 1993.
11 Jardine, op cit. p. 26.
12 Eimerl, S. *The World of Giotto*, New York: Time-Life Books, 1967.
13 Robertson, I. *Understanding Art Markets*, London: Routledge, 2016, p. 187.
14 Honig, E. *Painting and the Market in Early Modern Antwerp*, New Haven: Yale University Press, 1998, p. 110.
15 Hulst, T. (Ed.).' *A History of the Western Art Market*, Berkeley: University of California Press, 2017, p. 204.
16 Hook, P. *Rogues' Gallery*, New York: The Experiment, 2017, p. 9.
17 Ibid, p. 18.
18 Hamilton, J. *A Strange Business*, London: Atlantic Books, 2014, p. 5.
19 Ibid, pp. 23/4.
20 Bayer, T.M. and Page, J.R., *The Development of the Art Market in England*, London: Pickering and Chatto, 2011, p. 145.
21 Ibid, p. 146.
22 Hook, p. 62.
23 Ibid, p. 67.
24 Ibid, p. 80.
25 Ibid, p. 84.
26 Ibid, p. 126.
27 Hughes, R. *The Shock of the New*, New York: Knopf, 1981.
28 See for example Wolfe, T. *From Bauhaus to Our House*, New York: Farrar, Straus and Giroux, 1981.
29 Hamilton, op. cit.
30 Hook, p. 154.
31 Ibid, p. 200.
32 Ibid, pp. 219/220.
33 Ibid, pp. 228–9.
34 Quoted in Adam, G. *Big Bucks: The Explosion of the Art Market in the Twenty-First Century*, Farnham: Lund Humphries, 2014, p. 56.
35 Woodham, D. *Art Collecting Today*, New York: Allworth Press, 2017, pp. 52–3.
36 Adam, G. *The Dark Side of the Boom*, Farnham: Lund Humphries, 2017, p. 75.
37 Wealth-X, *World Ultra Wealth Report*, 2018.
38 McAndrew, C., *The Art Market 2018*, Art Basel/UBS 2018, p. 265.
39 Adam, 2017, p. 134.
40 Gerlis, M. *Art as An Investment*, Farnham: Lund Humphries, 2014.
41 Ibid.
42 Adam, 2017, p. 132.
43 Adam, 2017, p. 133.
44 Quoted in Adam, 2017, p. 132.
45 Korteweg, A.G., Kräussl, R. and Verwijmeren, P. 'Does It Pay to Invest in Art? A Selection-Corrected Returns Perspective', *Stanford Business School Working Paper No. 3124*, October 15, 2013, Stanford University.
46 Helperin, J. and Kinsella, E. "The 'winner takes all' art market," *Artnet*, September 20, 2017.
47 Adam, 2017, p. 141.
48 Adam, op cit.
49 Zaniol, G. "Brand art sensation," in *Cultural Politics*, January 12, 2016, p. 49.
50 See Berthon, P., Leyland, P., Parent, M. and Berthon, J.P. "Aesthetics and ephemerality: Observing and preserving the luxury brand," *California Management Review*, 52, 1, pp. 45–66.

7

FINE WINE

Creating Luxury in a Bottle

Where there is no wine there is no love.

Euripides

Good wine is a necessity of life for me.

Thomas Jefferson

In victory you deserve Champagne. In defeat you need it.

Napoleon Bonaparte

Go, eat your food with gladness, and drink your wine with a joyful heart, for it is now that God favours what you do.

Ecclesiastes, 9:7

Wine is a fascinating beverage that smells and tastes good, is a natural complement to food because it enhances the various flavors, and is a product that, in moderation, promotes good health.[1] It has a long and interesting history with evidence that it played an important role in normal everyday life as well as being a ceremonial product. In this respect it is quite ubiquitous in many societies. As wine economist James Thornton argues, "it is a complex and intriguing product that makes it different from a typical manufactured good. It arouses the intellect, pleases the sense."[2] For our ancestors who imbibed wine on a regular basis, it undoubtedly brought sensory pleasures to what for many was probably a very bland diet. For others it was a ritualized beverage that conferred dignity to a particular activity. In either case it was enduringly culturally significant.

Wine might have been simultaneously a rare and expensive product as well as one that was widely available and affordable to the common man – one can only speculate where and when such distinctions occurred. However, today wine covers many price points and numerous types (varietals). For example, one can currently buy inexpensive bottles of wine in many countries. Such commodity wines dominate the market and account for most of the sales by volume. They are the "everyday" wines that many people drink as a way of enhancing a meal or sharing a social event with friends. Generally uncomplicated, often generic tasting, they nonetheless satisfy the basic beverage needs for most people.

But there are other wines that fall into the category of "fine" wines – wines that have attained the highest quality ratings and reputation and often have a long and storied history. They are often more complex and refined than basic wines and provide nuanced characteristics that the discerning few are able to identify. Such wines are produced in very small quantities for oenophiles whose appreciation and wallet enable them to purchase what are very expensive and difficult to obtain wines. They are the quintessential luxury product because they remain exclusive and confer an element of sophistication upon the owner as well as possibly being a valuable asset until they are drunk. This chapter examines such wines but in addition to a brief description of traditional wine regions such as Bordeaux and Burgundy (which have been extensively discussed elsewhere),[3] I examine how a new wine region (Napa, California) has gained legitimacy and oenological credibility through concerted market building and luxury brand development strategies by a handful of what are referred to as cult wineries.[4] This is the story of how an exclusive wine region developed in a relatively short period of time, how part of its success relied upon external validation by new quality markers, plus the innovations associated with a technologically mediated approach to winemaking that provided greater consistency and enhanced finesse to the finished product whose availability was ultimately heavily restricted.

The wines that are discussed have been purposefully crafted to very high standards, often benchmarking famous Old World estates but with a distinctiveness in flavor and boldness (often described as big, fruit forward wines) that denote their specific locational attributes. They are the embodiment of a very scientific approach to winemaking even though their producers might invoke the importance of "*terroir*" in a paean to Old World traditions. These wines are expensive to make and priced accordingly. Such high prices denote status for producers and consumers alike (the so-called "Veblen good"). They are the product of resource rich new winery owners with the passion and financial wherewithal to make an exceptionally high-quality wine produced in limited amounts whose target customers are new groups of wealthy individuals developing an appreciation for fine wine (sometimes as a status good). Given the relative newness of these wines, whatever insecurities consumers might have had about buying them (the uncertainty factor), particularly doubts about quality, have been alleviated by the validation of acknowledged experts whose opinions and ratings confer legitimacy and a certain transparency on the products. Such experts constitute an important intermediary in the market for a finely crafted product that cannot invoke luxury markers such as heritage and tradition. Furthermore, they give transparency to the market structure by validating the wine and reinforce the brand building luxury strategy that underlies their evolving "iconic" status.

Evaluating Wine

Wine is an experience good – in other words, one has to actually drink it to know what it is like. For most table wines, making such a choice involves minimal investment and for cheap wines people appear willing to risk trying one since the cost is small. Expensive wines are a different matter since the significant upfront cost can deter most people unless they can rely upon accepted markers that signal the wine's basic quality and properties. This means that reputational aspects and brand identity are important components of such wines.[5] In other words the value of the wine must be authenticated by those who have consumed it and are knowledgeable enough and respected to provide a quasi-official judgment of the product. Such people can be wine experts whose credentials are acknowledged to have significant impact upon the eventual status of fine wines. Their role will be explained later in this chapter since they have been partly responsible for legitimizing Napa California's elevation to a respected wine region. That they have succeeded in placing some new wine regions alongside those in the Old World that were traditionally seen as the markers of excellence is testament to their role in conferring explanatory (and sensory) significance to many wine drinkers whose purchasing insecurity might preclude them from trying an expensive wine.

The difference between a good wine and an excellent one is not easily perceptible. High price and limited availability can, and often do, signify high quality but many people who can afford the most expensive wines nevertheless search for expert validation.[6] Famous wine critics such as the American Robert Parker and the respected wine magazines *Wine Spectator* and *Decanter* offer evaluations of many wines and have become the *de facto* "stamp of approval" for iconic wines.[7] In this respect they have firmly placed certain wines in the category of a luxury good, available to a small percentage of the population whose incomes and taste preferences extend to what after all is essentially an ephemeral product (eventually it is consumed).[8] How extensive is the phenomenon of fine wine given that the products are made in small quantities?

One way of documenting the growth of a fine wine marketplace can be seen in the increasing amount of wine sold at auctions. These could be charity events such as those held annually in Burgundy and Napa. Most often however, they are the regular auction events that bring collectors of fine wine together with sellers in an institutional setting of an auction house. It is from such events that one is able to gain an insight into the monetary value placed on fine wine and see that wines in such categories are clearly not a commodity product but almost an investment grade asset.

For many people, fine wine immediately conjures up classic Bordeaux and Burgundy estates with track records that extend hundreds of years.[9] Iconic brands and vintages of certain well regarded wine estates in these areas have set the pace at recent auctions following the growth of interest in fine wines.[10] For example, four bottles from the 1998, 1999, 2000 and 2003 vintages from famed Bordeaux estate *Petrus* recently went up (2018) for auction at Christie's with estimates of US$9500–$13,000. At that same auction a case (twelve bottles) of that estate's 1989 vintage had estimates in the £30,000–40,000 range. But in recent decades, fine wines from the New World have also acquired iconic status and set records at auctions. In addition to Australian brand *Penfolds Grange* (with certain vintages retailing at US$700–800 a bottle and a 1961 vintage at US$2123 a bottle), that same Christie's auction listed above had a case of *Heitz Martha's Vineyard Cabernet Sauvignon* 1974 (from Napa, California) with estimates of US$15,000–20,000.

Whereas Old World wines have a pedigree that comes from decades if not centuries of perceived quality and status, and are seen as the product of locational specificity (*terroir* driven), New World wines without such a track record must rely upon external validation of their product and a conscious effort to create their own delimited market space. This brings us back to the role of the aforementioned critics. To build brand recognition quickly is difficult since history and tradition are most often used to confer status on a product. However, in the case of wine, a new producer can possibly acquire the necessary credentials of excellence (prime vineyard site, famous winemaker, internationally renowned wine consultant) and very quickly elevate oneself to the pinnacle of oenological excellence if and when awarded the highest ratings (scores) from recognized experts. Wines in this category transcend the notional everyday drink and become a product to be revered and extolled for its uniqueness and exclusivity.

Wine's Early History

We can trace wine's origins to Europe and the Middle East. The earliest records can be found in 8000-year-old stoneware and pottery drinking vessels with traces of wine from that period that have been unearthed in what is now Bulgaria. Much of the discoveries of early wine cultures come from that part of the world. For example, wild grapes appear to have grown in Georgia, Armenia, Azerbaijan, plus coastal regions of Turkey and this strain of *vitis vinifera* (Europe's signature grape) was first fermented in these regions.

What motivated such an act? One can only speculate that our ancestors picked grapes and whilst keeping them for several days discovered that they fermented and could be transformed into a pleasurable beverage. As an agricultural product, wine is transformed from grapes via the fairly natural process of fermentation which requires minimal human intervention.[11] Since humans have long appreciated the joys of fortified beverages, this was nature at its most beneficent!

What appears to be the world's oldest winery was recently discovered in Armenia. The 6100-years-old site includes a pressing vat, fermentation jars, cups and bowls, plus the remains of crushed grapes and *vinis vinifera* vines.[12] The Bible is replete with references to wine (including the famous "turning water in wine" claim), suggesting that it played an important role in that part of the world. Meanwhile in Persia evidence of wine's presence can be seen in carvings in Persopolis in which soldiers from subjected nations brought vessels containing wine to be given to the Persian kings. What any of this early wine was and even how it tasted, however, is impossible to know. We can surmise as to its function as a ritualistic beverage and ponder how much our ancestors enjoyed it on a regular basis, possibly as a complement to meals. The fact that it was alcoholic suggests a further possibly illicit aspect to its enjoyment.

Wine was an important part of ceremonial life in ancient Egypt. Tomb walls contain images of wine vessels as a product deemed an essential accompaniment to the departed souls. However, it was in ancient Greece that a winemaking culture first systematically appeared with an aromatic white wine called *retsina*, a wine that is still associated with Greece.[13] The Greeks were also possibly the first to recognize the economic impact of wine since they exported the product (in amphoras that have been discovered in the area) to neighboring countries such as Sicily, Italy and even France.[14] Wine's centrality to Greek life and culture is best seen in the elevated status of the god Dioynsus who oversaw grape harvests, wine making and wine, plus activities that some still associate with excessive wine consumption (fertility and ecstasy for example). He came to be associated, somewhat pejoratively perhaps, with excess consumption and assumed cult-like status with some of his adherents. It was the Romans, however, who put viniculture and oenology firmly on the map in the first century AD as well as adding their own glorification of alcohol excess in the form of the wine god Bacchus (who incidentally was also the god of fertility). They refined production techniques and wine became more pervasive than on previous societies. Wine was integral to Roman society, as a beverage that was consumed by ordinary people as well a drink that was crucial in ceremonial events. The fact that the emperor Domitian passed the first recorded wine laws in AD 92 that banned the planting of new vineyards and uprooting many others suggests that drunkenness was becoming endemic. Whether or not he succeeded in curbing the Roman enthusiasm for wine is difficult to determine. However, during that same period, other rules were introduced to classify various regions according to the quality of their wine (the precursors to today's appellations) and new techniques adopted that improved winemaking. The gradual growth of Christianity in the next few centuries brought a further refinement to grape growing and wine making, since wine was central to Catholic masses and monks were tasked with ensuring adequate quantities and appropriate quality.

Wine became a common beverage across most sections of society in the southern parts of Medieval Europe where grapes were extensively cultivated. As Chapuis and Charters note, after the fall of the Roman Empire, the best vineyards were owned by the church who safeguarded viticulture in the turbulent times of that period.[15] Monks at Benedictine and then Cistercian monasteries further refined wine making, infusing it with new techniques and an organizational efficiency that prefigured many current wineries.[16] Their abiding commitment to excellence was borne out of their provision of hospitality and meals for pilgrims, the need for wine in the Eucharistic mass, plus their own daily libations. Furthermore they had the resources and patience to experiment with new techniques such as larger presses and vats (and storing wine in barrels) that could improve the finished product and were able to acquire the requisite land for such endeavors. In addition to vineyard consolidation which permitted scale efficiencies, they also divided vineyards into distinct plots to examine site variation – experimental analysis that presages the notion of terroir.

Quality Control

In northern Europe during the seventeenth century further innovations in viticulture resulted from a more "scientific" approach to winemaking as indicated by publications such as that of Olivier de Serres' manual entitled *Theatre of Agriculture and Field Management* (1600). He advocated new techniques for destemming, vat storage and appropriate varietals for specific areas. It was during this time that certain wines were seen to improve with age, as opposed to being drunk almost immediately.[17] If that was the case, then quality improvement must have occurred as traditionally wine turned very quickly to vinegar if not consumed quickly after production. Much of this experimentation was occurring in south western France, around the city of Bordeaux.

Bordeaux has been an important commercial center since the Gallo-Roman era, and wine has traditionally played a central role in that region's export trade. Initially much of this trade was with England but by the middle of the seventeenth century that had switched to the Netherlands. Dutch tastes favored richer, more robust wines than the lighter bodied (claret) wines preferred by the English.[18] This newer style of wines was the product of revised winemaking and vineyard management techniques that were spreading throughout the region plus the recognition that certain areas (soil types, micro-climates, etc.) could produce wines of outstanding quality. This territorial criterion, associated with the term *terroir*, became an important pricing component for wineries that strongly identified with a specific sense of place. High quality was associated with increased demand which meant wineries could charge a price premium for the wine. The forerunners of iconic estates such as Lafitte and Latour were established around this time and built their reputations by fully articulating this locational specificity.[19]

As the overall quality of wine improved and demand soared, some wineries began to designate their best wines via usage of the estate name. In Bordeaux, Arnaud III de Pontac, owner of Haut Brion explicitly used his winery's estate name rather than his own to sell his wine in London. The so-called "Ho Bryan" (sic) was popularized by Samuel Pepys in 1663 in his descriptions of tavern life in the capital.[20] The wine writer Hugh Johnson attributed Pontac's success to these innovative marketing skills plus his commitment to improved wine-making techniques.[21] A form of territorial brand, meanwhile, was developing at the same time in the champagne region of north east France. The monk Dom Pérignon was one of the first people to market his sparkling wine, first as a proprietary brand and then as a territorial brand (Champagne), leveraging the growing success of other producers in the area. The collective champagne brand was subsequently formalized as a type of intellectual property that under European law has a legal personality of its own. This has enabled champagne growers to protect their identity by preventing others from outside the demarcated region from using the name champagne and ensuring a certain product consistency (types of grapes used and how they are grown) for their wine.[22] Again, this provides pricing power for incumbents as well as formalizing the industry structure in the region.

We return to Bordeaux in the nineteenth century where official attempts to address variations in quality had led to informal classifications in which wines were ranked according to taste. In 1855, at the behest of Emperor Napoleon III who was seeking to extol the virtues of French agriculture and industry at the Imperial Universal Exposition in Paris, the president of the wine brokers association in Bordeaux was tasked with classifying the region's sixty-one greatest producers into five "grand crus" classes: 1st–5th growths.[23] The idea behind what is now known as the 1855 Classification was to formally recognize the best wines in the region. But somewhat ironically, the criteria chosen for the ranking was simply price (high-priced wines received higher classifications).

Value-based classifications had a long history in the Bordeaux wine trade in part because of difficulties in determining quality parameters plus frequent errors in judgment over what exactly is a quality wine. Since price and quality were closely related in the public eye, the classification simply organized what most people recognized as the best wineries (and most expensive wines) into a formal ranking. This classification reinforced the collective reputation of many Bordeaux wines plus elevated a few to iconic status. No additional wineries have been added to the classification since then in part because incumbents have no incentive to change a system in ways that could be disadvantageous to them. A similar but more thorough classification that included quality measures as well as reputation was introduced for Saint-Emilion wines (known as the right bank) in 1959.[24] By then better indicators of quality had been introduced and flaws were more easily documented so price was no longer the sole determinant.

Both sets of rankings have become firmly institutionalized through the *Place de Bordeaux*, the marketplace that structures most of the fine wine sales in the region. In recent decades the status of these classified growths has been consolidated by favorable scores from critics. Such endorsements provide transparency to brand value, minimizing uncertainty and risk on the part of consumers. They have also reinforced the market value of brand authenticity and heritage, a crucial component in luxury products, by allowing classified growth wineries to constantly invoke their stories and commitment to the creation of a natural product as opposed to one that is mass produced.[25] As a result, the returns to status over time, for both producers and consumers who buy the wine, becomes more predictable with an increased flow of information about the product's inherent quality.[26]

The legacy of these activities lies in how wine is now made and perceived by the general public. Historically wine was a beverage that was safe to drink (prior to the widespread availability of potable water) as well as an everyday foodstuff. It had been made by smallholders and peasant farmers often for their own consumption or for exchange in a local market. For many such producers, trial-and-error methods persisted with some good harvests accompanied by ones that resulted in flawed wines. On the other hand, as viticultural techniques and oenology practices became more professionalized and technically proficient, and resources were injected into the industry, much higher quality wines were produced on sites that acquired reputations for excellence. In other words a market segment of luxury wines emerged. Such wines are often associated with specific locations (classified growths in Bordeaux and Burgundy, for example), increasingly under the ownership of individuals with extensive resources, and within the institutional framework of governance structures designed to protect the "brand." In addition to the recognized quality dimensions, the success of such wines is based on the purposeful crafting of their brand authenticity.[27] Deliberate attempts by wineries to extol heritage and artisanal production features, whether real or imagined, have become crucial parts of subtle marketing techniques. They bestow the virtues of traditional craft production techniques, stylistic consistency and their cultural relevance as part of a process that legitimizes their core distinctiveness.

In recent decades new entrants to this exclusive world have come from regions outside those normally associated with wine production and in markets where wine consumption is increasing. In what is referred to as the New World, the United States is notable, particularly California where a chequered history of wine production has been significantly transformed in the past fifty years. Unable to play the heritage card of history and culture, wineries in such regions have developed strategies that focus upon crafting new styles of traditional wines. Specifically they have relied more heavily on technical intervention in the winemaking process in order to achieve greater consistency and quality. Their approach has been to emphasize a strong product orientation that optimizes marketing their uniqueness within a constructed niche.[28] This is particularly notable amongst the top wineries who have pursued a resource-driven commitment to quality together with high prices and limited availability to formalize their authenticity. They have, in a few decades, successfully built a luxury brand by purposefully extolling technical skills and a unique sense of place from which their product is made.

California's Early Wine History

As missionaries spread along the California coast in the late eighteenth century they brought from Europe grapes as well as other crops to plant. Wine was an important item in the life of these early settlers and its use in the missions became pervasive. It was a beverage that the priests were familiar with, as a drink with meals as well as its use in communion. When the missionaries moved north to the San Francisco Bay area they found land in what is now Sonoma County that was ideal for grape growing and subsequently wine making.[29] The wines they produced have been referred to generically as "Mission wines" because of their association with the missions there. We do not know much about the specifics of this wine, although one of the earliest documents on them, a letter by Father Narciso Duran to the California Governor, José Figueroa in 1833, lists four types – two reds and two whites with one of the latter fortified with the addition of brandy.[30] These wines came from the San Gabriel mission. In terms of quality Father Duran was renowned for producing good wine and brandy at his San Jose mission but others were already commenting on the quality of wine produced at the small Sonoma mission.[31] Unlike Burgundy where Cistercian and Benedictine monks were the oenological gatekeepers, it seems that in California the Franciscans were the driving force behind wine making. We do know that Mission grapes were a very dry, raisined fruit with much sugar and low in acid (a product of the sunny and dry conditions of California) and were probably fortified with brandy to make them palatable. The winemaking process was undoubtedly quite simple but it remains difficult to determine how much wine was made, how well it might have been distributed and what its overall quality was like.[32]

Following the Gold Rush of 1849, demand for wine grew as the city of San Francisco became an important trading center and its population increased. When it was recognized that there were almost perfect growing conditions in the coastal parts of the state, especially the area surrounding the San Francisco Bay, interest in wine shifted to experimentation with different grape varietals that might flourish and produce better quality wine than that found in Mission grapes. To encourage such experimentation and to avoid individual trial and error approaches, the recently established California State Agricultural Society (1854) disseminated information on viticulture and general growing practices.[33]

One of the early pioneers in this new approach to grape growing was Hungarian immigrant Agoston Haraszthy who argued (apparently without much prior knowledge!) that European varietals should replace Mission grapes because they could offer better-quality wine. To prove his claim, he bought 560 acres of land just north of the town of Sonoma and planted 14,000 vines that comprised 165 varieties. As an experiment it appeared to pay off since his widely disseminated "Report on Grapes and Wine of California," commissioned by the California State Agricultural Society in 1858, was soon seen as the definitive guide to grape growing in the region. Following his impetus, subsequent immigrants imported cuttings and vines from the Bordeaux region, particularly the signature varietals of Cabernet Sauvignon, Sauvignon Blanc, Carignan and Semillion.[34] Another report by the State Agricultural Society in 1861 ("Commission on the ways and means best adapted to promote the Improvement and Growth of the Grape-vine in California") indicates that at an institutional level, the state was beginning to play a role in providing the requisite knowledge for would-be winery owners to better understand the fundamentals of viticulture and oenology.[35] That, together with the arrival of more immigrants with winemaking experience (and wealth), added significant acreage under vine as people sought out plots in the hilly terrain of what is now Sonoma and Napa counties where growing conditions (particularly topography and climate) proved far more amenable to quality wine production than in the south around Los Angeles, where some of the early vineyards had been established.[36]

When George Crane planted a 300-acre vineyard just south of the town of St Helena in Napa Valley in 1861, he did so in area that was dominated by orchards. Similarly another immigrant and friend of Haraszthy, German Charles Krug, had acquired 540 acres north of that same town the previous year. They experimented with different grape varietals, ripping out the orchards and replacing them with vines. In the space of twenty years (from 1872 to 1892) Krug's production went from 250,000 to 800,000 gallons annually. Both eventually demonstrated that the area could produce good quality wine, especially if grape growers could be persuaded to abandon their commitment to maximizing the quantity of harvested grapes. Since many growers were paid a fixed price per ton for their grapes by bulk buyers and merchants who marketed the wine, the financial incentive induced a quantity over quality approach to harvesting. However, as marketers of their own wines, Krug and Crane were demonstrating that lower yields would produce much better-quality grapes.

A further advocate for the superior quality of *vinifera* grapes and better yield management was University of California Agriculture Professor Eugene Hilgard. In an important presentation to the State Vinicultural Society in 1875, he forcefully argued for a focus on quality over quantity.[37] Pruning vines and removing some grape clusters to reduce density would, he claimed, result in better quality grapes. During that same speech he also identified the phylloxera infestation that was destroying vines across the area and recommended crossing *vinifea* with American rootstocks to prevent the disease. Even though many growers remained skeptical (about both his claims) his ideas eventually found traction and Napa's potential for producing better wines than in other areas of Northern California was realized.

When the seven largest wine merchants in the state formed the California Wine Association (CWA) in 1894, they encouraged a more scientific approach to winemaking and part of this involved changing the payment practices to growers. Now growers would be paid in accordance with the quality in addition to the quantity of their fruit. Some growers balked at the changes but it did eventually lead to an overall improvement in the quality of wines produced and the subsequent low yield/high quality formula has since become widely accepted.[38] By the turn of the century the CWA (and Krug) became important voices that articulated the collective interests of growers at the state level. In doing this they were further consolidating the reputation of Napa as a pre-eminent site for wine making and beginning the process of building Napa's brand recognition. When tariffs were imposed on imported wines in 1873 and again in 1883, more people shifted their wine consumption to domestic wines (including those grown in the Mid-West and East coast as well as California) and this further boosted production.[39] There was a fourfold increase in wine production between 1877 and 1887 and by 1889 it was estimated that there were 5000 vineyards in California.[40]

At the World Exposition in Paris in 1889, Napa wineries collected eleven of the twenty-one medals awarded to California wineries – a clear indication that others were recognizing the growing quality of wine in that region. [41] In 1900 a small but very high-quality vintage produced wines that have subsequently become associated with Napa; ones that were fruit forward, rich and powerful wines. This style of wine was a product of long hot sunny days with grapes left to almost over-ripen which resulted in increased sugar levels, more alcohol content and an enhanced sensory richness. Yields were low but the resulting quality was very high. Winemakers were discovering that this type of wine was so notable that it stood out in competitions with other wines from the state (and even Europe) and they realized that they could charge a price premium for such a product. In the ensuing years Napa wines continued to win other awards and the area's reputation further improved.

When Frenchman Georges de Latour established his Beaulieu Vineyards in 1902, he located it next to an existing vineyard known for producing good wine. The latter, Inglenook Estate in Oakville, was founded by Finnish sea captain Gustav Niebaum in 1880. With extensive resources he created an expansive, professionally managed vineyard and paid particular attention to ensuing his winery was scrupulously clean (to avoid contamination that easily tainted wine). He was also the first person to provide a distinctive image for his wine with his diamond trademark and Latour was quick to imitate with his own branding and a determination to consistently make a premium quality wine. Both produced wines mainly for the discerning East Coast market and both became *de facto* benchmarks for what were considered Napa's best wines in the 1900s.[42]

Despite these successes, periodic boom and bust cycles inevitably hurt the embryonic industry, as did the persistent challenges of getting the wine to the East Coast where the major population centers and markets were. Glass bottles were expensive and difficult to obtain and most wine was shipped in barrels to be bottled at the destination with the almost inevitable problems of good wines being mixed with bad ones. Furthermore pests frequently damaged crops and thus lowered yield. However, just as the industry was beginning to overcome these problems and gaining broader recognition, Prohibition (the Volstead Act) was introduced in 1919 and took effect in 1920. This effectively shut down the wine industry as only small amounts of wine for home consumption were permitted. Of the approximately 700 wineries in California prior to Prohibition, only 130 existed shortly before the Act's repeal in 1933.[43] Subsequent efforts to rebuild the industry were plagued by shortages in skilled winery workers (vineyard managers, winemakers, technicians etc.), a collapse in the market for wine (many people had shifted their alcohol consumption to hard liquor which was easier to obtain during Prohibition or to poor quality but inexpensive homemade wine), and then finally the lingering recession years of the 1930s which constrained consumer spending. With wines sales depressed through the 1940s and 1950s, sales amongst premium producers such as Beaulieu and Inglenook continued to struggle and the number of California wineries declined by more than a third between 1950 and 1967.[44]

Napa's Rebirth

Two things were instrumental in Napa's post-World War II resurgence: the arrival of individuals with either wine making experience or a passion for entering the industry and with the financial resources to do so, and the growth of systematic and codified knowledge about viticulture and oenology that was occurring at the nearby University of California Davis. The latter became the center for research into improved wine making techniques and it offered degree programs in which many of the eventual Napa winemakers enrolled. Graduates from this program became technical specialists armed with templates on general techniques. Science increasingly became the *modus operandi* for wineries, trumping what some saw as outdated Old World veneration for *terroir*. Such techniques also involved a more active intervention in viniculture designed to achieve a predetermined taste, smell and appearance profile. A certain stylistic consistency resulted which subsequently became the hallmark of wines from Napa, although some have criticized such wines as being overly manipulated. Despite dramatic improvement in overall quality of wines from the region, such techniques were anathema to old-world producers who minimized intervention, preferring to allow nature to take its course.[45]

Wine consumption increased in the United States in the 1960s and there were several notable individual arrivals in Napa who were intent on making quality wine to serve this burgeoning market. These included Andre Tchelistcheff who took over at the recently revived Beaulieu vineyard, Croatian immigrant Mike Grgich who went to Souverain, and Robert Mondavi who built his now iconic Mission-style winery in 1966 in Rutherford.[46] They were followed by others who were trained in the new University programs and who brought a level of expertise and understanding of local conditions that enabled them to realize what sorts of wines could be made in the area.

One of the key figures of this group was Tchelistcheff who recognized the potential to make great wines providing the requisite skill sets amongst incumbent winemakers could be improved. And he argued that the more great wines that were made, the better Napa's reputation would become. He had been instrumental in forming the Napa Valley Technical Group with the aim of "providing a cooperative effort to exchange practical information on the production of high-quality wines."[47] Part of his goal was to encourage a cooperative spirit amongst winemakers to facilitate the exchange of information and best practices. Eventually more and more newcomers to the industry and area would participate in this often informal group, meeting regularly to share each other's wines and critique them.[48] This form of *de facto* "organizational capital" would be crucial to the industry's evolution since it enabled individuals to identity and then rectify problems before they damaged the collective image. Much detailed site-specific information was shared, including issues such as planting, canopy management, harvesting and fermenting techniques, as well as ideas as to which varietals were best suited to the area. Individual expertise was thus transformed into a collective good via a process of collective organizational learning and cluster development.[49]

New groups of owners revitalized the Napa Valley Vintners (originally formed in 1944) in the late 1970s and in 1975 the Napa Valley Grape Growers Association was created to exchange best practices amongst growers. At one level both of these groups were an important conduit of information about tacit skills that were quickly becoming community knowledge. They were also developing a *de facto* governance role designed to protect the embryonic Napa brand and its reputation for producing high quality wines. Information hoarding amongst winemakers was discouraged and a commitment to professional credentials was increasingly endorsed as a way to leverage extant knowledge. Both associational groups endorsed the scientific and technological approaches to viniculture advocated by UC Davis as the latter disseminated progressively formulaic and standardized ways of maximizing Napa's climatic potential over inherent soil properties. For as I have argued elsewhere, "No longer was the industry one of hard working amateurs pursuing trial and error alongside a few hardened professionals. The new benchmark was quality conditioned by scientific training."[50]

Napa's credibility received a significant boost in the late 1970s when wines from the area were favorably compared to the best in France. Napa wines were entered into a blind tasting competition in Paris in 1976, and a panel of French judges with extensive wine experience chose two of them – *Chateau Montelena's* Chardonnay and *Stag's Leap* Cabernet Sauvignon – over several famous French first growths. Subsequently known as the "Judgment of Paris," this tasting elevated Napa to the pantheon of oenological respectability and shocked the wine world, especially in France where experts in the past had been dismissive of California wine.[51] It also repudiated many of the French claims for the primacy of *terroir* and its unique presence in the Old World as the basis for fine wine (and therefore the ability to charge a price premium for it). It was a strong argument yet again in favor of a dedicated, and largely regulation free, scientific approach to winemaking. Californians were able to intervene in many ways banned in France (use of irrigation for example as well as no formal limits on yields) which meant they could mitigate problems to which French vineyards often succumbed. Given Napa's predictably consistent wine-friendly climate, there was little yearly variation in harvests. When combined with the primacy of science in vinicultural techniques, the result could be a wine of consistent high quality – unlike the annual fluctuations that characterized many old-world producers who were captives of vintage variations.

With the technical mediation firmly in place, in 1981 the Napa Valley AVA (*American Viticultural Association*) was created as a way of recognizing the soil and climate specificity of the region. It was the first to be designated in California and subsequently was divided into sixteen nested AVAs that identified further specific characteristics for grape growing. Napa winemakers could and often did introduce subtle stylistic characteristics to differentiate their wine to discerning consumers. In doing this they were often exploiting the sub regions in the valley that had become famed for their growing potential, thus allowing the notion estate distinctiveness. Some notable valley floor locations were highlighted (*To Kalon* being one of the most famous vineyards) whilst hillside sights were preferred by others. Estate designation enabled wineries to differentiate themselves but retain the overall Napa Valley designation that provided the overarching legitimacy.

Cult Napa: Luxury Wines from the New World

Researchers have shown how many new winery owners in the 1980s were purposeful in their strategy of emphasizing a niche for handcrafted, small-lot, vineyard-designated wine from the best land in the valley.[52] Their aim was exclusivity and limited availability, plus a high price that covered their high production costs. Scrupulous attention to detail and the evocation of crafts-manship across all aspects of production endowed the finished product with an aesthetic appeal that would capture the attention of wealthy individuals. The wine was restricted in distribution, largely sold via allocation to a small number of select individuals who often waited patiently to get on the list. This manufactured scarcity furthered the exclusivity of the wine. When critics awarded these wines very high scores, it was an acknowledgment that wines of exceptional character and finesse, comparable to the best from Bordeaux, could be produced in Napa.

Since wine is an experience good, expensive wines can be daunting for consumers unwilling to pay a large sum for an unknown product. Napa's brand reputation had been improving but at the high, luxury end where prices were in the hundreds of dollars, quality markers were necessary. Wine from Bordeaux and Burgundy had history, tradition and legacy to legitimize the high prices; Napa lacked any of these. However, when various critics whose oracular role in reviewing and classifying wines brought attention to Napa in general as well as certain specific wineries, it catapulted several wineries to virtual "cult" status.

Numerous publications and websites worldwide have provided evaluations and ratings of the quality of wines, but it was Robert Parker's quantitative 100-point quality scale that became the most important when it was introduced in 1978. Under this system, a wine that scores more than 95 is considered excep-tional, 90–94 is superior, 85–89 is seen as above average and so on down the scale to 65 where a wine is considered to be of poor quality. His quantitative scores are accompanied by a bimonthly newsletter (*The Wine Advocate*) in which he offers detailed descriptions of the various facets of the wine that was tasted. Other monthly periodicals such as *Wine Spectator* and *Wine Enthusiast* offer a similar scoring system and the former had a taster (*Jim Laube*) whose focus was specifically upon Napa Valley wines. Whilst there has been extensive debate as to how subjective such tasters are, whether they prefer a certain style of wine (e.g., big, rich fruit forward wines) that might stand out in blind tastings, it is acknowledged that a very high score can add significantly to the price of and demand for a specific wine.[53] In an interview I had with a prominent Napa winery manager on the day after his wine was named *Wine Spectator* "Wine of the Year," he said the phone hadn't stopped ringing and he had "discov-ered" many new Distributor "friends" who wanted to get access to this wine. Demand soon outstripped supply and he was able to significantly raise the price of that wine in subsequent years.

Regardless of hedonic studies that attempt to evaluate measures of sensory quality, and the accuracy of critics, consumers use scores as a way of inform-ing their purchasing decisions. This is especially the case with high-scoring expensive wines where consumers gain confidence in buying and cellaring a wine that has a 95 plus score. High scores are also used in auctions as well as the secondary market for wine as a way of bestowing appropriate status levels to the product and legitimates the high retail price. Whilst Chardonnay is widely planted in Napa and of excellent quality, by the 1990s it had become clear that Cabernet Sauvignon was the signature grape for the valley, the one that could command the highest prices. But who was buying these wines and who was making them? Answering precisely the first question is difficult; the second however is reasonably clear.

Starting a winery has always been an expensive proposition, especially since the returns to one's investment do not typically occur until on average seven years later. Some of the notable names from Napa's past were often wealthy individuals who used capital from prior successful businesses to fund their start up. That was less the case in the 1970s as many newcomers with limited means, but viticulture experience or a science background, entered the industry. However, since the late 1980s many of the new investors come from industry backgrounds such as technology, real estate or finance. The price of vineyard land increased dramatically, pricing out those with winemaking experience but not the financial resources. The new resource-rich owners are however, passionate about wine and owning a winery and are able to hire the best winemakers, vineyard managers as well as world famous consultants (such as the Frenchman Michel Rolland) to work with land that has often cost in excess of $300,000 an acre. They include *Harlan Estate, Araujo Eisele Vineyard, Colgin, Bryant Family, Screaming Eagle, Schrader, Ovid* and *Staglin* to name the most famous. Each sells a limited quantity of wine at prices that can exceed $1000 a bottle – if one can get hold of one.

Wealth has often been a feature behind winery purchases. For centuries in Bordeaux, it was wealthy families who were able to buy the best land and apply extensive resources to produce the best wine. They also used their political influence to shape regulations that best suited their properties, particularly in the increasingly social and political aspects of terroir classifications.[54] This pattern has persisted into the twentieth and twenty-first centuries as corporations as well as many wealthy foreign buyers have acquired some of the best estates in Bordeaux (vineyards are much smaller and fragmented in Burgundy, are more likely to be family owned for generations).

In bestowing vast sums to achieve the level of excellence they desire, do new owners in Napa display a different business model to ones that privilege simple profit motives? Researchers Fiona Scott Morton and Joel Podolny analyzed price and quality relationships amongst firms operating in the luxury California wine market. In addition to the normal profit maximizing behavior one experts of rational actors, they found that some firms pursued utility-maximizing strategies.[55] In other words such firms derive utility from securing lifestyle benefits and status that accrue from winery ownership and are prepared to eschew profits in the short run. Enjoyment of owning a winery trumps positive revenue streams. As a result such winery owners can focus upon producing excellent quality wines without the worry of profit; and they can charge higher prices for their wine because they have higher marginal costs. As Scott Morton and Podolny argue, increasingly the luxury segment of the market in Napa is occupied by such utility maximizers who enjoy producing high-quality wine. Eventually they might need to be profitable if the cross-subsidies from their other investment activities diminish but in the short run they have raised the quality bar in such a way that even profit maximizers have been forced to focus more upon their own quality parameters.

Their entry into the industry has generated much critical discussion especially as to whether they have priced out of the market others without deep pockets and are merely making Napa Valley a playground for the rich.[56] Unquestionably their presence has changed the dynamic in the Valley by creating a niche for the production of high-quality wines that are marketed as a boutique product. Such wines have a distinctive identity and a symbolic value that derives in part from their extremely limited availability. Their high market valuation is a result of their quality but also the status that they have carefully manufactured. Whereas in the past Napa wines sometimes lacked a legitimate and positive image, these cult wines have built upon several decades of high scores by critics, victories in global competitions, increased technological and viticultural skills and have brought extensive resources to upgrade operations and make a wine of excellent quality. Furthermore they have assiduously focused upon this product integrity by leveraging such endorsements precisely because they lack the historical traditions to invoke. As Beverland has argued, such strategies are an important way in which new firms build their brands in unique ways and with a strong product orientation.[57] The result has been higher collective organizational status and enhanced reputation. They have successfully leveraged the growing Napa brand and added their own distinct and exclusive identity to their wine. In many respects their status has been socially constructed within an evolving institutional and market structure that highlights the symbolic value of their product.

By the beginning of the twenty-first century, Napa wines in general and the cult wines in particular have become increasingly notable for their stylistic characteristics. Distinctive vineyard and viticulture practices such as dense spacing, intensely harvested for low yields that are less than half of the standard European practices, maximum ripeness and the use of post harvesting techniques such as micro-managing fermentation have become commonplace. When several wines from the 1997 vintage were given 100-point scores by critics, it was argued that crafting such big, fruit-forward Cabernet Sauvignons was now essential if such accolades were to persist.[58] When English wine critic Jancis Robinson noted that cult cabernets had become *de facto* "America's first growths," she somewhat dismissively argued that they were "muscling out finesse" with their rich, highly flavored wines designed to meet the preferences of influential critics.[59] Yet despite her concerns and comments, the practice of making big and bold wines has persisted because these wines were garnering the highest scores and prices and many acknowledged that they were in fact wines of exceptional quality. The pricing power bestowed by critics continues to remain a disincentive for producers to change their style of wine. Furthermore such wines were inextricably associated with Napa and were the ones for which consumers were willing to pay a considerable price premium. Markets subsequently valorized such wines as the epitome of quality with status effects characterizing both production and consumption. Utility maximizing wineries were charting a luxury strategy predicated upon a manufactured heritage and artisanal attributes. Wealthy individuals were purchasing such wines because they recognized both the exceptional quality and the prestige of ownership of such a rare item.

Historically expensive wines were the preserve of nobility and wealthy landowners followed in recent centuries by industrialists. In the last few decades a global elite has entered the market for fine wines, especially in the Asia Pacific region where demand mainly from China and Hong Kong has risen sharply.[60] By 2020 China is set to become the world's second-largest wine market with demand for luxury wines driven by rising disposable incomes, westernization, aspirational consumption and the rise of sophisticated drinking rituals.[61] In the United States, Burgundy and Bordeaux wines remain popular with connoisseurs, whether for their investment potential or for eventual drinking. The Liv-ex 100 Fine Wines Investible Index tracks the market for the most investible wines (200 wines from the top twenty-four Bordeaux châteaux) but in recent years auctions of top Napa wines have increased in visibility. Wine Spectator has an index of the average prices for eight multiple vintage cabernet sauvignon wines from Napa (plus sixteen from Bordeaux, five from Italy and three vintage Ports) that are the top selling wines at auctions. Other indexes exist for exclusively cult wines from Napa. Whilst it is impossible to know exactly who is buying these wines,[62] one has a rough guide by reviewing purchases at some of the charity auctions. In most cases it is ultra-high net worth individuals, that small group of people whose financial means and oenological interest drive sales.

In attempt to further break down consumers and their purchasing rationale, over the years I have asked winery owners in Napa in my research "who buys your wine?" The answers fall into two distinct categories. All were wealthy but one group had an appreciation for fine wine (so-called "wine geeks"). These were individuals who were knowledgeable and passionate about trying the best wines. They regularly drank expensive wine and saw it as quite natural to do on an everyday basis (the famous line of "life is too short to drink bad wine" was mentioned on numerous occasions). The second group was somewhat different. It comprised those for whom there were clear status benefits derived from ownership of notable wines or others who merely bought cases of fine wines as part of their investment strategy.[63] Both typically collected wines that scored in excess of 95 points but those who were driven by the aura of sophistication that accompanied ownership were likely to want to display them to friends and colleagues in lavishly designed cellars. This group were sometimes derogatively referred to as "stamp collectors" by winery owners since they bought solely wines that garnered the highest scores and were deemed the most valuable.

These comments are consistent with those of Spawton who classified luxury wine buyers into connoisseurs and aspirational consumers.[64] The former are clearly well informed about wine and seek the pleasures that are derived from its performance. In their pursuit of a gustatory and vinous lifestyle, they rely upon their own judgment to guide their purchases. Pleasure trumps price. Aspirational consumers on the other hand are more likely to seek external validation, whether from price as an indicator of quality, critic scores or if the wine has limited availability. Each is used as an indicator of status and prestige and purchases become part of self-conscious desires to impress others.[65] As with the connoisseurs, this group generally has the financial means to make the purchases although they use price as a qualifier in a decision making.

A recent special issue in *Wine Spectator* on creating an ideal cellar captures the essence of such behavior when it stated, "the lure of wine collecting can be intoxicating. Visions of gleaming wood, pristine glass and rough–hewn stone often come to mind."[66] Other wine periodicals provide images of luxurious cellars with bottles of top vintages visibly displayed; seating and ambience redolent of a sumptuous refuge for the elite. Such cellars are not the dark, damp, and musty basements of old buildings where wine is sometimes stored in their original boxes and in which visits are solely designed to retrieve the wine for consumption. These are climate controlled settings whose purpose is as much visual display as preservation. As Wine Enthusiast's Marshall Tilden III stated, "a wine cellar has to look beautiful and be a show stopper."[67] For many they are the manifestation of a person's passion for wine and by extension a reward for that passion. They are designed to be ostentatious because the owner is in some sense seeking validation of his/her ownership. It is also testament to the experiential aspect of luxury – one can sit comfortably in the cellar drinking some of the wines and reflecting on the sheer opulence of the ambience. But it also important to note that for many such collectors, a suitably designed cellar is a way of protecting their investment in wine. As such it is not entirely a work of vanity. But then such sites rarely take center stage as visible paragons of sophistication and respectability for which some collectors strive.

Conclusion

Luxury wine brands are the epitome of exclusivity. Certain producers in Napa valley have created deliberate strategies over the past few decades to elevate themselves to this hallowed vinous status. About 150 years ago the valley was home to orchards and nut growers with a few wineries producing wine of dubious provenance and quality. Over the years, an influx of individuals with ambition, passion and resources has transformed the area from producing commodity products to one equated with wines of excellent quality. A strong product orientation, capitalizing upon the uniqueness of the area to produce a certain style of wine, and the ability to sustain brand development over years without financial returns to their investment have enabled a small number of wineries to become elevated to iconic status. Their success has been validated by respected critics which has enabled them to appeal to connoisseurs as well as aspirational buyers. Whilst eschewing deliberate marketing strategies, their rigid control over distribution and product allocation has engineered the scarcity that nonetheless accentuates their exclusivity and value. As a value proposition, they appeal to the small segment of global high net worth individuals who either appreciate the experience of drinking a finely crafted wine or whose purchase and eventual consumption is part of attempts to enhance social status and self-image.

Demand continues to outstrip supply, hence pricing power remains in the hands of producers who can continue to manipulate the market by carefully monitoring output. The absence of history and tradition for Napa wineries has been supplanted by an alternative emphasis that focuses upon product integrity.[68] Part artisanal in their evocation, but also solidly scientific and technically proficient in their daily practices, these wineries have focused upon quality and consistency, scarcity and high price, as their *modus operandi*. They have successfully built a brand on a product that is intrinsically ephemeral. They have done this by appealing to the experiential interests of wealthy consumers as well as to those whose situational uncertainty can be assuaged by temporary ownership of the product. Understanding these consumers, gaining relevant information about them and building relationships with them has been an important part of their brand development. Endorsements from wine experts have cemented the consensus on quality and together with informal classifications has enhanced the authenticity of the product. Napa cult wines have become powerful brands by continuously emphasizing the traditional markers of luxury (quality, price and scarcity) that are implicit in their product, and building a culture of respect amongst wine professionals. External validation and legitimation has not only increased transparency of what is an experience good, it has also secured confidence amongst status seekers who see fine wine as a mark of sophistication. It has removed much of the uncertainty over making the wrong purchasing decision.

Notes

1 Thornton, J. *American Wine Economics*, Berkeley: University of California Press, 2014, p. 8.
2 Ibid., p. 8.
3 Coates, C. *Grand Vins: The Finest Châteaux of Bordeaux and Their Wines*, Berkeley: University of California Press, 1995; Simpson, J. *Creating Wine: The Emergence of a World Industry, 1840–1914*, Princeton: Princeton University Press, 2011; Faith, N. *The Winemasters of Bordeaux: The Inside Story of the World's Greatest Wines*, London: Prion Books, 1999.

4 Taplin, I.M. "Crafting an iconic wine: The rise of 'cult' Napa," *International Journal of Wine Business Research*, 2016, 28/2, pp. 105–19; Taplin, I.M. "Bottling luxury: Napa Valley and the transformation of an agricultural backwater into a world class wine region," *Luxury: History, Culture and Consumption*, 2015, 2/1, pp. 81–100.

5 See Malter, D. "On the causality and cause of returns to organizational status: Evidence from the Grands Crus classes of the Medoc," *Administrative Science Quarterly*, 2014, 59/2, pp. 271–300, for a full discussion of status transactions and reputational effects amongst top wines in Bordeaux.

6 Taplin, 2016.

7 See McCoy, E. *The Emperor of Wine: The Rise of Robert Parker Jr. and the Reign of American Taste*, New York: HarperCollins, 2005, for a full discussion of the role of critics in evaluating and subsequently validating wine.

8 Berthon, P., Leyland, P., Parent, M. and Berthon, J.P. "Aesthetics and ephemerality: Observing and preserving the luxury brand," *California Management Review*, 2009, 52/1, pp. 45–66.

9 For example, Chateau D'Issan, west of Bordeaux, notes that its wine was served at the wedding of Eleanor of Aquitaine to King Henry II of England in 1152.

10 Beverland, M. "An exploration of the luxury wine trade," *International Journal of Wine Marketing*, 2004, 16/3, pp. 14–28.

11 Ibid, p. 34.

12 Furer, D. "Armenia find is 'world's oldest winery,'" *Decanter*, January 12, 2011.

13 The history of wine in ancient Greece. Greek wine makers.com [http://www.greekwinemakers.com/czone/history/2ancient/shtml].

14 Sandler, M. and Pinder, R. (Eds.). *Wine: A Scientific Explanation*, London: CRC Press, 2002.

15 Chapuis, C. and Charters, S. "The world of wine," in Charters, S. and Gallo, J. (Eds.), *Wine Business Management*, Paris: Pearson France, 2014, pp. 13–14.

16 Seward, D. *Monks and Wine*, London: Mitchell Beazley Publishers, 1979.

17 Chapuis and Charters, p. 14.

18 Ouvrard, S. and Taplin, I.M. "Trading in fine wine: Institutionalized efficiency in the Place de Bordeaux system," *Global Business and Organizational Excellence*, 2018, 27/5, p. 15.

19 Ibid.

20 Chapuis and Charters, p. 15.

21 See Matthews, M. *Terroir and Other Myths of Wine Growing*, Berkeley: University of California Press, 2015, p. 158.

22 Charters, S. and Spielmann, N. "Characteristics of strong territorial brands: The case of champagne," *Journal of Business Research*, 2014, 67/7, p. 1463.

23 Markham, D. *1855: A History of the Bordeaux Classification*, New York: Wiley, 1998.

24 Chauvin, P.M. *Le Marché des Réputations. Une Sociologie du Monde des vins de Bordeaux*, Bordeaux: Féret, 2010.

25 Beverland, M.J. "Crafting brand authenticity: The case of luxury wines," *Journal of Management Studies*, 2005, 42/5, pp. 1003–29.

26 Podolny, J. "A status-based model of market competition," *American Journal of Sociology*, 1993, 98, pp. 829–72.

27 Beverland, p. 1025.

28 Beverland, M. "Uncovering 'theories-in-use': Building luxury wine brands," *European Journal of Marketing*, 2004, 38/3/4, pp. 446–66.

29 Pinney, T. *The History of Wine in America: From the Beginnings to Prohibition*, Berkeley: University of California Press, 1989.

30 Ibid., p. 240.

31 Ibid.

32 Archibald, A. *The Economic Aspects of the California Missions*, Washington, DC: Academy of American Franciscan History, 1978.

33 Taplin, 2015, p. 83.

34 Pinney, pp. 265–6.

35 Carosso, CV.P. *The California Wine Industry*, Berkeley: University of California Press, 1951, p. 50.

36 Pinney, pp. 266–7.

37 Sullivan, C.L. *Napa Wine: A History*, San Francisco: Wine Appreciation Guild, 2008.

38 For a fuller discussion of the debate on the relationship between yield and quality see Matthews, Chapter 1.

39 Simpson, op. cit.

40 Ibid.

41 *Reports of the United States Commissioners to the Universal Exposition at Paris*, Washington, DC IV.1891, pp. 726–32.

42 Sullivan, p. 80.

43 Taber, G. *The Judgement of Paris*, New York: Scribner, 2005.

44 See Matthews, Chapter 4, for a full discussion of the multiple and evolving definitions of terroir.

45 Thornton, p. 273.

46 See Heimoff, S. *New Classic Winemakers of California*, Berkeley: University of California Press, 2008, for a full discussion of these and other key figures in the industry's resurgence during this period.

47 Sullivan, p. 246.

48 See Shafer, D. *A Vineyard in Napa*, Berkeley: University of California Press, 2012, for more details on these informal and formal gatherings.

49 See Taplin, I.M. "Network structure and knowledge transfer in cluster evolution: The transformation of the Napa Valley wine region," *International Journal of Organizational Analysis*, February 9, 2011, pp. 127–45, for a full discussion of how clusters developed in the area. Also see Guthey, G.T. "Agro-industrial conventions: Some evidence from the northern California wine industry," *The Geographical Journal*, 2008, 174/2, pp. 138–18.

50 Taplin, 2015, p. 92.

51 See Taber for a full discussion of the event and its aftermath. A 2008 film called *Bottle Shock* provided a Hollywood spin on some of the principal Napa characters in the event.

52 Taplin, I.M. "Crafting an iconic wine: The rise of 'cult' Napa," *International Journal of Wine Business Research*, February 28, 2016, p. 111.

53 Thornton, pp. 254–56; Hodgson, R. "An examination of judge reliability at a major wine competition," *Journal of Wine Economics*, February 3, 2008, pp. 105–13; Goldstein, R., Almenberg, J., Dreber, A., Emerson, J.W., Herschkowitsch, A. and Katz, J. "Do more expensive wines taste better? Evidence from a large sample of blind tastings," *Journal of Wine Economics*, 2008, 3/1, pp. 1–9; Haeger, J. and Storchmann, K. "Prices of American Pinot Noir wines: Climate, craftsmanship, critics," *Agricultural Economics*, 2006, 35, pp. 67–78.

54 Matthews, M. *Terroir and Other Myths of Wine Growing*, Berkeley: University of California Press, 2015.

55 Scott Morton, F. and Podolny, J. "Love or money? The effects of owner motivation in the California wine industry," *Journal of Industrial Economics*, 2002, 50/4, pp. 431–56. See also the discussion in Thornton, pp. 186–89.

56 See Conaway, J. *The Far Side of Eden: New Money, Old Land and the Battle for Napa Valley*, Boston: Houghton Mifflin, 2002.

57 Beverland, 2004, p. 462.

58 Bonné, J. *The New California Wine*, Berkeley: Ten speed Press, 2013.
59 Quoted in Sullivan, 2008, p. 390.
60 Bär, J. "Luxury Wine Feature," *Wealth Report Asia*, Zurich: Julius Baer Group, 2018.
61 Ibid, p.1.
62 Annual wealth reports such as those published by UBS, Deloitte and Knight Frank provide an overview of spending patterns amongst ultra-high net worth individuals, often with a continent-based break down. However, they do not itemize expenditures by specific categories so it one is left to surmise actual purchases or rely upon anecdotal information from auctions. Alas major auction houses such as Christie's and Sotheby's that conduct Wines and Spirits auctions preserve considerable anonymity for their buyers.
63 These are the terms several winery owners in Napa used when referring to what are distinct categories of consumers.
64 Spawton, T., "Marketing planning for wine," *European Journal of Marketing*, March 24, 1991, pp. 6–48.
65 Vigneron, F. and Johnson, L.W., "A review and a conceptual framework of prestige-seeking consumer behavior," *Academy of Marketing Science Review*, January 9, 1999, p. 1; Beverland, 2004, p. 450.
66 Meltzer, P. "The path to wine collecting," *Wine Spectator*, July 31, 2017, p. 43.
67 Quoted in Friedman, R.A. "How to stash your wine," *Wall Street Journal*, September 14, 2018, M3.
68 See Beverland, 2004, p. 462.

8

CONCLUSION

Pilgrims on the Luxury Road

Most of us have a notion of what luxury is and what it typically entails. We see images of it almost every day or hear stories that reveal the sort of material excesses in which only a few can indulge. Perhaps not surprisingly a pervasive sense of envy lingers in our minds, largely inspired by media reports, advertisements, and the visible accoutrements of the wealthy. Whether it be luxury cruises, luxury real estate, luxury watches, luxury cars, luxury spas – the list is apparently endless. In each case the promise offered is of the consummate perfect good, something of exquisite quality or performance and probably not widely available. It refers to something extremely special and undoubtedly expensive yet often its promotional narrative is pitched broadly enough for many more people to see who could possibly afford it. In a way this is rather puzzling. Or is it? Have we been made increasingly aware of what luxury is so we can experience it vicariously? In a consumer society permeated by an increasing materialist ideology, is the idea of luxury dangled in front of us to stimulate our imagination as well as suggesting what might be ours if only things could be different? Does it for some suggest an attainable goal, a potentially realistic achievement if our investments pan out or we win the lottery?

What is so interesting about these scenarios is the notion that even if luxury is undoubtedly inaccessible, its manifest presence conjures all sorts of fantasies. The average person thinks about it from time to time ("if only I had this or that I could realize my dreams" is a common refrain) and contemplates what life might be like if there were fewer financial restraints. For some of us it constitutes a dream and whilst we recognize that it is unattainable, that it is not a palpable goal, we still harbor transient thoughts that nurture such sentiments. So despite such ruminations, whilst luxury has become a ubiquitous part of twenty-first-century life, its exclusivity will ultimately deny all but a very small segment of the population from taking advantage of it.

Admittedly in today's consumer society, more middle-class and even poorer people are spending increasing amounts of their discretionary spending on conspicuous consumption.[1] Such indulgences include what are commonly referred to as entry level luxury products like small bags with appropriate designer logos; spas that promise to pamper you for a brief period so that you can imbibe the thrill and pleasure of a luxury indulgence once in a while. But these are small indulgences that perhaps provide a sentient escape from the mundane routine of everyday life. They are part of the identity politics and an obsession with wealth that have become pervasive. Luxury firms might use these goods to entice future customers providing them with a step on the low rung of the luxury ladder.

What remains evident is the way inequality has always fueled luxury and how current patterns and apparent increases in inequality have neither stymied those for whom the lifestyle is an unrealistic goal or those whose material wealth provides them with the resources to flaunt their positional status. Despite the internal contradictions that might have conjured discontent, in the past inequality was firmly circumscribed by rigid hierarchies that provided moral as well as cultural jurisdiction for elite behavior. It was rarely questioned in part because it was sanctified by tradition, custom and even religion. As those hierarchies eroded with material and economic progress plus secularization, inequality did not disappear. Instead it became a feature of more fluid social structures where individual effort and achievement permitted entrance for a select few to an otherwise exclusive elite. The manifestations of luxury did not necessary change; merely the means whereby one could attain the position to exercise it. The maximization of wealth coupled with increased opportunity became ideologically legitimized in the twentieth century in many societies. Even though social mobility might not be the great equalizer that some had anticipated, it nevertheless remains sacrosanct in the minds of many, thus implicitly legitimizing inequality and disproportionate allocations of wealth.

The Bible reminds us that "the poor are always with us." But then so are the rich. Today they might constitute a different group to aristocrats and princes of the past, and the realization of their wealth derived by different means; how they express and rationalize that wealth might also have changed. They nonetheless remain the embodiment and expression of structural inequality that continues to fuel a culture of excess for a small minority whose sense of entitlement mirrors those of ages past. In a world awash in commodities, the extravagance that surrounds luxury reminds us how elegance can be appropriated by a few to signify their distinctiveness from the many. And status continues to be a preoccupation of many in a market society where materialism remains the *sine qua non* of success.

Making sense of luxury, as a material good as well as an abiding lifestyle, is fraught with ambiguity and contentious claims. It appears to have meant different things at different times in history. Its rationale has apparently changed over the centuries in terms of its function and its principal actors. The justification and legitimization of it has varied through the ages; however, the one abiding feature is the continued pervasiveness of inequality as the *deus ex machina* behind its persistence. In many respects luxury has always been the material expression of wealth and status disparities. What has changed is the way in which these differences are articulated, modified to meet the exigencies of socio-cultural changes and altered economic circumstances.

In the previous pages I have endeavored to outline not so much a trajectory of these changes as an apparent pattern. If we define luxury in its most basic terms as referring to products that are rare, of high quality and very expensive, then one can identity key periods in history where a select group of individuals had the resources to indulge in such material acquisitiveness. The institutional context and cultural parameters that frame such behavior inevitably led to varied behavioral patterns. Furthermore exogenous forces also changed the socio-economic dynamic in ways that altered market activity. Nonetheless, we can sketch how luxury was experienced, articulated and even formalized by elites and the wealthy over the ages. From this, discernible patterns emerge. Something that was occasionally scorned eventually became acceptable provided individual motivation was in line with cultural mores. The subsequent removal of moral sanctions followed since wealth was now a product of hard work and initiative. Currently excessive wealth is beginning to be cast as ethically questionable behavior as inequality has become pronounced but this has failed to gain sufficient traction for universal condemnation. Possibly this is because there are those in the bulk of the population who continue to harbor fantasies about becoming rich themselves – or else they have become resigned to recognizing that some people will inevitably have much more than themselves.

It was never my intention to write an exhaustive history of luxury as that has been discussed by other scholars who have provided comprehensive assessments of its multifaceted nature. However, their rich histories have provided me with useful information which I have endeavored to build upon and embellish in my own narrative. For me the question revolves around the link between luxury and inequality, specifically the moral and cultural framework that sanctions such patterns as well as the organizational processes that facilitate it. Pervasive as inequality has been in all societies, many studies have merely taken it for granted and focused upon the various manifestations of luxury or the rationale behind spending. We are well aware of the hierarchical and often formally structured societies of pre-industrial eras where a wealthy elite exercised disproportionate power and influence and used their access to fine objects as a means to embellish their status and remind people of their positional power. We have also noted how formal restrictions were frequently imposed on the majority of the population from attempting to emulate this behavior (through so-called sumptuary laws). The exercise of wealth was a circumscribed right; it endowed the owner with exclusive powers to utilize in ways that were consistent with societal norms as well as an expression of his/her own dispositions. The wealthy were not denied agency, but they did generally conform to the broad societal expectations that endorsed their position. Because medieval societies had such closed and tight social hierarchies, tastes and general displays of consumer behavior were quite scripted and designed to reinforce the prevailing social order.[2] Any inherent impulse towards accumulation was generally subsumed under the panoply of civic duty and an often complex obligational structure that rendered opportunistic behavior immutable. In other words wealth wasn't really questioned or seen as overly contentious because it was widely accepted as normative. Providing the wealthy fulfilled societal expectations their elite positioned was generally condoned. The majority of the population might have harbored envy, but they also recognized wealth as part of a sanctified hierarchical order and thus were passively attuned to its existence.

As we saw in Chapter 2 any moral opprobrium over luxury indulgences was excised providing the owner displayed the appropriate motivations in the acquisition of expensive products. Indulgences to churches via art, erection of public buildings that demonstrated civic responsibility, and suitable endowments to charitable causes displayed how the elite discharged their duties. This did not entail dispersing all of their wealth, merely sufficient discretionary material objects or money that could publicly demonstrate their virtuosity.

The moral order that sanctified these hierarchies gradually began to crumble following the growth of commerce in seventeenth-and eighteenth-century Europe. It was further de-legitimized when the Protestant Reformation laid bare some of the hypocrisy associated with elite dealings with the Roman Catholic Church. Questionable behavior regarding motives behind donations undermined the sanctity of the relationship and diminished the credibility of the donors or patrons. The glorification of God was an acceptable justification for patronage but not when gifts were a subtle way of leveraging one's own path to salvation. Distinguishing between the two was inevitably difficult as motives are notoriously opaque. Yet as we saw in earlier chapters, sufficient members of the elite appear to have embraced this sacred utilitarian path and thus tainted the moral imperatives of their position.

As the sacred façade dissipated, the wealthy were less likely to be admonished for gratuitous self-indulgence. In fact the incentive to accumulate for one's own private means was gaining traction. Increased market transactions and the availability of a wide variety of goods, often associated with colonialism and increased long distance trade, fostered an emerging materialist mentality and an ideology that implicitly encouraged accumulation for its own sake. This was particularly evident in the growing merchant classes who were taking advantage of more fluid social structures that economic wealth had given them. As merchants gained wealth, they could easily justify it on the basis of their work ethic and commercial insights. Wealth became less a birth right than the product of individual initiative. An aristocratic elite persisted and wielded political power, but an emerging merchant class was leveraging their economic power to challenge the rigid hierarchy of the past. Increased economic exchanges fostered even greater competition between groups leading to, as Sassatelli argues, "the speeding up and expansion of the dynamics of taste, freeing them from the constrictions of the medieval period."[3] With more money circulating, commercial activity became more legitimate and the exchange of goods framed increases in both production and consumption. As the demand for material goods increased, production was rationalized which gave rise to a further expansion of market activities as well as new sources of wealth.

Heightened market activity and the attendant production revolution has come to be seen as the genesis of an emerging consumer culture. Whilst the former was shaped by economic developments as well as political trends associated with colonialism, the latter is a social phenomenon that suggests a qualitative dimension with significant cultural implications. The rise in a culture of consumption has often been seen as the inevitable result of fundamental economic transformations that subsequently became a derivative of mass production in the industrial era. However, without necessarily subscribing to an anti-productivist view of consumer agency,[4] it does appear that new wealthy groups were embracing a material acquisitiveness hitherto not so evident in the past and it was not simply caused by the availability of more objects. In other words, their drive to consume constitutes a demand dimension that studies which view consumption as a mere product of increased production ignore. The interrelationship of economic and cultural processes thus frame a more complex dynamic than that of a simple one way causality.

Werner Sombart argued that the growth of trade with colonies was a pivotal moment in a new phase of luxury consumption.[5] He saw the creation of markets in high value goods as a driving force behind capitalist development. The growth of a material culture associated with such developments underlines the importance of acquisitiveness amongst the new bourgeoisie and merchant class. Their enthusiasm for the possession of often exotic products complemented their drive to accumulate the vestiges of high status that they identified with the old aristocratic elite. This heightened individualism gave greater credence to displays of wealth that simultaneously reflected individuals' indulgence in the joy of possession as well as positional markers of their new found status. Sombart argues that this new form of consumption from the late eighteenth century onwards is indicative of a hedonistic attitude that explicitly rejected the old moral order of disguised enjoyment. In this sense, consumption became de-moralized as the old vestiges of elite acquisition of luxury goods was washed away in a flurry of material appropriation for personal pleasure.

Social distinction which was always a feature of pre-industrial societies was now vested with a more fungible dimension. If wealth could be attainable through the operation of a transformed economic culture and a market rationality that endorsed the material value of goods, could the new class of wealthy inject a different dimension to luxury? In other words, if the pursuit of luxury was no longer circumscribed by moral restraints on possessions, does this entail a rethinking of luxury's role in society?

It appears that the relaxation of religious rules and institutions – the slow secularization that we associate with the Reformation and the emerging institutions of capitalism that Max Weber discussed – permitted the use of luxuries as part of a more hedonistic culture. The broader consumer society that developed later in the nineteenth century was thus the logical extension of this reframing of attitudes towards materialism; one that markedly legitimized and even canonized commercialism and acquisition. We now firmly enter theoretical territory marked out by Sombart and Veblen inasmuch as luxury begins to be viewed as both a product sought by the newly rich as well as a catalyst for further market growth. Rationalized industrial production of high value goods facilitated a broadened availability of expensive products to meet the increased demand from an expanded wealthy class. This entailed both a qualitative as well as a quantitative increase in the types of goods available. For Sombart this was part of the growing capitalist spirit that was becoming more pervasive in industrializing societies, leading to greater rationalization of economic activity.[6] Luxury goods would not necessarily be mass produced but they could be created according to a new economic logic that fostered a broadening of scope for what constitutes luxury. One-of-a-kind products (paintings, large houses, etc.) continued to be scarce phenomenon, but alongside these rare products were others that met the high-quality, high-price characteristics but were now more widely available. These goods were demanded by the wealthy to complement their general lifestyle accessions that arose from their emulation of previous elite behavior.

The consumer revolution of the early twentieth century transformed markets, providing an extensive range of products that were affordable to a population that benefitted from employment in the manufacturing sector. In the subsequent decades of economic growth, especially after World War II, a vibrant middle class was taking advantage of the proliferation of goods that improved everyday life (washing machines, dishwashers, etc.) as well as indulging in a much greater range of non-essentials than ever before. This has occurred several decades later in many emerging economies. Whether this market functioned to satisfy needs or was instrumental in creating those needs has been extensively discussed elsewhere. Herbert Marcuse's *One-Dimensional Man* for example argued that late capitalism systematically created false needs through an ideology of consumption disseminated through numerous information networks and advertising in particular.[7] Others have seen the creation of a "culture industry" that relies upon the mass marketing of cultural goods, particularly in the fashion industry where styles are systematically promoted as *de rigueur* accoutrements of success.[8]

These and other studies, either explicitly or implicitly, present a referential dimension to consumer behavior. Despite the growing privatization of consumption associated with increased agency (and financial means), twentieth-century marketers have bombarded consumers with lifestyle images designed to stimulate emulation and envy. In many cases this involved precisely the luxury goods that are beyond the financial means of the average person. Such images unambiguously suggest refinement and sophistication, even the enrichment of social life. They became success markers for a population enjoying unprecedented prosperity.

Unlike previous centuries, where luxury goods were acquired subtly, now they were actively marketed. Since its marketplace presence was now pervasive, luxury was no longer an abstract concept materially enjoyed by an elite. Mass society could now imagine luxury even if they could not actually afford it. Perhaps what is most telling about such visual narratives is that luxury was increasingly seen as legitimate and even beneficial. Yet it still remained beyond the reach of the vast majority of the population. However, what might seem a destabilizing contradiction appears to have actually reinforced the credibility of luxury. Persistent inequality paradoxically appeared to fuel desire rather than dampening it, creating an ambiguous marketplace for luxury goods. For some, so-called aspirational products provided a foot on the luxury ladder. For many however, the idea of luxury rather than the reality of its possession was what resonated. This was part of a commodified consumer culture that continued to prey upon a population already satiated with material goods. Even if not attainable, luxury constituted a reference point that benchmarked lifestyles. It pervaded consumer culture rather than being morally and ideologically separate. But it would always remain a distant possibility to all but a few whose position and status were in some respects solidified by this heightened awareness.

What has emerged from more fluid social structures, widespread material progress and a luxury goods industry that blankets the media with images of ostentatious beauty, especially in fashion, is a reframing of consumer ideology and behavior that endorses accumulation as a right. This applies to both rich and poor alike. The average consumer has become a private economic hedonist, seeking individual pleasures within a socio-cultural framework that condones and encourages consumption as a way of defecting other concerns that might be social disruptive. Meanwhile, the wealthy's pursuit of luxury continues unabated, albeit now with a greater range of available products. Free from any moral constraints of their behavior, they are a potent driving force behind a rejuvenated luxury goods industry, even in times of recession which stymies other consumer activities. They have reaffirmed luxury as a mark of refinement and cultural sophistication and enjoyed the excesses that their wealth permits. Consumer theorist Roberta Sassatelli sums it up quite eloquently when she states,

> This de-moralization was based on the idea that luxury was no longer the gauge of the unhealthy conflict between commercial and political activity (and in particular civic virtue). Commercial activity itself had come to appear more beneficial and legitimate, and so luxury had come to be valued on the basis of the effects it had on economic and commercial life.[9]

Not only could luxury be enjoyed by the wealthy, it had a positive economic benefit for society as a whole. This further subtle legitimation merely adds to the general assumption that consumption drives economic growth. If a small percentage of the population has the means to acquire lavish products, then their behavior is consistent with current materialist norms in which increasingly acquisitiveness appears to be the default option.

The persistence of inequality in the twenty-first century is now a feature of emerging economies where there has been a dramatic increase in wealth creation, especially for a small, privileged segment of the population. By the end of 2019 the UHNW population is expected to increase by 22 percent in the next five years with the fastest growth occurring in Asia. In China specifically (including Hong Kong) there have been significant increases in inequality in the past two decades as economic growth has not only created a large middle class of avid consumers but also provided vast fortunes for those best able to take advantage of increased market opportunities often associated with political connections. Eschewing the harsh economic discipline of Maoism, and despite the absence of free markets, significant numbers of Chinese people have channeled their activities into entrepreneurialism and have been able to take advantage of the re-introduction of monetary incentives.[10] In one way this taps into the Confucian heritage, which saw material wealth as enhancing moral life, especially since currently personal liberty remains subject to restrictions as in the past.[11] Whilst previously making money via one's office was viewed as morally dubious, contemporaries have now been given tacit approval to exploit connections and links with state enterprises. Thus wealth creation has gained universal acceptance and despite recent crackdowns on lavish gifting, has nurtured a culture that embraces materialism. Whatever political restraints have been imposed on freedom of expression, individuals have been given opportunities to maximize their financial gains providing they are unquestioning of the political order.

There is widespread recognition that UHNW individuals in this region display similar patterns of material acquisition as their western counterparts. Their behavior resonates with Sombart's hedonism, since the focus is on property, art, fine wine and watches. The difference, however, is the rationale for such actions and how they evaluate their purchases. Increasingly many invoke the language of investment strategies and asset yield, as well as acknowledging the vicissitudes of currency movements and interest rate fluctuations. This is the semantics of wealth management and the consideration that products have use value plus the potential for financial gain in the future. Arguably some of this reframing is a result of concerns over global economic instability and political upheavals – individuals are hedging against uncertainty. But luxury goods are also being seen in terms of "asset values," identifying those products that might yield greater financial returns. The positional status that accrues from ownership is now given a further tangible financial dimension.

As one might expect in a market economy, services catering to such interests and goals have emerged. For example, there are multiple luxury goods indexes to help the wealthy track and evaluate their possessions or future purchases. One such index is the Knight Frank Wealth Annual Report, which for 2019 noted a rise of 7.5 percent in 2018 driven by a mix of the normal scarcity, local demand and intrinsic quality.[12] They also note how the growth of non-financial assets such as real estate is one of the leading factors driving UHNW growth.

Whether it be purchases of rare whiskies and fine wines at a 2018 Sotheby's auction that have appreciated 9 percent since then for those fortunate enough to procure them, to other blue-chip collectibles whose prices have been accelerating, certain goods continue to offer a multi-purpose benefit to the discerning few. In terms of lifestyle, key cities such as London and New York continue to be attractive to the super rich because they offer stability and a plethora of cultural activities (restaurants, museums, etc.) that are congruent with their social pursuits. The experience of luxury is also increasing, with a 6.5 percent annual increase in luxury entertainment.[13] Cruise ships that are closely stratified according to price paid with exclusive decks for the rich; resorts with stratospheric prices designed to attract the discerning few and segregate them from the masses; these are all part of what is now seen as an experiential aspect of luxury. Instead of ownership that ultimately can sound like a commodity, we are talking about enjoying a particular event, albeit one that is extremely exclusive. For many this constitutes the new luxury, a complement to their possessions but also the apotheosis of their luxury entitlement.

In this story we have examined several manifestations of luxury against a background of its sometimes contentious role in society. I have shown how the medieval elite used indulgences as a way to sanctify their wealth. Eventually this led to the democratization of indulgences unleashed by twentieth-century industrial capitalism. Whilst the latter ordained a rapacious materialism, made possible by production efficiencies that lowered the costs of goods hitherto deemed luxurious as well, it was also a response to changing consumer demands as income levels rose and an ideology of acquisitiveness emerged. At the same time, enhanced inequality, in both the west and in emerging economies, has continued to differentiate the lifestyles of the UHNW individuals from the majority. As with their counterparts in the past, this group uses their wealth in positional terms as a way of demonstrating their status. They continue to do it more confidently given the pervasiveness of material ideologies legitimizing wealth. But they have also given it a further dimension by viewing it through the lens of investment strategies. Art, wine and other luxury products have become asset classes; a way for the elite to potentially realize further financial gain or, cynically, perhaps merely a way to justify their material accumulation. Whatever the truth, this financialization of luxury provides an added dimension to how luxury has evolved over the centuries.

In each age, it appears the wealthy have appropriated the requisite legitimation to consolidate their status and material possessions, sometimes sanctimoniously adhering to the received morality and at other times relishing if not glorifying their indulgences by invoking the ideology of success in an age of mobility. The range of goods deemed luxurious continues to expand, but they continue to be marked according to the age old definition of rarity, high cost and limited availability. The demand for them comes from that small segment of society who confidently assume the mantle of privilege. As with their counterparts in generations past, their self-justification for wealth remains sacrosanct. And presumably they will continue to be envied by some and their behavior abhorred by others. Plus ça change! The more things change, the more they stay the same.

Notes

1 See Currid-Hackett, E. *The Sum of Small Things: A Theory of the Aspirational Class*, Princeton: Princeton University Press, 2018.
2 Sassatelli, R. *Consumer Culture*, London: Sage Publications, 2007, p. 10.
3 Ibid, p. 10.
4 See Sassatelli for an interesting discussion of this. Also the work of Colin Campbell, *The Romantic Ethic and the Spirit of Modern Consumerism*, Oxford: Basil Blackwell, 1987, highlights the aspirational nature of early modern consumer behavior.
5 Sombart, W. *Luxury and Capitalism*, Ann Arbor: University of Michigan Press, 1967.
6 Ibid.
7 Marcuse, H. *One-Dimensional Man*, Boston: Beacon Press, 1967.
8 See for example Hirsch, P. "Processing fads and fashions: An organization-set analysis of cultural industry systems," in *American Journal of Sociology*, 1972, 77:639–59.
9 Sassatelli, p. 36.
10 Coase, R. and Wang, N. *How China Became Capitalist*, Basingstoke: Palgrave Macmillan, 2012, p. 31.
11 See Duncan, H. "The role of the Confucian gentleman," in *Symbols of Social Theory*, Oxford: Oxford University Press, 1969.
12 Knight Frank, *The Wealth Report, 2019*. London: Knight Frank, 2019.
13 Kelly, K. *The Inevitable*, New York: Penguin, 2016, p. 190.

BIBLIOGRAPHY

Adam, Georgina. 2014. *Big Bucks: The Explosion of the Art Market in the Twenty-first Century*. London: Lund Humphries.

Adams, William. 2012. *On Luxury*. Washington, DC: Potomac Books.

Allen, Robert. 2009. *The British Industrial Revolution in Global Perspective*. Cambridge: Cambridge University Press.

Anthony, Amanda and Ian M. Taplin. 2017. "Sustaining the retail pilgrimage: Developments of fast fashion and authentic identities." *Fashion, Style and Popular Culture* 4/2: 33–50.

Archibald, Robert. 1978. *The Economic Aspects of the California Missions*. Washington, DC: Academy of American Franciscan History.

Atkinson, Anthony. 2015. *Inequality*. Cambridge: Harvard University Press.

Bain and Company. 2013. *Bain Survey of Chinese Luxury Goods Consumer*. http://www.bain.com.

———. 2016. *Luxury Goods Worldwide Market Study. Fall-Winter 2016*. Boston: Bain and Company.

Belk, R., Ger, G. and Askegaard, S. 1996. "Metaphors of consumer desire." *Advances in Consumer Research* 23: 19, 369–373.

Berry, Christopher. 1999. *The Idea of Luxury*. Cambridge: Cambridge University Press.

Berthon, Pierre, Pitt, Leyland, Parent, Michael and Berthon, Jean-Paul. 2009. "Aesthetics and ephemarility: Observing and preserving the luxury brand." *California Management Review* 52, 1: 45–66.

Beverland, Michael. 2004a. "Uncovering 'theories-in-use': Building luxury wine brands." *European Journal of Marketing* 38, 3/4: 446–466.

———. 2004b. "An exploration of the luxury wine trade." *International Journal of Wine Marketing* 16, 3: 14–28, 34.

———. 2005. "Crafting brand authenticity: The case of luxury wines." *Journal of Management Studies* 42, 5: 1003–1029.

Bevolo, Marco, Gofman, Alex and Moskowitz, Howard. 2011. *Premium by Design*. Farnham: Gower.

Bordieu, Pierre. 1984. *Distinction*. London: Routledge.

Boston Consulting Group (BCG). 2003. *Opportunities for Action in Consumer Markets: Trading Up*. Boston: Boston Consulting Group.

Budd, M., Craig, S. and Steinman, C. *Consuming Environments: Television and Commercial Culture* (2nd ed.). New Brunswick: Rutgers University Press.

Campbell, Colin. 1987. *The Romantic Ethic and the Spirit of Modern Consumerism*. Oxford: Basil Blackwell.

Carosso, Vincent. 1951. *The California Wine Industry*. Berkeley: University of California Press.

Carroll, Glenn and Swaminathan, Anand. 2000. "Why the micro-brewery movement? Organizational dynamics of resource positioning in the U.S. brewing industry." *American Journal of Sociology* 3: 715–762.

Carruthers, Bruce C. and Babb, Sarah L. 2000. *Economy and Society*. Thousand Oaks: Pine Forge.

Chada, Radha and Husband, Paul. 2006. *The Cult of the Luxury Brand*. London: Nicholas Breely.

Chapuis, Claude and Charters, Steve. 2014. "The world of wine." In *Wine Business Management*, ed. Steve Charters and Jerôme Gallo. Paris: Pearson France.

Charters, Steve and Spielmann, Nathalie. 2014. "Characteristics of strong territorial brands: The case of champagne." *Journal of Business Research* 67, 7: 1463.

Chauvin, Pierre-Marie. 2010. *Le Marché des Réputations. Une Sociologie du Monde des vins de Bordeaux*. Bordeaux: Féret.

Clarke, Katherine. 2018. "War of the Megamansions!" *Wall Street Journal*, April 4.

Clouthier, David. 2015. *The Vice of Luxury*. Washington, DC: Georgetown University Press.

Coase, Ronald and Wang, Ning. 2012. *How China Became Capitalist*. Basingstoke: Palgrave Macmillan.

Coates, Clive. 1995. *Grand Vins: The Finest Châteaux of Bordeaux and Their Wines*. Berkeley: University of California Press.

Coates, David. 2016. *Capitalism, a Brief Introduction*. Abingdon: Routledge.

Cotterill, J. 2016. "Blue-chip bosses' £5.5m pay packets bolster UK premier's crackdown calls." *The Financial Times*, 8 August: 1.

Csaba, Fabian. 2008. "Redefining luxury: A review essay." *Creative Encounters Working Paper* 15 (November): 18–19. Copenhagen: Copenhagen Business School.

Currid-Halkett, Elizabeth. 2017. *The Sum of Small Things*. Princeton: Princeton University Press.

D'Arienzo, William. 2016. *Brand Management Strategies*. London: Bloomsbury.

Dalton, M. 2018. "Building buzz off the runway." *Wall Street Journal*, September 27: A14.

Davis, Fred. 1992. *Fashion, Culture and Identity*. Chicago: University of Chicago Press.

de Vries, Jan. 2008. *The Industrious Revolution: Consumer Behavior and the Household Economy, 1650 to the Present*. Cambridge: Cambridge University Press.

Deaton, Angus. 2013. *The Great Escape*. Princeton: Princeton University Press.

Deloitte. 2014. *Global Power of Luxury Goods*. Washington, DC: Deloitte.

———. 2016. *Global Power of Luxury Goods*. Washington, DC: Deloitte.

Dirix, Emanuelle. 2016. *Dressing the Decades*. New Haven: Yale University Press.

Duncan, H. 1969. "The role of the Confucian gentleman." In *Symbols of Social Theory*. Oxford: Oxford University Press.

Edwards, Tim. 2011. *Fashion in Focus*. London: Routledge.

Elias, Norbert. 1994. *The Civilizing Process*. Oxford: Basil Blackwell.

―――. 1998. *On Civilization, Power, and Knowledge*, ed. S. Mennell and J. Gouldsblom. Chicago: University of Chicago Press.

English, Bonnie. 2013. *A Cultural History of Fashion in the 20th and 21st Centuries*. London: Bloomsbury.

Evans, S. 2016. "Treasury Wine's $800 million pot of gold in luxury wines as Asia booms." *Sydney Morning Herald*, August 16.

Ewen, Stuart. 1976. *Captains of Consciousness*. New York: McGraw-Hill.

Faiers, Jonathan. 2014. "Editorial introduction." *Luxury: History, Consumption and Culture* 1/1: 5–13.

Faith, Nicholal. 1999. *The Winemasters of Bordeaux: The Inside Story of the World's Greatest Wines*. London: Prion Books.

Featherstone, Mike. 1990. "Perspectives on consumer culture." *Sociology* 24, 1: 5–22.

―――. 2014. "Luxury, consumer culture and sumptuary dynamics." *Luxury: History, Consumption and Culture* 1/1: 50, 52.

Fionda, A. and Moore, C. 2009. "The anatomy of the luxury fashion brand." *Journal of Brand Management* 16 (May): 162–167.

Fulcher, Jeffrey. 2004. *Capitalism, a Very Short Introduction*. Oxford: Oxford University Press.

Furer, D. 2011. "Armenia find is 'world's oldest winery.'" *Decanter*, January 12.

Girouard, Mark. 1978. *Life in the English Country House*. New Haven: Yale University Press.

―――. 1981. *The Return to Camelot: Chivalry and the English Gentleman*. New Haven: Yale University Press.

Goldstein, Robin, Almenberg, Johan, Dreber, Anna, Emerson, John W., Herschkowitsch, Alexis, and Katz, Jacob. 2008. "Do more expensive wines taste better? Evidence from a large sample of blind tastings." *Journal of Wine Economics* 3, 1: 1–9.

Goldthwaite, Richard. 1993. *Wealth and the Demand for Art in Italy, 1300–1600*. Baltimore: Johns Hopkins University Press.

Gordon, Robert. 2016. *The Rise and Fall of American Growth*. Princeton: Princeton University Press.

Greek wine makers. http://www.greekwinemakers.com/czone/history/2ancient/shtml.

Gregory, Brad. 2012. *The Unintended Reformation*. Cambridge, MA: Belknap Press/Harvard University Press.

Guillen, Mauro. 2006. *The Taylorized Beauty of the Mechanical*. Princeton: Princeton University Press.

Haeger, John and Storchmann, Karl. 2006. "Prices of American Pinot Noir wines: Climate, craftsmanship, critics." *Agricultural Economics* 35: 67–78.

Halle, David. 1993. *Inside Culture: Art and Class in the American Home*. Chicago: University of Chicago Press.

Han, Young Jee. 2010. "Signaling status with luxury goods: The role of brand prominence." *Journal of Marketing* 44: 15–30.

Heimoff, Steve. 2008. *New Classic Winemakers of California*. Berkeley: University of California Press.

Heine, Klaus, Atwal, Glyn and Ates, Zelal. 2014. "Luxury wine marketing." In *Wine Business Management*, ed. S. Charters and J. Gallo. Paris: Pearson France, pp. 235–244.

Hirsch, Paul. 1972. "Processing fads and fashions: An organization-set analysis of cultural industry systems." *American Journal of Sociology* 77: 639–659.

Hodgson, Robert T. 2008. "An examination of judge reliability at a major wine competition." *Journal of Wine Economics* 3, 2: 105–113.

Holmes, Stephen. 1993. *The Anatomy of Anti-Liberalism*. Cambridge: Harvard University Press, pp. 3–4.

Hughes, Robert. 1981. *The Shock of the New*. New York: Knopf.

Hume, David. 1739. *A Treatise on Nature*, London: Longmans Green & Co (1874).

Ingham, Geoffrey. 2008. *Capitalism*. Cambridge: Polity.

Jacobs, L. 2018. "Timelessly elegant, yet avant-garde." *Wall Street Journal*, November 28: A18.

Jardine, Lisa. 1996. *Worldly Goods: A New History of the Renaissance*. New York: WW Norton.

Kapferer, Jean-Noêl. 2012. "Abundant Rarity: The key to luxury growth." *Business Horizons* 55: 453–462.

———. 2015. *Kapferer on Luxury*. London: Kogan Page.

——— and V. Bastien. 2009. *The Luxury Strategy: Break the Rules of Marketing*. London: Kogan Page.

Karpik, Lucien and Scott, Nora. 2010. *Valuing the Unique*. Princeton: Princeton University Press.

Kawamura, Yuniya. 2005. *Fashion-ology*. Berg: Oxford.

Kay, John. 2015. *Other People's Money*. New York: Public Affairs.

Kelly, Kevin. 2016. *The Inevitable*. New York: Penguin.

Knight Frank. 2016. *The Wealth Report, 2016*. London: Knight Frank.

———. 2019. *The Wealth Report, 2019*. London: Knight Frank.

Ko, Eunju, Costello, John P. and Taylor, Charles R. 2017. "What is a luxury brand?" *Journal of Business Research* 1–9.

Kovesi, Catherine. 2002. *Sumptuary Law in Italy, 1200–1500*. Oxford: Oxford University Press.

———. 2015. "What is luxury?: The rebirth of a concept in the early modern world." *Luxury: History, Culture and Consumption* 2/1: 30–33, 85.

Lamont, Michelle. 1992. *Money, Manners and Morals*. Chicago: University of Chicago Press.

Lewis, Justin. 2013. *Beyond Consumer Capitalism*. Cambridge: Polity Press.

Lurie, Alison. 1981. *The Language of Clothes*. New York: Vintage Books.

Makkar, Marian and Yap, Sheau-Fen. 2018. "Emotional experiences behind the pursuit of inconspicuous luxury." *Journal of Retailing and Consumer Services* 44: 228.

Malter, Dolores. 2014. "On the causality and cause of returns to organizational status: Evidence from the Grands Crus classes of the Medoc." *Administrative Science Quarterly* 59, 2: 271–300.

Marcuse, Herbert. 1967. *One Dimensional Man*. Boston: Beacon Press.

Markham, Dewey. 1998. *1855: A History of the Bordeaux Classification*. New York: Wiley.

Marks, Robert. B. 2015. *The Origins of the Modern World* (3rd ed.). New York: Rowman and Littlefield.

Marshall, Peter. 2017. *Heretics and Believers: A History of the English Reformation*. New Haven: Yale University Press.

Matthews, Mark. 2015. *Terroir and Other Myths of Wine Growing*. Berkeley: University of California Press.

McCoy, Elin. 2005. *The Emperor of Wine: The Rise of Robert Parker Jr. and the Reign of American Taste*. New York: HarperCollins.

McKendrick, Neil. 1982. "The commercialization of fashion." In *The Birth of a Consumer Society*, ed. N. McKendrick, J. Brewer and J.H. Plumb. Bloomington: Indiana University Press, pp. 9–194.

McNeill, Peter and Riello, Giorgio. 2016. *Luxury: A Rich History.* Oxford: Oxford University Press.

Merton, Robert. 1973. *The Sociology of Science.* Chicago: University of Chicago Press.

Micklethwait, John and Woolridge, Adrian. 2003. *The Company.* New York: The Modern Library.

Milanovic, Branco. 2016. *Global Inequality.* Cambridge, MA: Belknap Press.

Mokyr, Joel. 2017. *A Culture of Growth.* Princeton: Princeton University Press.

Montgomery, Scott and Chirot, Daniel. 2015. *The Shape of the New.* Princeton: Princeton University Press.

Moore, Barrington. 1966. *Social Origins of Dictatorship and Democracy.* Boston: Beacon Press.

OECD. 2008, 2011. *Perspectives on Global Development.* Paris.

Okonkwo, Uche. 2007. *Luxury Fashion Branding.* New York: Palgrave Macmillan.

Ouvrard, Stephane and Taplin, Ian M. 2018. "Trading in fine wine: Institutionalized efficiency in the Place de Bordeaux system." *Global Business and Organizational Excellence* 27, 5: 15.

Peterson, Richard A. and Kern, Roger M. 1996. "Changing highbrow taste: From snob to omnivore." *American Sociological Review* 61: 900–907.

Picketty, Thomas. 2014. *Capital in the Twenty First Century.* Cambridge: Harvard University Press.

Pinney, Thomas. 1989. *The History of Wine in America: From Beginnings to Prohibition.* Berkeley: University of California Press.

Piore, Michael and Sabel, Charles. 1984. *The Second Industrial Divide.* New York: Basic Books.

Plato. 1968. *Politeia.* Ed. J. Burnett, 1902. Oxford: Clarendon Press.

Polanyi, Karl. 1944. *The Great Transformation: The Political and Economic Origins of Our Time.* Boston: Beacon Press.

Poldolny, Joel. 1993. "A status-based model of market competition." *American Journal of Sociology* 98: 829–872.

Prendergrast, Gerard and Claire Wong. 2003. "Parental influence on the purchase of luxury brands of infant apparel: An exploratory study in Hong Kong." *Journal of Consumer Marketing* 20 (Feb): 157–169.

Rachman, Gideon. 2016. "Trump and Brexit feed off the same anger." *Financial Times,* August 1.

Reports of the United States Commissioners to the Universal Exposition at Paris. Washington, DC: IV. 1891: 726–732.

Robert Parker Wine Advocate, https://www.robertparker.com/.

Rothenberg, Julia. 2014. *Sociology Looks at the Arts.* New York: Routledge. P213–P214.

Ryan, Carol. 2018. "Italy's the IT place for some luxury shopping." *Wall Street Journal,* November 17/18.

Sanderson, Rachel. 2018. "Europe's leaders in luxury have their designs on smaller groups." *Financial Times,* October 16: 13.

Sandler, Merton and Pinder, Roger. (Eds.) 2002. *Wine: A Scientific Explanation.* London: CRC Press.

Sassatelli, Roberta. 2007. *Consumer Culture: History, Theory, Politics.* London: Sage Publications.

Schwadel, Philip. 2016. "Social Class." In *Handbook of Religion and Society,* ed. David Yamane. Boston: Springer.

Scott, George Gilbert. 1857. *Secular and Domestic Architecture.* London.

Scott Morton, Frances and Podolny, Joel. 2002. "Love or money? The effects of owner motivation in the California wine industry." *Journal of Industrial Economics* 50, 4: 431–456.

Seo, Yuri and Buchanan-Oliver, Margo. 2017. "Constructing a typology of luxury brand consumption practices." *Journal of Business Research*, 1–8.

Seward, Desmond. 1979. *Monks and Wine*. London: Mitchell Beazley Publishers.

Shafer, Doug. 2012. *A Vineyard in Napa*. Berkeley: University of California Press.

Shaw, Jenny. 2010. *Shopping: Social and Cultural Perspectives*. Cambridge: Polity Press.

Silverstein, Michael J., Fiske, Neil and Butman, John. 2008. *Trading Up: Why Consumers Want New Luxury Goods and How Companies Create Them*. New York: Penguin.

Simpson, James. 2011. *Creating Wine: The Emergence of a World Industry, 1840–1914*. Princeton: Princeton University Press.

Simmel, G. *The Philosophy of Money*. (3rd ed.), London: Routledge Kegan Paul, 2004.

Slater, Don. 1997. *Consumer Culture and Modernity*. Cambridge: Polity Press.

Smart, Barry. 2010. *Consumer Society: Critical Issues and Environmental Consequences*. London: Sage.

Smil, Vaclav. 2013. *The Rise and Retreat of American Manufacturing*. Cambridge: The MIT Press.

Smith, Adam. 1984. *The Theory of Moral Sentiments*, ed. D.D. Raphael and A.L. Macfie. Indianapolis: Liberty Fund.

Smith, R.A. 2019. "Hermés wants to hang out." *Wall Street Journal*, April 4.

Snyder, C.R. 1992. "Product Scarcity by Need for Uniqueness Interaction: A consumer catch-22 carousel?" *Basic and Applied Social Psychology* 13, 1: 9–24.

Solca, L. 2016. "The rich don't drive the luxury sector." *Business of Fashion* 23, 1.

Som, Ashok and Blanckaert, Christia. 2015. *The Road to Luxury*. Singapore: John Wiley & Sons.

Sombart, Werner. 1967. *Luxury and Capitalism*, translated by W.R. Ditmar. Ann Arbor: University of Michigan Press.

Srinivasan, Bhu. *Americana: A 400 Year History of American Capitalism*. New York: Penguin Books.

Statista.com. 2017.

Stillerman, Joel. 2015. *The Sociology of Consumption*. Cambridge: Polity Press.

Strasser, Susan. 1989. *Satisfaction Guaranteed: The Making of the American Mass Market*. Washington, DC: Smithsonian Institution Press.

Sullivan, Charles. 2008. *Napa Wine: A History*. San Francisco: Wine Appreciation Guild.

Taber, George. 2005. *The Judgement of Paris*. New York: Scribner.

Taplin, Ian M. 1989. "Segmentation and the organization of work in the Italian apparel industry." *Social Science Quarterly* 70 (February): 408–424.

———. 2011. "Network structure and knowledge transfer in cluster evolution." *International Journal of Organizational Analysis* 19, 2: 127–145.

———. 2015. "Bottling luxury: Napa Valley and the transformation of an agricultural backwater into a world class wine region." *Luxury: History, Culture, and Consumption* 2, 1: 81–100.

———. 2016. "Crafting an iconic wine: The rise of 'cult' Napa." *International Journal of Wine Business* 28, 2: 105–119.

Thomas, Dana. 2007. *DELUXE: How Luxury Lost Its Lustre*. New York: Penguin Press.

Thompson, E.P. 1991. *The Making of the English Working Class*. London: Penguin.

Thornton, James. 2014. *American Wine Economics*. Berkeley: University of California Press.

Thurley, Simon. 2013. *The Building of England*. London: William Collins.

Tombs, Robert. 2014. *The English and Their History*. London: Penguin Books.

Trentmann, Frank. 2006. "The modern genealogy of the consumer: Meanings, identities and political synapses." In *Consuming Cultures, Global Perspectives: Historical Trajectories, Transnational Exchanges*, ed. J. Brewer and F. Trentmann. Oxford: Berg Publishers.

———. 2016. *Empire of Things*. New York: HarperCollins.

Turner, Aidair. 2016. *Between Debt and the Devil: Money, Credit, and Fixing Global Finance*. Princeton: Princeton University Press.

Turunen, Linda. 2017. *Interpretations of Luxury*. London: Palgrave Macmillan.

UBS. 2017. "New value creators gain momentum." *Billionaire Insights*. Zurich.

Vinofolio. https://www.vinfolio.com/producer/drc.

Galloni, Antonio. Harlan estate vertical at the Naples Winter Wine Festival, Vinous, https://www.vinous.com, September 26, 2017.

Waring, Steve. 1991. *Taylorism Transformed*. Chapel Hill: University of North Carolina Press.

Wealth-X. 2017. *Applied Wealth Intelligence*. London.

Weber, Max. 1958. *The Protestant Ethic and the Spirit of Capitalism*. New York: Scribners.

Wetlaufer, Suzy. 2001. "The perfect paradox of star brands." *Harvard Business Review* 79, 9: 116–123.

Wilson, Bastos and Levy, Sidney J. 2012. "A history of the concept of branding: Practice and theory." *Journal of Historical Research in Marketing* 4, 3: 347–368.

Wolfe, Tom. 1981. *From Bauhaus to Our House*. New York: Farrar, Straus & Giroux.

Wu, Kane. 2016. "Luxury ride hailing service gains speed." *Wall Street Journal*, August 5: B6.

Yurchisin, Jennifer and Johnson, Kim. 2010. *Fashion and the Consumer*. Oxford: Berg.

Zaniol, G. 2016. "Brand art sensation." *Cultural Politics* 12, 1: 49.

Zukin, Sharon. 2005. *Point of Purchase*. London: Routledge.

INDEX

Note: Page numbers in bold refer to tables.
Page numbers followed by n refer to notes.

Abstract Expressionism 12, 118–19
advertising 9, 59, 65–6, 70, 72–4, 76,
   81–2, 98, 154; *see also* branding;
   corporate 65; provocative 9
agricultural labor 37, 48, 55
Alibaba 100
Allen, Robert 48
Al Thani, Hamad bin Jassim bin Jaber 1
Amazon 100–1
annual wealth 147n62
Araujo Eisele Vineyard 140
Aristotle 24
Armani 88
Armani, Giorgio 102n50
Arnaud III de Pontac 131
Arnault, Bernard 10, 85–6, 92, 99
art 10–13, 103–23; *see also* Dadaism;
   specific names of artists, e.g., Titian;
   auction houses and dealers 110–14;
   see also Christie's; Sotheby's;
   changing role 106–10; investment
   120–2; new marketplace 114–17;
   revitalized auction houses and
   dealers become galleries 117–20
Artnet 121
Aston Martin 80
auction houses 1, 10, 12–13, 19, 110,
   112, 117–18, 121–2, 128, 147n62;
   see also Christie's; Sotheby's

automobile industry 2, 9, 67–8, 70–1,
   76, 79; *see also* Ford, Henry; Ford
   Motor Company

Bacon 32
Bader bin Abdullah bin
   Farhan al-Saud 122
Bain & Company 79
bankruptcy 23, 57
Basquiat, Jean-Michel 1
Benjamin, Walter 60
Bentley 2, 20n26, 76
Berenson, Bernard 114
Berry, Christopher 19, 25–6, 32, 34
Bethlehem Steel Company 68
Beverland, Michael 141
Beyeler, Ernst 117
billionaires 17, 78, 119
Biltmore House 57
Birkin, Jane 2
Birkin bag 2, 95
BMW 20n26
Bonaparte, Napoleon 125
Bon Marché 60
Bourdieu, Pierre 16, 62, 75–6, 104
Bourdieu wine region 2, 14–15, 95,
   126, 128, 130–2, 134, 139–40,
   142, 145n5, 145n9

branding 66, 72, 76, 80, 82, 84–90,
    98, 136
Brexit 5
British Rail Pension Fund 120
Bruegel, Pieter the Elder 111
Bryant Family 140
Buchanan-Oliver, Margo 86
Burberry 9, 66, **93**
Burgundy wine region 1–2, 14, 126–8,
    132–3, 139–40, 142

Cabernet Sauvignon 128, 134, 138,
    140–2
California State Agricultural Society 134
California Wine Association (CWA) 135
Calvinism 46
Campbell, Colin 46
Canal, Giovanni Antonio (Canaletto) 108
capitalism 19, 47, 50; advent 35–9;
    consumer 37–8, 51; growth 46;
    industrial 6, 9, 37, 71–2, 91, 156;
    institutions 153; managerial 69;
    material advantages 45
cars 67–8; *see also* automobile industry;
    rail 69; rental 7
Cartier **93**, 102n50
Cassirer, Paul 117
Castelli, Leo 118
Cato the Elder 22, 26
Chanel 66, **93**
Chanel, Coco 66–7
Chapuis, Claude 130
Chardonnay 138, 140
Charles I 109
Charmet 94
Charters, Steve 130
Château Cheval Blanc 95
Chateau D'Issan 145n9
Château D'Yquem 95
Chateau Montelena 138
Chirot, Daniel 3
Chow Tai Fook 93
Christian Dior 86, **93**, 102n50
Christianity 27–32, 36, 130
Christie, James 112
Christie's 1, 110–12, 118, 128, 147n62
Church 7; *see also* Roman Catholic
    Church
Church of Santa Croce in Florence 107
Cicero 25; *Pro Sexto Roscio Amerino* 22
Clarke, Katherine 81
Clouthier, David 24
Coach **93**

Colgin Cellars 95, 140
commodity production 12, 53, 55,
    128, 143
consolidation and growth 66, 96–101
conspicuous consumption 2–3, 16, 19,
    44, 54, 57, 77, 89, 149
consumerism 6, 9, 18, 31, 47, 51, 66, 75,
    77, 106, 108–9, 112
consumer society 16, 23, 43, 148–9, 153
consumption 13, 42, 47, 49–50,
    62–3, 70–1, 73, 75–6, 103,
    142, 144, 152–5; alcohol 136;
    commodity 90; conspicuous
    2–3, 16, 19, 44, 54, 57, 77, 149;
    culture of 44–7, 49, 73, 81, 152;
    essentialism 74; excessive 30–1,
    129; habits 22, 72; hedonistic 79;
    high-price limited 10; household
    58; inconspicuous 89; increased
    7, 43, 59; inequality 79; luxury
    7–8, 16–17, 37, 50, 78; mass 2,
    18, 49, 51, 58–61, 66–70, 73,
    77, 81–2; material 45–6, 60, 85;
    modern 71; self-control 27; status
    seeking 99; stimulated 17; surge
    100; symbolic 84; wine 14, 129,
    132, 135–7, 143; worker fueled 49
"crafting" 89
Crane, George 134
Credit Suisse 97
Crivelli, Carlo 106
Crosby, A. 106
Csaba, Fabian 97
Cubism 114, 117
culture of consumption 44–7, 49, 73,
    81, 152

Dadaism 11, 114, 116
D'Arienzo, William 84
da Vinci, Leonardo: *Salvator Mundi* 122
Decanter 127
de Latour, Georges 135
de la Warr (Earl) 56
Deloitte 147n62
de-moralization 32, 34, 153, 155
department store 9, 59–60, 66–7, 91, 96
de Vries, Jan 48
Dirix, Emmanuelle 9, 91
discretionary spending 37, 70, 149
Dix, Otto 117
Domaine de la Romanee Conti, La
    Tâche: 2014 1
Dom Pérignon 95, 102n50, 131

Duchamp, Marcel: *Urinal* 12, 116
Duke of Urbino 11, 108
Dumas, Axel 2
Duran, Narciso 133
Durand-Rual, Paul 115
Duveen, Joseph 113–14

Ebel 94
effeminacy 22, 26
Elias, Norbert 62, 73
elites 7, 17, 26, 29–30, 43, 45, 63, 66–7,
    74–5, 80, 90, 151, 153–4, 157;
    aristocratic 37–8, 50, 152; art 118;
    artists 108; behavior 149; Brussels
    111; buyer 108; cloistered 109;
    clothing 9; contemporary 3, 8;
    criticism 6, 19; dress 8; entitlement
    44; exclusive 149; Florentine 107;
    global 82, 122, 142; lifestyle 61,
    75, 81; medieval 156; new 37,
    44, 50; old 30–1, 36–8, 42, 50,
    52, 61–2, 77, 79; post 2008 crash
    23; privileged 75; refuge 143;
    sensibilities 56; twentieth-century
    9, 91; wealthy 81, 84, 97, 150
Enlightenment 32, 34–5, 39, 46;
    post 62; pre- 24, 114
Establissments François Pinault 96
Etruria 105
Euripides 125
Ewen, Stuart 72–4
extravagance 3, 14, 22, 24, 28, 56, 149

false needs 18, 153–4
fashion 8–10; *see also specific names of
    individual companies*, e.g., Gucci;
    advertising 9; business 91–3
Federal Reserve 78
Ferragamo, Salvatore 88
Ferrari 2, 20n26, 100
Fiat 20n26
Figueroa, José 133
Filenes 60
fine wine 13–15, 125–44; *see also* wine
    regions; *specific names of wines
    and wineries*, e.g., Domaine de
    la Romanee Conti, La Tâche;
    California early wine history
    133–6; early history 128–30;
    evaluating 127–8; luxury wines
    from New World 138–43; Napa
    cult 138–43; Napa's rebirth 136–8;
    quality control 130–3

Flechtheim, Alfred 117
"flexible specialization" 102n21
Ford, Henry 67–71
Fordism 6, 9, 51
Ford Motor Company 67, 70–1; *see also*
    Model T
Frankfurt School 72
Freud, Sigmund 114
frugality 3, 29, 42, 66, 70

Gagosian, Larry 118
Gainsborough, Thomas 11;
    Mr. and Mrs. Andrews 52
Galeries Lafayette 67
galleries 13, 19, 113, 117–19, 121–3;
    see also National Gallery; mega
    10, 12
Gambart, Ernest 112–14
Gaultier, Jean-Paul 95
gender 7
Giotto di Bondone: Basilica of St
    Francis at Assisi 107; Church of
    Santa Croce in Florence 107;
    Santa Maria Novella 107;
    Scrovegni Chapel in Padua 107
Girouard, Mark 52, 54
globalization 6, 17, 77, 100
Gold Rush 133
Google 100
Great Depression 81
greed 3, 24–9
Gregory, Brad 29, 36, 47
Grgich, Mike 137
Grosz, George 117
Gucci 9, 87, 89, **93**, 96
Guidobaldo II della Rovere 108

Haraszthy, Agoston: "Report on Grapes
    and Wine of California" 134
Harding 60
Harlan Estate 140; 2011 2
Harris poll 5
Haut Brion 131
Heaven, kingdom of 27
hedonism 54, 155–6
Heitz Martha's Vineyard Cabernet
    Sauvignon 1974 128
Hennessy 92, 94
Hennessy, Richard 94
Hermès 9, 92, **93**, 96, 100, 102n50;
    Birkin bag 2, 95
Hermès, Charles-Emile 95
Hermès, Thierry 95

hierarchies 7, 23, 29, 31, 38, 62, 75, 99, 112, 114, 150; Catholic 32; fixed 3, 23, 27; fluid 46, 52; ordained imperial 28; pre-ordained 16; rigid 24, 33, 149, 152; sanctified 151; social 32, 151; traditional 42, 46, 61
Hilgard, Eugene 134
Hirst, Damien 12, 119
historical context 22–39; capitalism advent 35–9; Christianity 27–32; money, markets, and morality 32–5; vice 24–7
Holbein 11
home as domestic refuge and emblem of excess 51–68
Hook, Philip 111, 113, 115, 118
Houghton House 53
Howard, Peter 30
Howell & Co's Grand Fashionable Magazine 60
Hughes, Robert: *The Shock of the New* 12
Hume, David 61

Imperial Universal Exposition 131
Impressionism 114–15
Inclosure Acts 53
industrialism 11, 23–4, 43, 45, 47–51, 56, 60, 114, 116; birth 40
Industrial Revolution 8, 34, 42–3, 49, 53, 110; England 48
inequality 3–8, 10, 16–17, 19, 23–5, 27, 31, 33–6, 43–4, 77, 82, 89, 99–100, 122–3, 149–50, 154–5, 157; materialism 77–9
Inglenook Estate 135–6

Jacob, L. 35
Jameson, Frederic 12
Jardine, Lisa 106–7
Jefferson, Thomas 125
jewelry 31, 38, 50, 59, 76, 79, 90, 94–6
Johns, Jaspar 118
Johnson, Hugh 131
Jonghelinck, Nicolaes 111

Kahnweiler, Daniel-Henry 117
Kapferer, Jean-Noël 4, 81, 85, 97
Kay, John 6
Kelly, Grace 95
Kelly bag 95
Kent, William 55

Kering 9–10, 87, **93**, 95–6, 98; customers 89; mergers and acquisitions 92, 96, 101; sales growth 88
Knight Frank 147n62, 156
Koons, Jeff 12, 119
Kovesi, Catherine 30
Krug 95, 134–5
Krug, Charles 134

landownership 11, 42–3, 50, 53–6, 61, 109, 142
Laube, Jim 139
Lewis, Justin 66, 74
Liebow, Victor 44
Louis Vuitton 92, **93**, 94
Luxottica **93**
luxury: definition 4; goods firms 90–1
LVMH 9–10, 85–6, **93**, 94–5, 98–9, 101; advertisements 102n50; mergers and acquisitions 92; revenue 95–6; sales growth 88

Maezawa, Yusaku 1
Mallatier, Louis Vuitton 94
Manhattan Meatpacking District 97
mansions 81
Maoism 155
Marcuse, Herbert: *One-Dimensional Man* 153–4
Marshall, Alfred 58–9
Marshall, Peter 34
Marshall Fields 60, 67
Marx, Karl 46, 50, 53, 74
mass consumption 2, 18, 49, 51, 66–7, 77, 81–2; dawn 58–61; mass production 67–70, 73
mass distribution 9, 16, 51, 65, 70
mass production 2, 9, 16, 18, 23, 51, 58, 72–4, 76–7, 82, 84, 87, 105, 152; mass consumption 61, 65, 67–70, 73
material excess 23, 26–7, 39, 46, 148
materialism 23, 25, 44, 73, 99, 122, 149–50, 153, 155–6; consumer 17; inequality 77–9; middle class 61
McCloskey 35
McNeill, Peter 38, 105
meatpacking industry 69
media 66, 112, 148, 154; *see also* press; social 87, 101
median household incomes 5
Medici, Cosimo de' 30, 110–11

Mellon, Andrew 113
Messel, Ludwig 57
Meyer, Tobias 119
Michael Kors 88, **93**
Michelangelo 107
Milanovic, Branko 77
Millet, Jean-François 115
Model T 69–70
Modernism 12, 114, 116
Moët et Chandon 92, 94
Mokyr, Joel 32, 35, 40n41, 43
Mondavi, Robert 137
Montgomery, Scott 3
Montgomery Ward 59
morality 22, 36, 42, 108, 157; *de
    facto* 35; economics 33; excessive
    inequality 3; individual 34, 36;
    money and markets 32–5;
    regulating 27, 32; self-control 27;
    subjective individual 34
Mozart 11

Napa Valley AVA (American
    Viticultural Association) 138
Napa Valley Grape Growers
    Association 137
Napa Valley Technical Group 137
Napa Valley Vintners 137
Napa Valley wine region 2, 14–15, 95,
    126–8, 134–6, 146n51, 147n63;
    cult 138–43, 145n4; rebirth 136–8
Napoleon III 131
National Gallery: London 52, 106;
    Washington, DC 113
National Trust 56
new luxury 19, 99, 156
new rich 17, 31, 38, 44, 46, 58, 74,
    76–7, 112
Newton 32, 95
Niebaum, Gustav 135

Okonkwo, Uche 85
Old Masters 110, 112
Ovid 140

Parker, Robert 127, 139
Penfolds Grange 128
Pepys, Samuel 131
Petrus 128
Phillips Auctioneers 94
Picasso 117; *Guernica* 12, 116; *Les
    Femmes D'Alger (version O)* 1
Picketty, Thomas 78

Pieter Bruegel the Elder 111
Pinault, François 95–6
Pinault-Printemps-Redoubt (PPR) 96
Place de Bordeaux 132
Plato 22, 25
Podolny, Joel 140–1
polis 22–3, 25
Pop Art 12, 119
PPR *see* Pinault-Printemps-Redoubt
    (PPR)
Prada 9, 88, **93**
press 2, 4, 16
Prohibition 136
Protestantism 35; Reformation 151;
    Work Ethic 46
Puritans 35
pursuit of luxury 3, 23, 44, 153–4

rail cars 69
Ralph Lauren 90, **93**, 102n50
Raphael 107
rarity 10, 12, 19, 66, 80–1, 85, 89–90,
    99, 120–1, 157
real estate 87, 140, 148, 156
Reformation 31–2, 34, 153;
    Protestant 151
Renaissance 11, 31, 38, 43, 54–5, 79,
    104, 106–9, 115–17, 123
rental cars 7
Richemont 10, 92, **93**
Riello, Giorgio 38, 105
Robinson, Jancis 141
Rolex 10, **93**, 100
Rolland, Michel 140
Rolls Royce 2, 20n26, 76
Roman Catholic Church 28–9, 31,
    34, 151
Ruskin, John 112–13

Sassatelli, Roberta 152, 155
Sauvignon Blanc 134
Schrader 140
scientific management 68
Scott, Gilbert 55
Scott Morton, Fiona 140–1
Screaming Eagle 140; 2010 2
Scrovegni, Enrico degli 107
Sears Roebuck 59
self-betterment 43, 47
self-interest 3, 33–4, 39, 43, 46–7, 89
Selfridge, Gordon 60
Selfridges 67
Seo, Yuri 86

Serres, Olivier de: *Theatre of Agriculture and Field Management* 130
Simmel, Georg 74, 80, 104
Smith, Adam 3, 32–4, 36, 46–7; *The Wealth of Nations* 22
Smith, Joseph 108
social class 35, 40n43, 75
social order 25, 32, 35–7
Sombart, Werner 38, 79, 152–3, 155
Sotheby's 1, 110–12, 118–19, 147n62, 156
Srinivasan, Bhu 59, 69
Staglin 140
standard of living 3, 23, 36, 49, 51, 59
State Vinicultural Society 134–5
status 74–7
Stewart, A. T. 60
Stewart's Cast Iron Palace 60
sumptuary laws 3, 7, 16–17, 22, 27, 30–1, 37, 62, 151
super rich 8, 12–13, 81, 99, 122, 156
supply and demand 11, 42, 45, 89, 109
Swatch **93**

Tag Heuer 94
Taylor, Frederick 68–9
Tchelistcheff, Andre 137
Thomas Pink 94
Thornton, James 125
Thurley, Simon 54–5
Tiepolo, Giovanni Batista 108
Tiffany **93**
Tilden, Marshall, III 143
Tintoretto 108
Titian 38; *Venus of Urbino* 11, 107–8
trade up 14, 98
Trentman, Frank 47, 51, 59, 72–3

UBS 147n62
UHNW *see* ultra-wealthy high net worth (UHNW)
ultra-wealthy high net worth (UHNW) 4, 78–9, 85, 98, 120–1, 155–6
Unitarianism 35
United States Forest Service 57
University of California Davis 136–8
Urbino, Duke of 11, 108

Vallas 71
Vanderbilt, Cornelius 57
Vanderbilt, George 57–8
Van Eyck 11

Veblen, Thorstein 3, 16, 74–5, 77, 100, 153; "conspicuous consumption" 57; "Veblen good" 126
Vecellio, Tiziano (Titian) 38; *Venus of Urbino* 11, 107–8
Versace 88
Veuve Clicquot 96
vice 3, 24–9, 32
Vinfolio 1–2
viniculture 129, 136–8
virtue 32, 35, 61, 75, 84, 99, 116; Christian 30; civic 23, 155; craft production techniques 132; Edenic 54; French agriculture and industry 131; individual initiative 34; moral 29–30; *see also* morality; newness 115; painters 113; public 36

vitis vinifera 128–9, 134
Volstead Act 136
VW 20n26

wages 5–6, 48–51, 58, 71–2
Wall Street Journal 81
Walpole, Robert 53
Wanamakers 60
Warhol, Andy 118
wealth effect 58, 60
Weber, Max 46–7, 74, 153
Wilson, Peter 118
The Wine Advocate 139
Wine Enthusiast 139, 143
wine regions: Bordeau 2, 14–15, 95, 126, 128, 130–2, 134, 139–40, 142, 145n5, 145n9; Burgundy 1–2, 14, 126–8, 132–3, 139–40, 142; California 15; Italy 15; Napa Valley 2, 14–15, 95, 126–8, 134–6, 146n51, 147n63; Napa Valley cult 138–43, 145n4; Napa Valley's rebirth 136–8; Sonoma 133–4
Wine Spectator 127, 139, 142–3
World Exposition 135
World War II; post- 6, 84, 86, 117, 136, 153
Worth, Charles Frederick 8–9, 91
Wyeth, Andrew 12

Yoox Net-a-Porter 101

Zenith 94
Zwirmer, David 118–9

Printed in the United States
by Baker & Taylor Publisher Services